Long Overdue

LIBRARIAN. *n.f.* [*librarius*, Latin.]
1.   One who has the care of a library.
2.   One who transcribes or copies books.
    Charybdis thrice swallows, and thrice refunds, the waves:
this must be understood of regular tides. There are indeed but
two tides in a day, but this is the error of the *librarians*.
                                        Broome's Notes on the Odyssey

LIBRARY. *n.f.* [*librarie*, Fr.] A large collection of books, publick,
    or private.
        Then as they 'gan his *library* to view,
    And antique registers for to avise,
    There chanced to the prince's hand to rise
    An ancient book, hight Briton's monuments.   *Fa. Qu.*
        Make choice of all my *library*,
    And so beguile thy sorrow.   *Shakesp. Titus Andronicus.*
    I have given you the *library* of a painter, and a catalogue
    of such books as he ought to read.   *Dryden's Dufresnoy.*

                                        Samuel Johnson,
                            A Dictionary of the English Language, 1755

Well she got her daddy's car and she cruised through the
    hamburger stand now,
Seems she forgot all about the library like she told her old man
    now,
And with the radio blasting goes cruising just as fast as she can
    now,
And she'll have fun fun fun till her daddy takes the T–bird away

                            The Beach Boys, *Fun, Fun, Fun*, 1964

Long Overdue
A LIBRARY READER

Edited by
ALAN TAYLOR

LIBRARY ASSOCIATION PUBLISHING

in conjunction with

MAINSTREAM PUBLISHING
EDINBURGH AND LONDON

Copyright © Alan Taylor and the contributors, 1993

The moral rights of the authors have been asserted

Published jointly in 1993 by
LIBRARY ASSOCIATION PUBLISHING
7 Ridgmount Street, London WC1E 7AE
and
MAINSTREAM PUBLISHING COMPANY (EDINBURGH) LTD
7 Albany Street, Edinburgh EH1 3UG

ISBN 1 85158 596 6 (cloth)
ISBN 1 85158 577 X (paper)

A catalogue record for this book is available from the British Library

Typeset in Bembo by Litho Link Ltd, Welshpool, Powys
Printed in Great Britain by The Cromwell Press, Melksham, Wiltshire

ACKNOWLEDGMENTS

Why? was the common response when it leaked out that I was compiling this book. It was hard to convince people that an anthology about libraries and librarians could be as compelling as one on drink or seductions or soccer. If I had doubts myself these were quickly dispelled as I began to read potential pieces. Far from scraping the bottom of a barrel it was obvious that I would have to leave as much out as I would be able to include.

For this I am particularly grateful to many individual librarians around the globe who responded to requests in the professional press and elsewhere for suggestions. These include: Ian Allan, Bruce Anderson, Ann Baer, David Broomwich, Colette Coen, Glyn Davies, Lydia Gerend, Eric Heap, D. A. Hickling, Alan Hill, Jimmy Hogg, D. W. Hutchings, Colin Hynson, Anna Yardley Jones, Prof. R. MacGregor-Hastie, Alison Million, Alison Minns, Joan Newiss, Claire Pillar, Frank Rogers, Catherine Royce, Andy Sawyer, Paul Slinger, Margaret Sparks, Norman D. Stevens, J. M. Sweetland, John Taylor, E. S. Turner, Nigel Ward, Jane Whitnall and Hamish Whyte. A special acknowledgment must go to Peter J. Taylor who sent me two volumes he had compiled on the subject, which I have happily plundered.

A number of libraries have proved invaluable, principally Edinburgh City Libraries, National Library of Scotland and the Scottish Poetry Library.

Finally, I am grateful to Jill Davies, then of Library Association Publishing, for commissioning the book. Bill Campbell and Peter MacKenzie of Mainstream know full well the sub-text of the title. However, without the gentle but persistent prodding of Peter Frances, *Long Overdue* may yet have lived up to its billing.

The editor and publishers wish to thank the following who have kindly given permission for the use of copyright material: Daniel J. Boorstin and Random House Inc. for an extract from *The Discoverers*; Umberto Eco and Reed International Books Ltd for an extract from *The Name of the Rose*; Faber and Faber Ltd for an extract by Philip Larkin from *Required Writing*; Elias Canetti and Jonathan Cape Ltd for an extract from *Auto da Fé*; MacGibbon and Kee (an imprint of HarperCollins) for an extract from *The Best of Myles* by Flann O'Brien; Peters Fraser Dunlop for permission to reprint 'In a Library' by Edmund Blunden from *Collected Poems 1930–40*, published by Macmillan London Ltd; Garrison Keillor and Faber and Faber Ltd for an extract from *We Are Still Married*; Barbara Pym, Macmillan London Ltd and Dutton Signet (a division of Penguin Books USA Inc.), copyright © 1982 Hilary Walton, for an extract from *An Unsuitable Attachment*; Anita Brookner and A.M. Heath and Co. Ltd. for an extract from *Lewis Percy*, published by Jonathan Cape Ltd; Anthony Burgess and Reed International Books Ltd for an extract from *Little Wilson and Big God*; Nigel Williams and Judy Daish Associates Ltd for an extract from *Witchcraft*, published by Faber and Faber Ltd; Faber and Faber Ltd for permission to reprint 'The British Museum Reading-Room' from *The Collected Poems of Louise MacNeice*; David Lodge and Curtis Brown Ltd for an extract from *The British Museum is Falling Down*, copyright © David Lodge (1965), published by Secker and Warburg and Penguin; Jonathan Cape Ltd for permission to reproduce 'A Ticket for the Reading-Room' by William Plomer; Kate Morris and Solo Syndication and Literary Agency Ltd for permission to quote from her article in *The Evening Standard*, Kingsley Amis and Victor Gollancz Ltd for an extract from *That Uncertain Feeling*; Bernard MacLaverty and Jonathan Cape Ltd for an extract from *Cal*; The Woburn Press Ltd for permission to reproduce 'The Missing Page' from *Hancock's Half Hour* by Tony Hancock; Charles Addams and Hamish Hamilton Ltd for permission to reproduce a cartoon from *The World of Charles Addams*; Victoria Wood and Reed

CONTENTS

INTRODUCTION

Sitting in my Balham bedsit, lorries trundling loudly past on the High Road below, I pondered my next move. For a year I had been working in London as a civil servant. The office was in the City, a stone's throw from St Paul's. When I first arrived in London I lived in Ladbroke Road in Notting Hill in a hostel populated mainly by servants of Her Majesty's government. Some had been there for decades, others, such as myself and my room-mate, were passing through. 'Like a dose of the clap,' sniffed one disaffected long-term inmate, a languid Liverpudlian with pole-vaulter's legs and a mop of ginger hair.

I shared a room the shape and size of an up-ended wardrobe with a teenage Saudi Arabian who had come to England to learn the language. Omar was small, wiry and drank Coca-Cola to excess. Once a week he went to see *Lawrence of Arabia*, north or south of the river, wherever it was showing. Perhaps he was memorising the lines. I imagined him affecting Peter O'Toole's pukka accent and shouting 'Charge!' while waiting at Notting Hill Gate station for the train to Tottenham Court Road from where he walked every morning to a tutorial in Bloomsbury. Would the hordes of commuters stand aside and let him embark as if he were royalty? I was pretty sure they would until one morning a man tripped while rushing for his train. No one attempted to help him up; rather he was treated with the respect of a rugby player who has collapsed the scrum. As the train pulled out I watched the man get to his feet, brush himself down and adjust his bowler as if it were an everyday occurrence.

Since moving to Balham I had swapped the Central for the Northern line. It was quieter but dirtier. Balham, as Peter Sellers facetiously and famously remarked, was 'the gateway to the South'. At the office, Ron from Chelmsford, with a toothbrush moustache, and a regimental tie, preferred to call it 'darkest Balham'. Me, being Scottish, he dubbed David Livingstone. 'What good works are you up to this weekend, doc?' he'd invariably ask on a Friday afternoon as he silted his tea with sugar. 'Got anything planned for natives?' Mostly this went zooming over my head but something must have stuck because whenever I was asked in the street if I wanted to receive Christian literature I always said yes and gave Ron's address. He was inundated.

The office routine was suffocating. When the pay slips were issued at the end of the month it was like a bribe to a blackmailer.

'They may have abolished capital punishment,' Ron said, 'but what about people dying of boredom? What the papers wouldn't give to hear about that.' All that stopped him singing, he said, was the monthly cheque. Each break in the day was elaborately orchestrated, every anniversary meticulously observed. Leaving 'dos' were planned like Caesar's Gallic campaign. Wins at bingo were celebrated with lashings of synthetic cream. The annual leave allocation was measured by the carat. So stultifying was the daily grind that the office boy perked up his lunch-hour by running a discothèque in a near-by pub.

I was paid £72 a month. It wasn't a lot but it was more than I had ever had in my hand before at any one time. I was 19 with one presentable suit and an idea that every London pub had a Dylan Thomas on a bar-stool. By the time I had paid the rent, bought a monthly season ticket for London Transport and shopped for bacon and bread, I had just enough left over either to visit my girlfriend in Maidenhead or buy a few pints of Youngs' bitter over the weekend at a watering-hole on Clapham Common.

After work during the week I left the office as five struck. On wet November nights I would join the fleeing throng as it headed for the Bank Underground, black brollies gleaming like cockroaches beneath the wan street lights. Occasionally, to avoid the rush hour, I would kill time by going to Cannon Street library. It was a dull but functional place, a testimony to the municipal imagination. Everyone wanted to read *The Lord of the Rings* but no one could get his hands on it. The librarians were long suffering. 'Have you tried *Lord of the Flies*?' one asked an indignant reader who had been hanging on for a half a year in mute anticipation. 'What about buying it for yourself?' I wanted to say to him, but in those halcyon and ethically unchallenged pre-Thatcher days that would have been a heresy.

But Cannon Street library was so soulless a place that my visits were infrequent. I preferred the public library at Balham, round the corner from my curtainless room above a Polish barber and an Indian takeaway with an uninterrupted view of Sainsbury's. By early evening the library was bustling. As well as a large lending section, it boasted a room set aside for studying; desks were at a premium in an area where impecunious students found peace hard to come by in cramped lodgings. I was not as poor as them, I suppose, but I was not flush either. On a raw night the library provided warmth and entertainment free of charge and I was loath to leave it for my room with its two-bar electric fire and Hancockian décor.

For about nine months that library plied me with reading matter. I read structurelessly. Unlike Sheilah Graham who had Scott Fitzgerald to direct her, I followed my fancy, picking up the trail of one author after another. I read by serendipity, following the alphabet more than anything else: Hardy, Hemingway, Heyer, Huxley; Günter Grass, Henry Green and Graham Greene; Salinger, Scott, Simenon and Robert Louis Stevenson. I rarely read a newspaper and certainly never came across a books page. Hardly ever did I venture into a bookshop. Charing Cross Road was Mecca but to go there was to tempt the kleptomaniac in me. In my year in London I bought one book in Foyle's – 'the biggest bookshop in London' – Donne's *Sonnets* in a slim Penguin, priced 30p, which I have still though I have stopped pretending to read it on trains or on buses.

London then, at the onset of the seventies, was still trying to recover from the riotous party that had been the sixties. Once, in the King's Road, I spied a girl ambling along topless as if on walkabout in the outback. (At the time I thought she was a fashion victim; now I'm inclined to the view that she was a few crisps short of a packet.) People still sported flowery ties and purple jackets with oceanic lapels. My girlfriend wore an Afghan which when wet smelled of yoghurt that had turned. It was as if no one wanted to let go. But you could almost feel the spirit of the sixties ebbing away. People who previously had lived for today were looking towards tomorrow. Caution was blowing in the wind. Suddenly, it was no longer naff to contemplate a career in banking or insurance or, even, the civil service.

One night I caught the last tube. It moved reluctantly, like a goods train. When it pulled into Clapham Common and refused to go any further I contemplated a long walk home in driving rain. But when I got to the exit, the portcullis was down and the turnkey had called it a night. Three of us trudged along the underground track to Balham expecting at any minute a train to hurtle out of the darkness and drag us to our deaths. Emerging at midnight at Balham, I swore it would never happen again. I had been in London a year and I was tired of it. I had been to the Cheshire Cheese, drunk warm beer and written 'Johnson was here' above the urinal. Whatever the sage of Lichfield said, you don't need to be tired of life to have had a bellyful of London.

But what was I to do? I was offered a transfer to Glasgow, the only catch being that I would have to get my hair cut. Would a punk surrender his safety pins? I had never been to Glasgow and I didn't think I could face it with a short back and sides. In any case, I wanted to live at home for a while. Before I'd left for London I'd had an interview with the local librarian whose office was in a converted school building. He was a spindly man with bony knees; I know this because he was wearing a kilt. He recommended a year at the coal-face working as a dogsbody in a branch library, then a period of incarceration in an educational institution where I could qualify as a 'professional librarian'.

This advice was imparted gravely and without much enthusiasm. Maybe he discerned a lack of enthusiasm on my part. Whatever the reason, I was not wholly sold on the idea of becoming a librarian. Now though, the situation was different; beggars could not be choosers and studying my curriculum vitae it was obvious that my options were limited.

I wrote to the city librarian of Edinburgh and asked if there was anything going. I received a reply by return of post calling me to interview. It took place in the boardroom of the Central Library on George IV Bridge, the walls panelled in American walnut with the names of successive city librarians engraved in gold lettering. The personnel officer was Tony Shearman, who later became the city librarian, an angular man with a pronounced Adam's apple and the light tread of a long-distance runner. (Later I learned that he was a great walker and would measure his excursions with a pedometer. Once, he left it on the bonnet of his car and it was stolen, or rather swapped, for a tatting set. Why, has confounded detectives for two decades.)

What, he asked, was I reading? I mentioned *The Lord of the Rings* and we circumnavigated Middle Earth until the subject turned to ping-pong. I could see it was a sport that appealed to Mr Shearman and I talked as knowledgeably as I could about foam bats, top spin and the latest Chinese wunderkind until he made it clear the interview was over. Two days later he phoned offering me a job as a library assistant at McDonald Road branch library.

I didn't know what to expect there but I did expect someone to be expecting me. I arrived on my first morning five minutes early; a girl, name of Nancy, had turned up a few minutes earlier. She was expected. Apparently, I was not. By dint of her getting in the door first she was henceforth senior to me and allowed precedence when it came to taking holidays. The woman in charge that morning, the branch librarian's deputy, looked like a rep for Inter-flora. Her hair was close-cropped. She had a pink bow round her neck and wore an overall that had begun life as a bouquet. On her feet were lilac Hush Puppies. She moved like greased lightning and talked as if she had just been given 30 seconds to say all there was to say about what was expected of humble library assistants. Without hesitation, repetition or digression, she took Nancy and me round the Victorian building, finishing off with an explanation of how to shelve books, an activity, it seemed, as arcane as an apothecary's.

'Watch me,' she said, her voice fluttering like a bird's. First she took an armful of books and spread them spine upwards on a wooden trolley. With the dexterity of a croupier dealing at poker she sorted them into alphabetical order. 'By author.' I didn't know there was an option. 'If you have two or more books by the same author,' she said, 'arrange them alphabetically by title.' When these were sorted she scooped the books, 15 or so, into an elastic arm and raced round the shelves inserting them at a dizzying speed. Once books were added the spines had to lie flush to the shelves. In each bookcase the books on the shelves had to align so that everything was in its proper place and looking as smart as a squad on parade. This, one was given to understand, was housekeeping as a science.

McDonald Road library, like the rest of Edinburgh's public libraries, was arranged by the Library of Congress classification, which made it something of an anomaly in the profession. While most of Britain adhered to the Dewey Decimal classification, Edinburgh had Congress foisted upon it by one Ernest Savage, who lived up to his surname, at least when it came to enthusiasm for libraries. On a visit to America he witnessed Congress at work and immediately imported it to the bemusement of his staff. To me it was neither here nor there. In my career as a library user I had never paid much attention to how books were arranged. Certainly such hifalutin concepts as the organisation of knowledge had never crossed my mind, probably because I was only interested in fiction; any information I needed I gleaned from the *Encyclopaedia Britannica*. But even as I went about the daily business of returning books to their correct place on the shelves it never occurred to me that I was restoring order to chaos, harnessing the sum of the world's intellect in an Edinburgh suburb.

Perhaps I am doing them a disservice but I don't think it ever occurred to my colleagues either. Anne Laurie though, who had put me straight as far as shelving was concerned, was passionate about putting books in people's hands, as were most of the staff. In those days when asked why you worked in libraries, you chanted the mantra 'because I like books'. Later, much later, you might add 'and people'.

The branch librarian was 'Middie' Craise, a man of gnomish build who took a child's size of shoe, thus saving a small fortune. His face flushed like a strawberry when flustered, particularly when the 'issue' – the trays of cards recording which books were borrowed by whom and for how long – got into a muddle. Mr Craise, as we called him to his face, had stoutly resisted the modern urge to turn libraries into supermarkets. Occasionally he mounted a display of war books with the rubric 'Cry Havoc', which was about as far as he got to commercialising the premises. But as soon as he was out the door Anne took it down and put up something more to her liking. In any case, the most popular 'display' was the returned bookshelf which drew readers like sailors to a Siren. Catherine Cookson, then as now, was the mainstay of the public library, and I could reel off her titles as I could the names of England's World Cup winning 11.

McDonald Road was a library ruled by its regulars, stout women like Daisy Miller, the Ena Sharples of that part of Edinburgh, who with her entourage dropped by several times a week for a natter and a fix of Netta Muskett or Jean Plaidy. Romance was what these women in hairnets were after; there was no point trying to woo them away from Nora Lofts to Doris Lessing. 'I read all that years ago,' Daisy would say airily, if you tried to tickle her fancy with a name from Leavis's élite. On the other hand, men like the fishmonger from Leith Walk, or those from the nearby bus depot, were aficionados of Westerns which were bought by the yard as lairds used to buy leather-bound tomes for their never-used libraries.

Nevertheless the library was well stocked in the classics and there was a glass-cased annexe which housed forbidden books, including car manuals in washable covers and guides to tropical fish, kept out of the reach of the public because they were liable to 'walk'. There was also a newspaper reading-room where men with time to kill could play chess or draughts and dry their socks. Not long before I arrived it had been the practice to obliterate the racing section of newspapers with a stamp, which was still used by some library authorities where Presbyterian councillors could not countenance the thought that someone might make a few bob from the rates on the recommendation of the tipster on the *Daily Express*. Sometimes it was hard to believe this was 1972.

But if I was in any doubt I had merely to survey my colleagues, my future wife among them. If Germaine Greer had burned her bra for the feminist cause, women in libraries had embraced the spirit of the times by taking a stand over trousers, defiantly wearing them to work against the wishes of the branch librarians like the one at Morningside, which boasted that it was the busiest branch library in Britain thanks to its slightly superior readers who devoured the Sunday supplements and demanded the books reviewed therein be supplied toute de suite.

The mini-skirt too was much in evidence but what with all the bending and stretching it was not the ideal apparel for library work. From the Carnegie endowed Central Library came reports of readers wielding sticks with mirrors attached so they could get a better view as female assistants climbed steps to replace books on the top shelf. As is clear from many of the pieces which follow, libraries carry a peculiar erotic charge, and female library workers, chained to the issue counter, were fair game; one I worked with received a note inserted in a copy of Wilhelm Reich's *The Function of the Orgasm* asking for a date. She accepted.

Then as now, though the trend seems less apparent, libraries were largely the preserve of women. The two wars took away most of the able-bodied men, leaving behind those like Philip Larkin (the popular view of the librarian, to the chagrin of many in the profession) who to his delight failed his army medical with flying colours. In Edinburgh the theory was that for a woman, a job in the public library was on a par with that of a shop assistant in Jenners, the Scottish Harrods. It was the kind of occupation genteel folk with not too much on the top storey might aspire to, not too taxing physically or intellectually but respectable in a mysterious sort of way. It had the cachet of the esoteric, as if somehow handling books all day drew them into the academic bloodstream, like a bibliographic virus.

At McDonald Road everyone on the staff read, and at lunch and tea breaks in the staffroom conversation was often monosyllabic. Later, when working at another branch library, a girl who in homage to David Bowie had dyed her hair bilious green switched on a radio; the librarian, who still insisted the staff use fountain pens, switched it off with contempt.

We were a strange crew but a happy one, a mixture of spinsters, young men in brothel creepers and tank tops, and dizzy girls who didn't know what to do with themselves. We worked alternating shifts; from 8.45 a.m. to 4.30 p.m. and from 1.45 p.m. to 8.30 p.m. The day began by tidying up and that was what it mainly comprised, shelving and reshelving between bouts of stamping out books, an activity that is fast dying out with computerisation. After a Friday night or a Saturday morning when the library was mobbed you went home, as did Larkin at the fag-end of the war, with blistered hands from stamping out books. What perked up an otherwise tedious day was the wacky staff and readers' enquiries, a steady source of muffled guffaws.

'Have you got the complaint, son?'

'Which complaint would that be, Mrs McDougall?'

'*The* complaint. The one they're all talking about. My man wants to see it.'

'You mean' – lowering the voice to a whisper – 'venereal disease?'

'No, the book that was in a' the bestseller lists. By Portnoy, I think it is.'

'Ah *Portnoy's Complaint*, you mean, by Philip Roth.'

'Aye, that'll be it.'

Such exchanges were the norm rather than the exception. Library readers have a legendary capacity for forgetfulness of essential details and a diffident sense of imparting information. Wresting these from them is a large part of the fun of working in libraries, particularly reference libraries, where I landed after a sojourn at the library school at Robert Gordon Institute of Technology in Aberdeen, where I added the letters ALA (Associate of the Library Association) to my name. At Gordon's I encountered another peculiar species, the library school lecturer. In another life most of these men – and in my day they were all men – had been practising librarians but they had escaped and now taught cataloguing and classification, historical bibliography, library architecture and local government law.

'Work hard and play hard,' the head of the school told us, his eyes trained on the distance, like a golfer following a hooked drive.

'There is no crime,' he added, 'not murder or rape, worse than that of stealing a book.'

No one in the class demurred. 'Why do you want to be a librarian?' one of the few males in the room was asked. 'Because I never want any responsibility for money,' he replied, without so much as a smidgen of irony. In the forthcoming days, we were often accused of being on 'cloud nine' but it was the lecturers who flew us there. Intriguing as it was to learn of Thomas Wise's career as forger of nineteenth-century pamphlets at the British Museum

and his unmasking by Carter and Pollard, in one of my reveries I
wondered what it possibly had to do with Daisy Miller and the
denizens of McDonald Road. In the evening, killing an hour before
clocking in at the Prince of Wales, I tried to get to grips with
AACR, the Anglo-American Cataloguing Rules, to cataloguers
what a papal bull is to Roman Catholics. On autumnal afternoons
we played a version of *What's My Line?* in which two students
played a reference librarian and a reader, the object being to find
out what the reader wanted to know through a gentle form of
interrogation.

'Morning, sir, how can I help you?'

'Do you have any books on houses?'

'I'm sure we do. Do you have any particular kind of house in
mind?'

'Semi-detached.'

Thus the exchange proceeded until the reader finally revealed
that what he wanted was to have a bat removed from his loft. In
the real world my boss in the reference department of Edinburgh's
Central Library had long since dispensed with such shillyshallying,
confronting stammering members of the public with an unwaver-
ing stare and a tart, 'What exactly is it that you want to know?'
Less resilient enquirers turned and ran.

For those unused to its workings, it took courage to mount the
broad staircase and enter the hushed room with its row upon row
of catalogue drawers (British Museum rules, 1908). In the body of
the hall antique desks sat beneath the nineteenth-century dome.

One morning we noticed that the number of desks seemed to be
diminishing, a suspicion that was confirmed after a quick count.
Several desks had disappeared under our noses and were sold to
antique dealers in the vicinity. The deputy city librarian had to go
to court to get them back. I worked in the reference library for ten
years and more and throughout that time there were always some
repairs going on. Once a painter working on the ceiling over-
turned a tin of paint and it dripped from on high for an afternoon,
narrowly missing a reader who didn't budge for hours in case it hit
him. The reference library was a magnet to the city's eccentrics.
'Which of my ears do you think is higher than the other?' a regular
asked a colleague. He had a 50 per cent chance of getting it right
but chose wrongly. The man stomped off. One woman entered
the library wearing a pair of jeans and left in a dress. 'Get me that
book,' demanded a man peering through binoculars towards the
gallery. Later he rang to ask if anyone had handed in an aluminium
kitchen sink which he had left behind. Someone had.

The library staff did their best to keep up with readers. One, it
was reported, could be seen from the top deck of a bus in his home
conducting music in the nude. An assistant was discovered
overnight in the fiction library where she had set up home, feasting
on cold baked beans. She apparently was saving money on lodgings
to have a nose job after which she intended to woo Mick Jagger.

On the library vans, the gulags of the service, a hairy frustrated poet read obscene verses to girl assistants who were sent there 'on relief'. A newly married member of staff took to reading Alex Comfort's *The Joy of Sex* in his coffee break and passed it around asking for comments on the various positions. In the department where new books were ordered and processed, a stout fellow burped ostentatiously and passed wind as he went about his work.

At times lunacy undoubtedly ruled but though creaky the service was well loved and well used. By the beginning of the eighties, however, as it began to look as if public libraries might have survived the cranks advocating community librarianship, who wanted to turn librarians into book-wielding social workers, and to hell with the loyal 30 per cent of readers, another spectre loomed. One word sums it up: management. Suddenly librarianship seemed to be flooded with people who were more suited to running consultancies. There was talk of teams. Where in the past individual librarians bought books for their libraries, this now became the prerogative of the team. Meetings proliferated like measles. Ascetic-looking men wearing in suits you used only to see on Mormons wittered on about management by objective and time and motion studies. I found myself on a course run by the Industrial Society where we were asked to come up with as many uses for a paper clip as we could in a minute. One suggestion of mine would have grievously harmed one of the management clones; they could see I was not one of them.

The eighties was a bad decade for public libraries. Carnegie's libraries were beginning to show wear and tear. Librarianship as a profession seemed to have lost its way. Productivity and efficiency replaced service. The trinity of education, information and entertainment remained as an ideal but while the debate over charging for libraries began to grow more vociferous, thanks to an uninformed report of the Adam Smith Institute, and there was much talk at library conferences of the information rich and the information poor, one sensed librarians had lost grip of their philosophy, their reason for being. The aim now was to be all things to everyone. If the public demanded videos, videos they should have. Records, cassettes, computer games, cuddly toys, paintings; there was nothing you couldn't borrow from a library. It was a variation of *The Generation Game*. One nutty librarian enthused by the enterprise culture rented umbrellas. Wasn't there one library that lent out pets?

Somewhere books got lost in all of this and Tim Waterstone and others took their chance and boldly went where librarians were too timid to venture. His smart new bookshops found a public for good books, which many of my former colleagues had long given up on. I was asked to make a list of the best contemporary writers. I have a suspicion that this led to their proscription. Catherine Cookson continued to flood in, but the new teams went into interminable huddles to decide whether to buy one copy or two of the latest Iris Murdoch. They knew nothing about books or their contents but they had algebraic formulae to prove that Barbara Taylor Bradford was more cost effective than Saul Bellow.

It was time for me to bow out. I went with regret, knowing one thing for sure; that once a librarian, always a librarian. For librarians like priests cannot completely relinquish their vocation. I think of myself now as a lapsed librarian, grateful to have been initiated in the ways of what Umberto Eco calls the labyrinth. The book that follows expresses for that my long overdue thanks.

THE GOOD OLD DAYS

As soon as there were two tablets of stone the need for a library must have been apparent. Before the advent of printing there were extensive and efficiently run manuscript libraries; Julius Caesar, despite destroying the legendary library of Alexandria, was the first statesman to pronounce that a public library should be available to the populace. In 39 BC he built the first public library in Rome. Eventually imperial Rome had 28 libraries.

In the Middle Ages the great libraries were those of closed societies, monastic, episcopal or academic. But by the Renaissance, wealth and the printing press allowed many individuals to form private libraries. By today's standards these were small, a few thousand volumes at most, but from these grew the great libraries of today.

The Ambroisiana in Milan in 1609 was perhaps the first major library to be opened to the public. Others soon followed. In Britain this was bolstered by the Licensing Act of 1663 which determined that a select number of libraries (eventually limited to six: the British Museum, the national libraries of Scotland and Wales, the Bodleian, Cambridge University Library, and Trinity College, Dublin) receive free copies of every publication. Other countries followed this example and in the seventeenth and eighteenth centuries the foundations of several great national libraries were laid: the Prussian State Library in Berlin (1659), the Kongelige Bibliotek in Copenhagen (1661), the Biblioteca in Copenhagen (1661), the National Library of Scotland (1682), the Biblioteca Nacional in Madrid (1712), the Biblioteca Nazionale Centrale in Florence (1747), the British Museum (1759), and the Library of Congress in Washington (1800).

Boston, Massachusetts, pioneered the public library movement as early as 1653. But we had to wait much longer before public lending libraries were generally introduced. In the 1720s Allan Ramsay, a sometime wig maker and poet, added a circulating library to his Edinburgh bookshop but it was not until 130 years later that the public library was acknowledged as an essential adjunct to the education system. The spur in Britain came in 1850 when the MP for Dumfries, William Ewart, nursed through Parliament a bill establishing the right of every town to have a free public library. In the process he sparked off a debate that has been going on ever since, the arguments typified by the contributions that follow from M.D. O'Brien and Lady Janetta Manners. But by the time Philip Larkin arrived on the scene in 1943, public libraries, thanks largely to the benevolence and foresight of Andrew Carnegie rather than the machinations of municipal panjandrums, were part of the furniture of Britain.

DANIEL BOORSTIN

The Godfathers of Libraries

The Latin culture of medieval Europe could hardly have prospered without the enthusiasm, the passion, and the good sense of Saint Benedict of Nursia (480?-543?). The father of Christian monasticism in Europe, he was also the godfather of libraries. The preservation of literary treasurers of antiquity and of Christianity throughout the Middle Ages was a Benedictine. Saint Benedict himself, born of a good family at Nursia, near Perugia, in Umbria, had been sent to school in Rome where the ancient imperial power was in decay and the power of the papacy was on the rise. Troubled by the dissoluteness of the city, he retired for three years to a cave in the Abruzzi hills. When he became known for his holiness, he was invited to become abbot of a monastery, where he disciplined his fellow monks. When a disgruntled friar tried to poison him, he retired again to his cave. But his vision survived. He went on to found in that region alone twelve monasteries with twelve monks in each, all under his direction. He then went south, where, about 529, he founded the abbey of Monte Cassino. Sacked by the Lombards and the Saracens and shaken by earthquake, it still remained the spiritual headquarters of the monastic movement in Europe. It would finally be levelled by aerial bombing in World War II.

The Rule (*Regula*) of Saint Benedict offered a workable compromise between the ascetic otherworldly spirit and the weaknesses of human nature. After a year of probation the young monk vowed obedience to the Rule and lifelong residence on the same monastery. In each monstery the monks elected their abbot for life, and otherwise there was no hierarchy. Saint Benedict's sensible schedule for the monks' daily life spread across Europe, preserving and perpetuating Latin literary culture through the following centuries. According to chapter 48 of his Rule:

> Idleness is the enemy of the soul: hence brethren ought at certain seasons to occupy themelves with manual labour, and again at

---

A big book is a big nuisance.
Callimachis, head librarian at Alexandria (305–240 BC)

certain hours with holy reading. Between Easter and the calends of October let them apply themselves to reading from the fourth hour until the sixth hour . . . From the calends of October to the beginning of Lent, let them apply themselves to reading until the second hour. During Lent, let them apply themselves to reading from morning until the end of the third hour, and in these days of Lent, let them receive a book apiece from the library and read it straight through. These books are to be given out at the beginning of Lent.

Every monastery needed its library. 'A monastery without a library [*sine armario*]', a monk in Normandy wrote in 117, 'is like a castle without an armoury [*sine armamentario*]. Our library is our armoury. Thence it is that we bring forth the sentences of the Divine Law like sharp arrows to attack the enemy. Thence we take the armour of righteousness, the helmet of salvation, the shield of faith, and the sword of the spirit, which is the word of God.' In each monastery the precentor had the duty of checking out books and seeing that they were returned. It was customary for monasteries to lend their books to other monasteries and even, with proper security, to the secular public. The Benedictine pioneers in 'interlibrary loan' provided a kind of public lending library for the learned few.

Special curses were uttered against those who mutilated books or absconded with them. 'This book belongs to [the monastery of] St Mary of Robert's Bridge', warns a twelfth-century manuscript of Saint Augustine and Ambrose, 'whosoever shall steal it, or sell it, or in any way alienate it from this house, or mutilate it, let him be forever accursed. Amen.' Below this, in the manuscript, now in the Bodleian Library at Oxford, we can read in a fourteenth-century hand: 'I, John, Bishop of Exeter, know not where the aforesaid house is, nor did I steal this book, but acquired it in a lawful way.'

Wandering clerics and pious travellers entrusted their manu-script treasures to the monastic and cathedral libraries, which vied for the best collated versions of sacred texts and received substantial fees for the right to copy them. Constantine the African (*c*.1020–*c*.1087), who spent forty years collecting and translating into Latin scientific treatises from Egypt, Persia, Chaldea, and India, finally settled in Monte Cassino, where he deposited his great collection. When the library of the monastery of Novalsea was destroyed by the Saracens in 905, it was reported to have

---

Far more seemly to have thy Studie full of Bookes, than thy Purse full of Money.

John Lyly, *Eupheus* (1579)

contained more than sixty-five hundred volumes. Every manuscript copy of a learned work was unique, but one that has been
laboriously collated with others had special authority.

Monastic libraries, of course, included the holy Scriptures,
writings of the Church Fathers, and commentaries on them.
Larger collections, sometimes found in cathedral libraries, would
include chronicles like Bede's *Ecclesiastical History*, the writings of
Augustine, Albertus Magnus, Aquinas, and Roger Bacon. Their
secular books would include Virgil, Horace and Cicero. Plato,
Aristotle, and Galen, among others, were found in Latin translation. Such libraries across Europe were not only the armouries of
Christian crusaders but the treasuries of European culture.
Monkish students who had studied at Paris or Bologna would
bring back their lecture notes with the latest interpretation of
theology and the classics for their monastery library. It was in
these libraries that five books of the *Annals* of Tacitus, the *Republic*
of Cicero, and other ancient literary monuments survived.

Not only did the Benedictines collect libraries, but they created
them. The 'making' (i.e., the copying), like the reading, of books,
became a sacred duty, and the scriptorium, the scribes' copying
room, was a usual feature of their monasteries. In some ways they
were freer to reproduce books than were publishers in the later age
of the printing press. Of course, their 'publishing' list was limited
by orthodoxy and by dogma, but there was no law of copyright
and so no royalties to be paid to the author. Their whole stock-in-
trade was what the modern publisher would call a backlist. The
book was not expected to be, nor dared it be, a vehicle for new
ideas carrying messages from contemporaries to contemporaries.
Instead it was a device to preserve and amplify the treasured
revolving fund of literary works – the sacred scriptures and their
commentators, ancient classics of Greece and Rome, and a few
established texts in Hebrew or Arabic.

The age of 'authorship' had not yet arrived. When reading a
sacred *text*, medieval scholars were quite indifferent to the author.
The writers who were being transcribed had not always troubled
to 'quote' what they had taken from other writers. Even in an era
when students were taught to argue by citing 'authority' it was
practically impossible, even if it had been thought desirable, to
ascribe particular passages to particular authors. Writers of original
texts were reluctant to take the credit, or risk the more likely
blame, for innovation. In the great age of manuscript books,
anonymity was dictated by technology, orthodoxy and prudence.

Come, and take choice of all my library,
And so beguile thy sorrow.
    William Shakespeare, *Titus Andronicus* (1590)

Even the best modern scholars on the subject cannot devise a satisfactory scheme for arranging these manuscripts in a 'bibliography'. They must resort to lists arranged not by author but by opening words or other devices. Quotation marks first came into general use with the printed books of Italy and France in the fifteenth and sixteenth centuries, but this kind of punctuation, which guides the reader to the original author, did not receive its modern name or enter standard usage until the seventeenth century.

In the Middle Ages every monastery was its own publishing house, and a monk with writing desk, ink and parchment was his own publisher. 'A book should always be in your hand or under your eyes', advised Saint Jerome. The rich lore surrounding these scriptoria reminds us that long before the making of books was a business it had become a sacred enterprise. Saint Louis (Louis IX, 1214–1270) insisted that it was better to transcribe a book than to buy the original, because this helped diffuse the Christian gospel. Work in the scriptorium had as much dignity as labour in the fields. 'He who does not turn up the earth with a plough', a monk exhorted his fellows in the sixth century, 'ought to write the parchment with his fingers.' And in the ill–heated hall or cell these fingers were often numb. Many a monk gave his eyesight to provide the illuminated missals that our own eyes admire . . .

If Saint Benedict was the patron saint of the manuscript book in the Middle Ages, the worldly patron was Charlemagne (742–814). It was a happy coincidence for Western civilisation that so effective an administrator was also a devotee of the written word. The shadowy textbook figure who was crowned Holy Roman emperor on Christmas Day, 800, comes to life as the sponsor of bookish culture, reformer of the Latin language and the Roman alphabet. Charlemagne inherited his throne as king of the Franks in 768. A fierce man of ruthless ambition, he overrode the claims of rivals and relatives, subdued the Saxons, conquered Lombardy and finally organised an empire that included Northern Italy, France, and most of modern Germany and eastern Europe. As an ally of the Pope and a passionate Christian, Charlemagne was shocked by the decay of Christian learning. He was dismayed by the crude Latin in the letters he received, even from bishops and abbots. The Carolingian renaissance that he sparked was a Latin renaissance.

When Charlemagne met the personable English monk Alcuin (732–804) in Italy in 781, he persuaded him to come to Aachen (Aix-la-Chapelle) to organise a reform of language and of

---

Neither a borrower, nor a lender be;
For loan oft loses both itself and friend.
                                    William Shakespeare, *Hamlet* (1601)

education. In remote Yorkshire, Alcuin had set high standards that made his cathedral school famous across Europe. Charlemagne agreed, too, that the correct knowledge of Scripture required a correct command of Latin. In his famous edict of 789, written by Alcuin, Charlemagne ordered: 'In each bishopric and in each monastery let the psalms, the notes, the chant, calculation and grammar be taught and carefully corrected books be available.' Alcuin set the standards at his new school of calligraphy in Tours:

> Here let the scribes sit who copy out the words of the Divine Law, and likewise the hallowed sayings of the holy Fathers. Let them beware of interspersing their own frivolities in the words they copy, nor let a trifler's hand make mistakes through haste. Let them earnestly seek out for themselves correctly written books to transcribe, that the flying pen may speed along the right path. Let them distinguish the proper sense by colons and commas, and let them set the points each one in its due place, and let not him who reads the words to them either read falsely or pause suddenly. It is a noble work to write out holy books, nor shall the scribe fail of his due reward. Writing books is better than planting vines, for he who plants a vine serves his belly, but he who writes a book serves his soul.

Charlemagne's rich library in his palace at Aachen became a cultural centre drawing scholarly Christian refugees from the Moors in Spain, and even from the distant lands of Ireland. He ordered every school to have a scriptorium . . .

In the heyday of the medieval libraries books had been so valuable that they were chained to their shelf or to a horizontal bar above the desk where they were to be consulted. The symbol of the old library was the chained book. Hundreds of such captive volumes, called *catenati*, can still be seen neatly arrayed on the shelves of the library of Hereford Cathedral. None of the consequences of printing was more far-reaching than the power of the press to free books from these chains. As books became more numerous they no longer rested on their side, as had been the medieval practice, but instead were stood up close together displaying spine, title, and author.

The library of the Escorial near Madrid built in 1584 replaced the old monastic chapel-like bays by shelves that lined the walls, offering a large stock to users who might want to browse. Arranging books in a library became a science. In 1627 Cardinal

Me, poor man – my library
Was dukedom large enough.
                    William Shakespeare, *The Tempest* (1611)

Mazarin's librarian, Gabriel Naudé (1600–1653), who also served Cardinal Richelieu and Queen Christina of Sweden, wrote the pioneer treatise on librarianship. The Mazarin Library of 40,000 volumes, collected and organised by Naudé, was designed for a great private collector willing to make his treasures available 'to all who wish to go there to study'. Samuel Pepys followed Naudé's advice in his own elegant library, which still serves scholars in Magdalene College, Cambridge.

The multiplication of books on all subjects challenged philosophers to map the whole terrain of learning. The great German philosopher Leibniz supported himself as a librarian, and helped the dukes of Brunswick-Luneburg in Hanover arrange their collection of 3,000 volumes. Then he went on to organise the 30,000-volume Ducal Library of Wolfenbüttel, for which he provided one of the first comprehensive alphabetical author catalogues. His new fireproof library design put galleries and shelves around the supporting pillars. But the Duke rejected his plan and constructed the library of wood, with the result that scholars had to shiver in winter because it was too risky to have a furnace. Leibniz saw the library as a congregation of all knowledge, with the librarian as minister keeping the congregation up to date and freely communicating. He pioneered in classification schemes alphabetical finding aids, and abstracts to help the scholar. The library was his encyclopedia.

Leibniz signalled the transition from the royal and ecclesiastical collections for the privileged few to the public library serving everyone. In the next century his visions would be realised in the surprising career of the Italian émigré Sir Anthony Panizzi (1797–1879), a passionate Italian nationalist and energetic man of action. Forced to flee his native Brescello, in the Duchy of Modena, where he had joined a secret society conspiring against the Austrian occupiers, he had been sentenced to death in absentia. He found refuge in England, where he was named the first professor of Italian literature at the University of London. When students did not come, he gave up the honorific post to join the staff of the British Museum in 1831. For the next thirty-five years he dominated and invigorated that place to make it the model of a national library in the modern mode, reaching out to the new reading public.

'What a sad want I am in of libraries, of books to gather facts from!' Thomas Carlyle lamented as he moved from Scotland to London. 'Why is there not a Majesty's library in every county

---

Affect not to do as some do that bookish ambition to be stored with books and have well-furnished libraries, yet keep their heads empty of knowledge; to desire to have many books, and never to use them, is like a child that will have a candle burning by him all the while he is sleeping.
                              Henry Peacham, *The Compleat Gentleman* (1622)

town? There is a Majesty's gaol and gallows in every one.' The 'Majesty's library', the British Museum in London, to which Panizzi came, was ill equipped for Carlyle or for even less irritable scholars. Statuary, fossils, paintings, and maps were cluttered together with books and manuscripts. The extensive private library of George III brought to the museum in 1823 was joined with the old Royal library, and a new building was being built when Panizzi joined the staff. In 1837 Panizzi was appointed Keeper of the Museum's Department of Printed Books, and Principal Librarian in 1856. His fiery temperament was not one to soothe the stuffy trustees, who held a tight rein.

'I want a poor student to have the same means of indulging his learned curiosity', Panizzi told the Parliamentary Select Committee on the Museum in 1836, 'of following his rational pursuits, of consulting the same authorities, of fathoming the most intricate enquiry, as the richest man in the kingdom, as far as books go, and . . . Government is bound to give him the most liberal and unlimited assistance.' In 1849 Panizzi still boasted that he had 'never felt the skin of any reader' and treated them all alike. Of course Carlyle, who was no friend of democracy, considered himself entitled to very special treatment. It also happened that he was hypersensitive to physical discomfort, as he was to almost everything else. Living in Chelsea, he detested the long trip to Bloomsbury to use Panizzi's library, where all the books had to be consulted on the premises, which closed at five o'clock in the afternoon. Naturally, Carlyle became Panizzi's sworn enemy.

Then Carlyle made his clash with Panizzi the occasion for some library innovations of his own. In 1841 he responded to Panizzi's ruthless egalitarianism by organising the London Library. Carlyle called a public meeting to enlist his rich and noble friends. When the London Library opened in 1841, its five hundred subscribers had access to a collection of 3,000 volumes – and there was no alien radical in charge. The Earl of Clarendon was President, the Prince Consort was Patron, and Carlyle made sure that the first librarian was an amenable Scotsman. Carlyle continued to dominate the London Library, which grew into an unexcelled scholarly subscription library.

Meanwhile, Panizzi was making something quite new of the national library. Under him, librarians ceased to be underpaid clerks. He recruited scholars who were attracted by the secure tenure and the atmosphere of catholic learning. He provided comprehensive catalogues accessible to all, and he enforced the law

---

Libraries are as forests, in which not only tall cedars and oaks are to be found, but bushes too and dwarfish shrubs; and as in apothecaries' shops all sorts of drugs are permitted to be, so may all sorts of books be in a library.
William Drummond of Hawthornden (1585–1649),
On Libraries

of legal deposit, which entitled the Museum to a copy of every new British publication. Despite urging by his most respectable patrons, he refused to second-guess the future by collecting only 'worthwhile' books on 'important' subjects. The grand circular Reading Room of the British Museum was Panizzi's conception, destined to become an exhilarating model for the Library of Congress and other libraries. Devising his own ninety-one *Cataloguing Rules*, he insisted on a complete alphabetical name catalogue, and he refused to print the catalogue until all the library's collection was included. The trustees convened a Royal Commission to bring him to heel, but the Commission's final report in 1850 supported Panizzi.

The public library 'in every county town', which Carlyle demanded, was yet to come. Panizzi still required users to present letters of introduction to enter the Reading Room and his books did not circulate. Another Scotsman, Andrew Carnegie (1835– 1919), of a temperament very different from Carlyle's, would spread public libraries across a transatlantic continent-nation.

The Discoverers: A History of Man's Search to Know His World and Himself
(Random House, 1983; J. M. Dent, 1984)

Books that stand thinne on the shelves, yet
so as the owner of them can bring forth
everyone of them into use, are better than
farre greater libraries.
        Thomas Fuller, 'Of Books', *The Holy State* (1642)

UMBERTO ECO

The Librarian and the Labyrinth

I felt the abbot was pleased to be able to conclude that discussion and return to his problem. He then began telling, with very careful choice of words and with long paraphrases, about an unusual event that had taken place a few days before and had left in its wake great distress among the monks. He was speaking of the matter with William, he said, because, since William had great knowledge both of the human spirit and of the wiles of the Evil One, Abo hoped his guest would be able to devote a part of his valuable time to shedding light on a painful enigma. What had happened, then, was this: Adelmo of Otranto, a monk still young though already famous as a master illuminator, who had been decorating the manuscripts of the library with the most beautiful images, had been found one morning by a goatherd at the bottom of the cliff below the Aedificium. Since he had been seen by other monks in choir during compline but had not reappeared at matins, he had probably fallen there during the darkest hours of the night. The night of a great snowstorm, in which flakes as sharp as blades fell, almost like hail, driven by a furious south wind. Soaked by that snow, which had first melted and then frozen into shards of ice, the body had been discovered at the foot of the sheer drop, torn by the rocks it had struck on the way down. Poor, fragile, mortal thing, God have mercy on him. Thanks to the battering the body had suffered in its broken fall, determining from which precise spot it had fallen was not easy: certainly from one of the windows that opened in rows on the three stories on the four sides of the tower exposed to the abyss.

'Where have you buried the poor body?' William asked.

'In the cemetery, naturally,' the abbot replied. 'Perhaps you noticed it: it lies between the north side of the church, the Aedificium, and the vegetable garden.'

'I see,' William said, 'and I see that your problem is the following. If that unhappy youth, God forbid, committed suicide, the next day you would have found one of those windows open,

---

It is vanity to persuade the world one hath great learning, by getting a great library. As soon shall I believe that every one is valiant that hath a well-furnished armoury.

Thomas Fuller, 'Of Books', *The Holy State* (1642)

whereas you found them all closed, and with no sign of water at the foot of any of them.'

The abbot, as I have said, was a man of great and diplomatic composure, but this time he made a movement of surprise that robbed him totally of that decorum suited to a grave and magnanimous person, as Aristotle has it. 'Who told you?'

'You told me,' William said. 'If the window had been open, you would immediately have thought he had thrown himself out of it. From what I could tell from the outside, they are large windows of opaque glass, and windows of that sort are not usually placed, in buildings of this size, at a man's height. So even if a window had been open, it would have been impossible for the unfortunate man to lean out and lose his balance; thus suicide would have been the only conceivable explanation. In which case you would not have allowed him to be buried in consecrated ground. But since you gave him Christian burial, the windows must have been closed. And if they were closed – for I have never encountered, not even in witchcraft trials, a dead man whom God or the Devil allowed to climb up from the abyss to erase the evidence of his misdeed – then obviously the presumed suicide was, on the contrary, pushed, either by human hand or by diabolical force. And you are wondering who was capable, I will not say of pushing him into the abyss, but of hoisting him to the sill; and you are distressed because an evil force, whether natural or supernatural, is at work in the abbey.'

'That is it . . .' the abbot said, and it was not clear whether he was confirming William's words or accepting the reasons William had so admirably and reasonably expounded. 'But how can you know there was no water at the foot of any window?'

'Because you told me a south wind was blowing, and the water could not be driven against windows that open to the east.'

'They had not told me enough about your talents,' the abbot said. 'And you are right, there was no water, and now I know why. It was all as you say. And now you understand my anxiety. It would already be serious enough if one of my monks had stained his soul with the hateful sin of suicide. But I have reason to think that another of them has stained himself with an equally terrible sin. And if that were all . . .'

'In the first place, why one of the monks? In the abbey there are many other persons, grooms, goatherds, servants . . .'

'To be sure, the abbey is small but rich,' the abbot agreed smugly. 'One hundred fifty servants for sixty monks. But

---

Dr Tenison communicating to me his intention of Erecting a Library in St Martines parish, for the publique use, desird my assistance with Sir Chr: Wren about the placing and structure thereof: a worthy and laudable designe; He told me there were 30 or 40 Young Men in Orders in his Parish, either, Governors to young Gent: or Chaplains to Noble-

everything happened in the Aedificium. There, as perhaps you already know, although on the ground floor are the kitchen and the refectory, on the two upper floors are the scriptorium and the library. After the evening meal the Aedificium is locked, and a very strict rule forbids anyone to enter.' He guessed William's next question and added at once, though clearly with reluctance, 'Including, naturally, the monks, but . . .'

'But?'

'But I reject absolutely – absolutely, you understand – the possibility that a servant would have had the courage to enter there at night.' There was a kind of defiant smile in his eyes, albeit brief as a flash, or a falling star. 'Let us say they would have been afraid, you know . . . sometimes orders given to the simple-minded have to be reinforced with a threat, a suggestion that something terrible will happen to the disobedient, perforce something supernatural. A monk, on the contrary . . .'

'I understand.'

'Furthermore, a monk could have other reasons for venturing into a forbidden place. I mean reasons that are . . . reasonable, even if contrary to the rule . . .'

William noticed the abbot's uneasiness and asked a question perhaps intended to change the subject, though it produced an even greater uneasiness.

'Speaking of a possible murder, you said, "And if that were all." What did you mean?'

'Did I say that? Well, no one commits murder without a reason, however perverse. And I tremble to think of the perversity of the reasons that could have driven a monk to kill a brother monk. There. That is it.'

'Nothing else?'

'Nothing else that I can say to you.'

'You mean that there is nothing else you have the power to say?'

'Please, Brother William, Brother William', and the abbot underlined 'Brother' both times.

William blushed violently and remarked, 'Eris sacerdos in aeternum.'

'Thank you,' the abbot said.

O Lord God, what a terrible mystery my imprudent superiors were broaching at that moment, the one driven by anxiety and the other by curiosity. Because, a novice approaching the mysteries of the holy priesthood of God, humble youth that I was, I, too, understood that the abbot knew something but had learned it

---

men, who being reprov'd by him on occasion, for frequenting Taverns or Coffe-houses, told him, they would study and employ their time better, if they had books. This put the pious Doctor upon this designe, which I could not but approve of, and indeede a great reproch it is, that so great a Citty as Lond: should have never a publique Library

under the seal of confession. He must have heard from someone's lips a sinful detail that could have a bearing on the tragic end of Adelmo. Perhaps for this reason he was begging Brother William to uncover a secret he himself suspected, though he was unable to reveal to anyone – and he hoped that my master, with the powers of his intellect, would cast light on – what he, the abbot, had to shroud in shadows because of the sublime law of charity.

'Very well,' William said then, 'may I question the monks?'

'You may.'

'May I move freely about the abbey?'

'I grant you that power.'

'Will you assign me this mission coram monachis?'

'This very evening.'

'I shall begin, however, today, before the monks know what you have charged me to do. Besides, I already had a great desire – not the least reason for my sojourn here – to visit your library, which is spoken of with admiration in all the abbeys of Christendom.'

The abbot rose, almost starting, with a very tense face. 'You can move freely through the whole abbey, as I have said. But not, to be sure, on the top floor of the Aedificium, the library.'

'Why not?'

'I would have explained to you before, but I thought you knew. You see, our library is not like others . . .'

'I know it has more books than any other Christian library. I know that in comparison with your cases, those of Bobbio or Pomposa, of Cluny or Fleury, seem the room of a boy barely being introduced to the abacus. I know that the six thousand codices that were the boast of Novalesa a hundred or more years ago are few compared to yours, and perhaps many of those are now here. I know your abbey is the only light that Christianity can oppose to the thirty-six libraries of Baghdad, to the ten thousand codices of the Vizir Ibn al-Alkami, that the number of your Bibles equals the two thousand four hundred Korans that are the pride of Cairo, and that the reality of your cases is luminous evidence against the proud legend of the infidels who years ago claimed (intimates as they are of the Prince of Falsehood) the library of Tripoli was rich in six million volumes and inhabited by eighty thousand commentators and two hundred scribes.'

'You are right, heaven be praised.'

'I know that many of the monks living in your midst come from other abbeys scattered all over the world. Some stay here a short

---

becoming it: There ought to be one at St Paules, the West end of that Church, (if ever finish'd) would be a convenient place . . .

John Evelyn, *Diary*, 13 February (1684)

time, to copy manuscripts to be found nowhere else and to carry them back then to their own house, not without having brought you in exchange some other unavailable manuscript that you will copy and add to your treasure; and others stay for a very long time, occasionally remaining here till death, because only here can they find the works that enlighten their research. And so you have among you Germans, Dacians, Spaniards, Frenchmen, Greeks. I know that the Emperor Frederick, many and many years ago, asked you to compile for him a book of the prophecies of Merlin and then to translate it into Arabic, to be sent as a gift to the Sultan of Egypt. I know, finally, that such a glorious abbey as Murbach in these very sad times no longer has a single scribe, that at St Gall only a few monks are left who know how to write, that now in the cities corporations and guilds arise, made up of laymen who work for the universities, and only your abbey day after day renews, or – what am I saying? – it exalts to ever greater heights the glories of your order . . .'

'Monasterium sine libris,' the abbot recited, pensively, 'est sicut civitas sine opibus, castrum sine numeris, coquina sine suppellec- tili, mensa sine cibis, hortus sine herbis, pratum sine floribus, arbor sine foliis . . . And our order, growing up under the double command of work and prayer, was light to the whole known world, depository of knowledge, salvation of an ancient learning that threatened to disappear in fires, sacks, earthquakes, forge of new writing and increase of the ancient . . . Oh, as you well know, we live now in very dark times, and I blush to tell you that not many years ago the Council of Vienne had to reaffirm that every monk is under obligation to take orders . . . How many of our abbeys, which two hundred years ago were resplendent with grandeur and sanctity, are now the refuge of the slothful? The order is still powerful, but the stink of the cities is encroaching upon our holy places, the people of God are now inclined to commerce and wars of faction; down below in the great settlements, where the spirit of sanctity can find no lodging, not only do they speak (of laymen, nothing else could be expected) in the vulgar tongue, but they are already writing it in, though none of these volumes will ever come within our walls – fomenter of heresies as those volumes inevitably become! Because of man- kind's sins the world is teetering on the brink of the abyss, permeated by the very abyss that the abyss invokes. And tomorrow, as Honorius would have it, men's bodies will be smaller than ours, just as ours are smaller than those of the

---

In the library of a young prince, the solemn folios are not much rumpled; books of a lighter digestion have the dog's ears.

Charles Montagu Halifax (1661–1715)

ancients. Mundus senescit. If God has now given our order a mission, it is to oppose this race to the abyss, by preserving, repeating, and defending the treasure of wisdom our fathers entrusted to us. Divine Providence has ordered that the universal government, which at the beginning of the world was in the East, should gradually, as the time was nearing fulfilment, move westward to warn us that the end of the world is approaching, because the course of events has already reached the confines of the universe. But until the millennium occurs definitively, until the triumph, however brief, of the foul beast that is the Antichrist, it is up to us to defend the treasure of the Christian world, and the very word of God. as he dictated it to the prophets and to the apostles, as the fathers repeated it without changing a syllable, as the schools have tried to gloss it, even if today in the schools themselves the serpent of pride, envy, folly, is nesting. In this sunset we are still torches and light, high on the horizon. And as long as these walls stand, we shall be the custodians of the divine Word.'

'Amen,' William said in a devout tone. 'But what does this have to do with the fact that the library may not be visited?'

'You see, Brother William,' the abbot said, 'to achieve the immense and holy task that enriches those walls' – and he nodded toward the bulk of the Aedificium, which could be glimpsed from the cell's windows, towering above the abbatial church itself – 'devout men have toiled for centuries, observing iron rules. The library was laid out on a plan which has remained obscure to all over the centuries, and which none of the monks is called upon to know. Only the librarian has received the secret, from the librarian who preceded him, and he communicates it, while still alive, to the assistant librarian, so that death will not take him by surprise and rob the community of that knowledge. And the secret seals the lips of both men. Only the librarian has, in addition to that knowledge, the right to move through the labyrinth of the books, he alone knows where to find them and where to replace them, he alone is responsible for their safekeeping. The other monks work in the scriptorium and many know the list of the volumes that the library houses. But a list of titles often tells very little; only the librarian knows, from the collocation of the volume, from its degree of inaccessibility, what secrets, what truths or falsehoods, the volume contains. Only he decided how, when, and whether to give it to the monk who requests it; sometimes he first consults me. Because not all truths are for all ears, not all falsehoods can be recognised as such by a pious soul; and the monks, finally, are in the scriptorium

---

Unlearned men of books assume the care,
As eunuchs are the guardians of the fair.
Edward Young, *The Love of Fame* (1728)

to carry out a precise task, which requires them to read certain volumes and not others, and not to pursue every foolish curiosity that seizes them, whether through weakness of intellect or through pride or through diabolical prompting.'

'So in the library there are also books containing falsehoods . . .'

'Monsters exist because they are part of the divine plan, and in the horrible features of those same monsters the power of the Creator is revealed. And by divine plan, too, there exist also books by wizards, the cabalas of the Jews, the fables of pagan poets, the lies of the infidels. It was the firm and holy conviction of those who founded the abbey and sustained it over the centuries that even in books of falsehood, to the eyes of the sage reader, a pale reflection of the divine wisdom can shine. And therefore the library is a vessel of these, too. But for this very reason, you understand, it cannot be visited by just anyone. And furthermore,' the abbot added, as if to apologise for the weakness of this last argument, 'a book is a fragile creature, it suffers the wear of time, it fears rodents, the elements, clumsy hands. If for a hundred and a hundred years everyone had been able freely to handle our codices, the majority of them would no longer exist. So the librarian protects them not only against mankind but also against nature, and devotes his life to this war with the forces of oblivion, the enemy of truth.'

'And so no one, except for two people, enters the top floor of the Aedificium . . .'

The abbot smiled. 'No one should. No one can. No one, even if he wished, would succeed. The library defends itself, immeasurable as the truth it houses, deceitful as the falsehood it preserves. A spiritual labyrinth, it is also a terrestrial labyrinth. You might enter and you might not emerge. And having said this, I would like you to conform to the rules of the abbey.'

'But you have not dismissed the possibility that Adelmo fell from one of the windows of the library. And how can I study his death if I do not see the place where the story of his death may have begun?'

'Brother William,' the abbot said, in a conciliatory tone, 'a man who described my horse Brunellus without seeing him, and the death of Adelmo though knowing virtually nothing of it, will have no difficulty studying places to which he does not have access.'

William bowed. 'You are wise also when you are severe. It shall be as you wish.'

The Name of the Rose (Secker and Warburg, 1983)

Twenty-two acknowledged concubines, and a library of sixty-two thousand volumes attested the variety of his inclinations; and from the productions which he left behind him, it appears that both the one and the other were

What the Public Paid to Read in 1838

Novels by Walter Scott, and Novels in imitation of him; Galt, etc.	166
Novels by Theodore Hook, Lytton Bulwer, etc.	41
Novels by Captain Marryat, Cooper, Washington Irving, etc.	115
Voyages, Travels, History, and Biography	136
Novels by Miss Edgeworth, and Moral and Religious Novels	49
Works of a Good Character, Dr Johnson, Goldsmith, etc.	27
Romances, Castle of Otranto, etc.	76
Fashionable Novels, well known	439
Novels of the lowest character, being chiefly imitations of Fashionable Novels, containing no good, although probably nothing decidedly bad	1008
Miscellaneous Old Books, Newgate Calendar, etc.	86
Lord Byron's Works, Smollett's do., Fielding's do., Gil Blas, etc.	39
Books decidedly bad	10

From a list compiled by the London Statistical Society from a survey of ten circulating libraries in three Westminster parishes. Richard Altick: *The English Common Reader* (Chicago University Press, 1957)

---

designed for use rather than for ostentation.
Edward Gibbon, of the Emperor Gordian the Younger,
The Decline and Fall of the Roman Empire (1776–88)

M. D. O'BRIEN

God-Sends to the Town Loafer

The enormous amount of light reading indulged in by the frequenters of Free Libraries leads us to expect that these places are largely used by well-to-do and other idlers. And that is exactly what we find. Free Libraries are perfect 'god-sends' to the town loafer, who finds himself housed and amused at the public expense, and may lounge away his time among the intellectual luxuries which his neighbours are taxed to provide for him. Says Mr Mullins, the Birmingham librarian, 'No delicacy seemed to deter the poor tramp from using, not only the news-room, but the best seats in the reference library *for a snooze*. Already the Committee had to complain of the use of the room for *betting*, and for the transaction of various businesses, and the exhibition of samples, writing out of orders, and other pursuits more suited to the commercial room of a hotel.' And referring to another Free Library, the same authority continues: 'In the Picton Room of the Liverpool Library, alcoves were once provided with small tables, on which were pens, ink, etc., but it was found that pupils were received in them by tutors, and much private letter-writing was done therein; so that when a respectable thief took away £20 worth of books they were closed.'

After the nonsense usually indulged in by the officials of library pauperism such candour as this is positively refreshing. It is seldom the high priest allows us to look behind the curtain in this fashion. As a rule, the admission is much less direct, and can only be gathered from a careful analysis of the statistics. According to the Bristol Report for last year, there were 416,418 borrowers during the twelve months preceding 31 December 1889: of these 148,992 are described as having 'no occupation'. At the same town, in the years 1887–8, there were 641 who, according to the report, were without any occupation, out of a total of 1481. According to the annual report of the Leamington Free Public Library for 1888–9, 187 made a return 'no occupation' out of a total of 282 applicants. In the Yarmouth Report for the same year, out of a total of 3085

A man might as well turn his daughter loose in Covent-Garden, as trust the cultivation of her mind to A CIRCULA-TION LIBRARY.

George Colman the Elder, *Polly Honeycombe* (1760)

new borrowers, 1044 are described as of 'no occupation'; the
report for the previous year states the proportion as follows: total
of borrowers, 2813; 'no occupation', 1078; in the year before the
total was 3401; 'no occupation', 1368.

Some reports give a fuller analysis of the different classes of
people who use the libraries to which they refer. In the Wigan
Report for last year we are told that 13,336 people made use of the
reference library in that town during 1889–90. The largest items of
this amount are given as follows: solicitors, 1214; clergy, 903;
clerks and bookkeepers, 1521; colliers, 961; schoolmasters and
teachers, 801; architects and surveyors, 418; engineers, 490;
enginemen, 438. At Newcastle-on-Tyne, last year, there were
11,620 persons who used the reference library, and only 3949 of
these were of 'no occupation'. Yet, notwithstanding the numerical
weakness of the latter, they managed to consult nearly half the
books that were consulted that year. The total number consulted
was 316,000; and 16,800 were used by people, who had 'no
occupation'. And this is legislation for the Working Classes!

Free Libraries, in *A Plea for Liberty*,
Edited by Thomas Mackay (John Murray, 1892)

In order to check the previous excessive concourse in the
best manner possible, anybody who wants to inspect a
book has to apply to the librarian who then will show and, if
need be, even allow him to read it.

Librarian of Gotha (1774)

LADY JANETTA MANNERS

What Women Should Read

In free libraries women can share the advantages of the books; and it has been found desirable to have some works specially intended for women who wish to be really helpful to their husbands and their families. I name a few: Mrs Valentine's *Domestic Economy*; *Enquire Within upon Everything*; Miss Nightingale's *Notes on Nursing*; Miss Octavia Hill's *Homes of the London Poor*; Lady Hope's *Our Coffee Room*; Miss Weston's *Our Blue-Jackets*; *The Early Choice*, a book for daughters; *Friendly Words for Our Girls*, by Lady Baker; *Thoughts for Young Women in Business* by Mrs W.H. Wigley. I must strongly recommend this most useful little book to the attention of shop-assistants; it is published by Messrs Hatchard, contains advice applicable to all young women; so do *Letters to Young Woman*, by J.M. Carr. *Common-Sense for Housemaids*, by Jane Tytler, is a really diverting and practical book (mistresses and maids ought to read it). *An Old Mother's Letter to Young Women*, by Mrs Bayley, is valuable; and so is her *Letter on Temperance Work*, addressed to our serving friends. *Lectures on Health*, by Caroline Hallett, may be bought for a shilling, and will save the purchaser many pounds, if understood. The Girls' Friendly Society papers should be placed in the room; Warne's *Cookery Book for the Million* contains two hundred useful recipes, and its cost is twopence; *Cooking Recipes for the Million*, published by the Ladies' Sanitary Society, are very good. The *Life of Princess Alice*, if it comes into a cheap edition, would be most suitable; for it would show many busy, harassed women that their Queen's daughter washed for her children, nursed them devotedly, and found time to care for the sick and needy, while managing her household and cultivating her mind.

Free Libraries, in *A Plea for Liberty*,
Edited by Thomas Mackay (John Murray, 1892)

On Wednesday, April 3, in the morning I found him very busy putting his books in order, and as they were generally very old ones, clouds of dust were flying around him. He had on a large pair of gloves, such as hedgers use. His present appearance put me in mind of my uncle, Dr Boswell's

LADY JANETTA MANNERS

Why Men Should Be Allowed Out of the House

It has been urged that the existence of reading-rooms might draw men from their homes. To this objection I reply that, in very many places where reading-rooms have been established, the wives of the working men frequenting them have expressed their great satisfaction that they should have such resorts. When it is remembered that in a poor man's cottage one or two rooms serve for cooking, sleeping, washing, eating, and nursing the children, it will be conceded that a quiet hour for reading cannot very often be secured at home; and for the unmarried men who have no home, how doubly useful must the reading-room be.

Under Italian skies much enjoyment may be had in the open air in the evening; but there are many weeks in our year when we should like to lounge about, after a hard day's work, in the misty, rainy, or blustery evening? The public-house is often the only one to which the men are welcome. Even the most affectionate fathers and brothers in well-appointed 'rich men's dwellings', occasionally find the pattering of little feet and the ceaseless babbling of children, varied by occasional shrieks, roars, or wailing, rather jarring to the nerves. How thankful the mother of, say, three or four great boys, two girls of ten or twelve, and two or three small children, living in two rooms, must be if the boys can leave it for a comfortable reading-room, where they will not find temptations to drink. Colonel Fane, of Fullbeck, Grantham, has a night-school for the village lads, and occasionally social evenings for them. The lads are only too eager to avail themselves of opportunities given them to learn.

Some of the Advantages of Easily Accessible Reading and Recreation Rooms and Free Libraries (Wm Blackwood, 1885)

---

description of him, 'A robust genius, born to grapple with whole libraries.'

James Boswell, *Life of Johnson* (1776)

PHILIP LARKIN

Single-Handed and Untrained

In autumn 1943 the Ministry of Labour wrote to ask what I was doing. I could have answered that, having finished with the university and English literature, I was living at home writing a novel, but I rightly judged the enquiry to be a warning that I had better start doing something. Picking up the day's *Birmingham Post* (the paper we took in those days), I soon discovered an advertisement by a small urban district council for a librarian. The salary was £175 per annum (plus cost-of-living bonus, Whitley Scale, of £45 10s for men, £36 8s for women), and the duties included 'those usual to the operation of a Lending Library (open access), and Reading Room supervision'.

Recourse to a gazetteer revealed that the town was about twelve miles from a school where a college friend of mine had recently taken a job as a temporary assistant master and was also writing a novel. This seemed a good omen, and I applied. In due course I was asked to attend for interview, and it occurred to me I had better find out something about the operation of a lending library (open access). A friendly senior assistant at the local one was kind enough to spend a morning showing me how books were ordered, accessioned and catalogued, and then given little pockets with individual tickets in them that were slipped into borrowers' cards when the book was lent. 'Come back tomorrow,' she said, 'and I'll tell you about inter-library loans.'

My father, with remote amusement, handed me a green-covered report that had come out in the previous year entitled *The Public Library System of Great Britain*, and I took it with me in the train on 13 November, the day of the interview. Rain smashed against the carriage windows as I read the author's summary dismissals of sample libraries serving populations between 20,000 and 30,000: 'Old buildings, drab stocks and bad traditions of support . . . antiquated methods include a really filthy indicator [what was that?] . . . the reference library consists of two small cases of quite useless items. . . .' The account of library 'I' seemed particularly

---

The Bibliomania, or the collecting of an enormous heap of literature without intelligent curiosity, has, since libraries have existed, infected weak minds, who imagine that they themselves acquire knowledge when they keep it on their shelves. Their motley libraries have been called the *mad-houses of the human mind*; and again, the *tombs of books*,

intimidating: 'the children's books are much dirtier even than those provided for the adults. There is no proper counter; the single-handed librarian is untrained.' I fancied that the authority to which I had applied was in a smaller population category than this: would its library be worse? Certainly its potential librarian looked like being single-handed, and could hardly have been more untrained.

Mr McColvin, the author of the trenchant sentences just quoted, would not in all probability have been much kinder about it. The council had adopted the Library Acts, and built a library to celebrate the coronation of Edward VII. It was a simple two-storey building, with a reading room and a boiler room on the ground floor and a lending library, with a rudimentary office-cum-reference room, upstairs; its handsome stone façade was inscribed PUBLIC LIBRARY and recorded why it was erected and when (I think the date was 1903). A librarian-caretaker, son of a failed Wolverhampton bookseller, was appointed. When I turned up forty years later (for my application was successful), the astonishing thing was that almost nothing had changed. The librarian-caretaker was still there, by now a courtly old gentleman of at least seventy, who wore a hat indoors and uttered from time to time an absent-minded blowing noise, like a distant trombone. For many years he had washed the floors and lighted the boiler every morning in addition to his professional duties, and may have done so to the end. After leaving he never used the library, and I saw him only once again; he called when it was shut ('Anyone in? It's only the old blackguard'), and we chatted, mostly about his inadequate pension and his funeral arrangements ('I've told the wife to stay at home and drink whisky'). I wondered uneasily if my life would be anything like this.

In 1903 the library had, of course, been closed access; in the Thirties an effort had been made to modernise its methods, opening the doors to readers and constructing an issue desk. There had even been purchased a copy of the current edition of Dewey. Otherwise it remained antiquated. The boiler (which I had to stoke, if not light) did little to heat the radiators, which were in any case poorly placed; the real warmth of the building came from the gas lights, that had to be illumined with long tapers that dropped wax over the floors, and even on myself until I learned how to handle them. There was no telephone. The stock amounted to about 4,000 books, 3,000 of which were fiction and the rest non-fiction and juvenile (the admission of children had been a severe

---

when the possessor will not communicate them, and coffins them up in the cases of his library – and it was facetiously observed, these collections are not without a *Lock on Human Understanding*.
Isaac D'Israeli, *Curiosities of Literature* (1791–1834)

blow to my predecessor). The shelves were high, but even so layers of long-withdrawn books, thick with dust, were piled on top of them. I wish I had taken more detailed notes both of them and of the current stock: in all, it was like the advertisement pages of late nineteenth- and early twentieth-century novels come to life. A substantial body of the readers were elderly people, who found the stairs difficult, but were still prepared to face them for Mrs Henry Wood, Florence L. Barclay, Silas K. Hocking, Rosa M. Carey and many others. The rest were either children or hopeful adults, some of them strangers to the town and used to better things.

My day began with collecting the day's papers and journals and setting them out in the reading room in time to open its doors at 9 a.m. Then I retreated to the closed lending department and dealt with the post, such as it was, making out applications for inter-library loans and parcelling up volumes to be returned (the post office was, fortunately, directly opposite). From then until 3 p.m., when the first of the two-hour lending-library 'operations' began, my time was my own; landladies did not really want to provide fires in the morning, and I wrote my novel in the library before taking it back with me to work at after lunch. After another session from 6 to 8 p.m. I finished reshelving and sorted the issue in time to close the reading room at 8.30 p.m. It was a long day, and in some respects a tiring one. Quite early on I recorded a week when I issued 928 books in 20 hours, or one about every 77 seconds – not much, perhaps, but an equal number had to be reshelved, and some of the shelves could be reached only by ladder. At first my hand was blistered from stamping books.

It was clear that the premises, stock and staff of the library were totally inadequate for the potential, or even actual, demands of its readers. At the same time it was difficult to know what to do about it – difficult, because I really had no idea of how to come to grips with the council in order to, for instance, appoint a couple of assistants, double or treble the book grant (I don't think, in fact, that there was one), create a catalogue, modernise the building and so on, and even if I had there would have been, in the middle of the war, no money to do so. My committee, however, was sympathetic, chaired by a friendly and forward-looking headmaster, and they did what they could. New books began to appear on the shelves (I heard that I was 'filling the Library with dirty books' – not in the McColvin sense, but with Lawrence, Forster, Joyce, Isherwood, *et al.*), and after a year and three-quarters I got an assistant, enabling

When circulating libraries were first opened the booksellers were much alarmed, and their rapid increase, added to their fears, had led them to think that the sale of books would be much diminished by such libraries. But experience has proved that the sale of books, so far from being diminished

the lending library to 'operate' in the mornings. Readership increased to about twice the original number. Issues did likewise, from 3,000 to 6,000 a month. A most dramatic increase was in inter-library loans, from 68 in the year I came to 499 in the year I left: these were chiefly to sixth formers, and those readers with precise interests and courses of study. Most of the books came from the huge and generous Birmingham City Libraries, at that time presided over by H. M. Cashmore, surely one of the most indefatigable correspondents among chief librarians. Hardly a day passed when I did not receive a letter signed by him correcting me about the details of an application, or pointing out that a parcel had' been badly tied. Other librarians I met later confirmed this experience.

The library should, of course, have been absorbed into the county system, and the county was anxious to do this: it already sent us a consignment of perhaps 300 books that was changed every few months, and these alone kept readers from complete apathy. Since the council could not be compulsorily taken over, and there was enough local patriotism to believe that with 'the new young man' a proper library service could be offered. Of course improvements took place: almost anything one did was an improvement (one of my early reports states 'the library has joined the official waiting list for *The Times Literary* and *Educational Supplements*'), and readers responded so eagerly in those book-hungry days that I could never stop trying, but in fact little could be done compared with what was needed. I consoled myself with my novel (having finished the first, I had begun a second), and started a correspondence course for Library Association qualifications.

My appointment there lasted two and three-quarter years. About three years after I left, the council did, in fact, surrender its powers, and 'my' Library became a county branch. Subsequently it was remodelled and enlarged, and in 1962 became a headquarters; to my surprise, I was asked to open it. Usually I avoid such undertakings, but the implication that I was not regarded by those concerned as an unfortunate episode best forgotten was so gratifying that I gladly accepted. The architect had done his work well, so that it was impossible to see where the boiler room had been, or the poky stairs, or the cobwebbed and dingy lavatory, on the wall of which my aged predecessor had pencilled a series of dates, a reference to a brand of pills, and a name that looked like 'Marley Mount'. Split-level and splendid, the library now had

by them, has been greatly promoted, as from those repositories many thousand families have been cheaply supplied with books, by which the taste of reading has become much more general, and thousands of books are purchased every year by such as have first borrowed them

proper staff quarters, a record-listening room, a separate children's library and an electric book lift.

As I listened to the other speakers (my old chairman among them, still in office), I wondered what I had done to justify my presence at the ceremony. I had achieved nothing lasting: union with the county system had been delayed only a few years, and it might be said that I had made it inevitable. I found myself thinking of individual readers: the boy I had introduced to the Sherlock Holmes stories, the old lady who sent a messenger for her books and whose final note I still have: 'Owing to failing sight, I have decided no longer to be a Member of the "Free Library". Please accept of my grateful thanks for kindness choosing books for me during the past years . . .' and others, such as the lady who gave me ten 'Cogent' cigarettes at Christmas (product of the Scottish Co-operative Wholesale Society). I thought, too, of the know-ledgeable 'graduate trainees' of today, with their year in a university library followed by a year at library school, and wondered further if there were any libraries left as backward as this one had been, or any librarians as unqualified as myself when appointed to it. If not, as seemed probable, this was no doubt the most comforting reflection available.

Required Writing (Faber, 1982)

at those libraries, and after reading, approving of them, becoming purchasers.

James Lackington (1746–1815)

BOOK BLIGHT

Bibliomania is a disease like any other and those caught in its grip can seriously damage their bank balance. To be like Elias Canetti's Doctor Kien, a man so consumed with the desire to possess books that he dare not go out while the bookshops are still open, is to be in a very bad way, because once you've started to build a library you can never stop; no library is ever complete.

Anyone who owns more than a shelf or two of books knows that the rest of the population thinks he's a bit peculiar. 'Have you read all these books,' say some. The less polite tackle the problem head on: 'Why do you need all these books?'

It is not a question that is easily answered for it's true of the book collector that one book leads to another, and one doesn't have time to read everything. Even those who try to keep their libraries subject specific find themselves straying into areas common sense tells them it is better to avoid. Thus those who would have only football books in their library find themselves confronting the dilemma of whether or not they ought to admit Peter Handke's novel *The Goalkeeper's Fear of the Penalty*.

Gutenberg is directly to blame for the disease, for he was its first carrier. The invention of moveable type made a private library feasible for the first time in history. Before him a library was the preserve of men of wealth and learning who in the fifteenth and sixteenth centuries still stood a chance of containing the record of world knowledge under their own roofs. But as presses proliferated and book production rose from a few hundred volumes per decade to a few thousand it was clear that even the most avaricious collector must have some gaps on his shelves. In the eighteenth century the library of the landed gentry became a feature, in which ignorant aristocrats bought books by the shelf-load from furniture suppliers. The books, in well-polished leather, did indeed furnish rooms even if only a few of the pages were cut.

What a pity then that Myles na Gopaleen's book-handling service had not been on the go in those days; what status it would have conferred on those who took advantage of it. But there are pitfalls. As Myles was well aware, because a book looks well used it doesn't necessarily mean that it has been read. Is there anything worse than being confronted by an author, like Garrison Keillor's Dusty Pages, and being asked what one thought of his books?

ELIAS CANETTI

The Morning Walk

Professor Peter Kien, a tall, emaciated figure, man of learning and specialist in sinology, replaced the Chinese book in the tightly packed brief-case which he carried under his arm, carefully closed it and watched the clever little boy out of sight. By nature morose and sparing of his words, he was already reproaching himself for a conversation into which he had entered for no compelling reason.

It was his custom on his morning walk, between seven and eight o'clock, to look into the windows of every bookshop which he passed. He was thus able to assure himself, with a kind of pleasure, that smut and trash were daily gaining ground. He himself was the owner of the most important private library in the whole of this great city. He carried a minute portion of it with him wherever he went. His passion for it, the only one which he had permitted himself during a life of austere and exacting study, moved him to take special precautions. Books, even bad ones, tempted him easily into making a purchase. Fortunately the greater number of the bookshops did not open until after eight o'clock. Sometimes an apprentice, anxious to earn his chief's approbation, would come earlier and wait on the doorstep for the first employee whom he would ceremoniously relieve of the latch key. 'I've been waiting since seven o'clock,' he would exclaim, or 'I can't get in!' So much zeal communicated itself all too easily to Kien; with an effort he would master the impulse to follow the apprentice immediately into the shop. Among the proprietors of smaller shops there were one or two early risers, who might be seen busying themselves behind their open doors from half-past seven onwards. Defying these temptations, Kien tapped his own well-filled brief-case. He clasped it tightly to him, in a very particular manner which he had himself thought out, so that the greatest possible area of his body was always in contact with it. Even his ribs could feel its presence through his cheap, thin suit. His upper arm covered the whole side elevation; it fitted exactly. The lower portion of his arm supported the case from below. His outstretched fingers splayed out over

---

Sir: I have duly received your favor of Apr. 26, in which you are pleased to ask my opinion on the subject of the arrangement of libraries. I will communicate with pleasure what occurs to me on it. Two methods offer themselves. The one alphabetical, the other according to the subject of

every part of the flat surface to which they yearned. He privately excused himself for this exaggerated care because of the value of the contents. Should the brief-case by any mischance fall to the ground, or should the lock, which he tested every morning before setting out, spring open at precisely that perilous moment, ruin would come to his priceless volume. There was nothing he loathed more intensely than battered books.

Today, when he was standing in front of a bookshop on his way home, a little boy had stepped suddenly between him and the window. Kien felt affronted by the impertinence. True, there was room enough between him and the window. He always stood about three feet away from the glass; but he could easily read every letter behind it. His eyes functioned to his entire satisfaction: a fact notable enough in a man of forty who sat, day in day out, over books and manuscripts. Morning after morning his eyes informed him how well they did. By keeping his distance from these venal and common books, he showed his contempt for them, contempt which, when he compared them with the dry and ponderous tomes of his library, they richly deserved. The boy was quite small, Kien exceptionally tall. He could easily see over his head. All the same he felt he had a right to greater respect. Before administering a reprimand, however, he drew to one side in order to observe him further. The child stared hard at the titles of the books and moved his lips slowly and in silence. Without a stop his eyes slipped from one volume to the next. Every minute or two he looked back over his shoulder. On the opposite side of the street, over a watchmaker's shop, hung a gigantic clock. It was twenty minutes to eight. Evidently the little fellow was afraid of missing something important. He took no notice whatever of the gentleman standing behind him. Perhaps he was practising his reading. Perhaps he was learning the names of the books by heart. He devoted equal attention to each in turn. You could see at once when anything held up his reading for a second.

Kien felt sorry for him. Here was he, spoiling with this depraved fare an eager spiritual appetite, perhaps already hungry for the written words. How many a worthless book might he not come to read in later life for no better reason than an early familiarity with its title? By what means is the suggestibility of these early years to be reduced? No sooner can a child walk and make out his letters than he is surrendered at mercy to the hard pavement of any ill-built street, and to the wares of any wretched tradesman who, the devil knows why, has set himself up as a dealer in books. Young

---

the book. The former is very unsatisfactory, because of the medley it presents to the mind, the difficulty sometimes of recollecting an author's name, and the greater difficulty, where the name is not given, of selecting the word in the title which shall determine its alphabetical place. The

children ought to be brought up in some important private library. Daily conversation with none but serious minds, an atmosphere at once dim, hushed and intellectual, a relentless training in the most careful ordering both of time and of space – what surroundings could be more suitable to assist these delicate creatures through the years of childhood? But the only person in this town who possessed a library which could be taken at all seriously was he, Kien, himself. He could not admit children. His work allowed him no such diversions. Children make a noise. They have to be constantly looked after. Their welfare demands the services of a woman. For cooking, an ordinary housekeeper is good enough. For children, it would be necessary to engage a mother. If a mother could be content to be nothing but a mother: but where would you find one who would be satisfied with that particular part alone? Each is a specialist first and foremost as a woman, and would make demands which an honest man of learning would not ever dream of fulfilling. Kien repudiated the idea of a wife. Women had been a matter of indifference to him until this moment; a matter of indifference they would remain. The boy with the fixed eyes and the moving head would be the loser.

Pity had moved him to break his usual custom and speak to him. He would gladly have bought himself free of the prickings of his pedagogic conscience with the gift of a piece of chocolate. Then it appeared that there are nine-year-old children who prefer a book to a piece of chocolate. What followed surprised him even more. The child was interested in China. He read against his father's will. The stories of the difficulties of the Chinese alphabet fascinated instead of frightening him. He recognised the language at first sight, without having seen it before. He had passed an intelligence test with distinction. When shown the book, he had not tried to touch it. Perhaps he was ashamed of his dirty hands. Kien had looked at them: they were clean. Another boy would have snatched the book, even with dirty ones. He was in a hurry – school began at eight – yet he had stayed until the last possible minute. He had fallen upon that invitation like one starving; his father must be a great torment to him. He would have liked best to come on that very afternoon, in the middle of the working day. After all, he lived in the same house.

Kien forgave himself for the conversation. The exception which he had permitted seemed worth while. In his thoughts he saluted the child – now already out of sight – as a rising sinologist. Who indeed took an interest in these remote branches of knowledge?

arrangement according to subject is far preferable, altho' sometimes presenting difficulty also. For it is often doubtful to what particular subject a book should be ascribed. This is remarkably the case with books of travels, which often blend together the geography, natural history, civil history,

Boys played football, adults went to work; they wasted their leisure hours in love. So as to sleep for eight hours and waste eight hours, they were willing to devote themselves for the rest of their time to hateful work. Not only their bellies, their whole bodies had become their gods. The sky God of the Chinese was sterner and more dignified. Even if the little fellow did not come next week, unlikely though that was, he would have a name in his head which he would not easily forget: the philosopher Mong. Occasional collisions unexpectedly encountered determine the direction of a lifetime.

Smiling, Kien continued on his way home. He smiled rarely. Rarely, after all, is it the dearest wish of a man to be the owner of a library. As a child of nine he had longed for a bookshop. Yet the idea that he would walk up and down in it as its proprietor had seemed to him even then blasphemous. A bookseller is a king, and a king cannot be a bookseller. But he was still too little to be a salesman, as for an errand boy – errand boys were always being sent out of the shop. What pleasure would he have of the books, if he was only allowed to carry them as parcels under his arm? For a long while he sought for some way out of the difficulty. One day he did not come home after school. He went into the biggest bookstore in the town, six great show windows all full of books, and began to howl at the top of his voice. 'I want to leave the room, quick, I'm going to have an accident!' he blubbered. They showed him the way at once. He took careful note of it. When he came out again he thanked them and asked if he could not do something to help. His beaming face made them laugh. Only a few moments before it had been screwed up into such comic anguish. They drew him out in conversation; he knew a great deal about books. They thought him sharp for his age. Towards the evening they sent him away with a heavy parcel. He travelled there and back on the tram. He had saved enough pocket money to afford it. Just as the shop was closing – it was already growing dark – he announced that he had completed his errand and put down the receipt on the counter. Someone gave him an acid drop for a reward. While the staff were pulling on their coats he glided noiselessly into the back regions to his lavatory hide-out and bolted himself in. Nobody noticed it; they were all thinking of the free evening before them. He waited a long time. Only after many hours, late at night, did he dare to come out. It was dark in the shop. He felt about for a switch. He had not thought of that by daylight. But when he found it and his hand had already closed

---

agriculture, manufactures, commerce, arts, occupations, manners etc. of a country, so as to render it difficult to say to which they chiefly relate . . .

Thomas Jefferson, *Letter to Mr Watterson*, 7 May 1815

over it, he was afraid to turn on the light. Perhaps someone would see him from the street and haul him off home.

His eyes grew accustomed to the darkness. But he could not read; that was a great pity. He pulled down one volume after another, turned over the pages, contrived to make out many of the names. Later on he scrambled up on to the ladder. He wanted to know if the upper shelves had any secrets to hide. He tumbled off it and said: I haven't hurt myself! The floor is hard. The books are soft. In a bookshop one falls on books. He could have made a castle of books, but he regarded disorder as vulgar and, as he took out each new volume, he replaced the one before. His back hurt. Perhaps he was only tired. At home he would have been asleep long ago. Not here, excitement kept him awake. But his eyes could not even make out the largest titles any more and that annoyed him. He worked out how many years he would be able to spend reading in this shop without ever going out into the street or to that silly school. Why could he not stay here always? He could easily save up to buy himself a small bed. His mother would be afraid. So was he, but only a little, because it was so very quiet. The gas lamps in the street went out. Shadows crept along the walls. So there *were* ghosts. During the night they came flying here and crouched over the books. Then they read. They needed no light, they had such big eyes. Now he would not touch a single book on the upper shelves, nor on the lower ones either. He crept under the counter and his teeth chattered. Ten thousand books and a ghost crouching over each one. That was why it was so quiet. Sometimes he heard them turn over a page. They read as fast as he did himself. He might have grown used to them, but there were ten thousand of them and perhaps one of them would bite. Ghosts get cross if you brush against them, they think you are making fun of them. He made himself as small as possible; they flew over him without touching him. Morning came only after many long nights. Then he fell asleep. He did not hear the assistants opening up the shop. They found him under the counter and shook him awake. First he pretended that he was still asleep, then he suddenly burst out howling. They had locked him in last night, he was afraid of his mother, she must have been looking for him everywhere. The proprietor cross-questioned him and as soon as he had found out his name, sent him off home with one of the shopwalkers. He sent his sincerest apologies to the lady. The little boy had been locked in by mistake, but he seemed to be safe and sound. He assured her of his respectful attention. His mother

---

As to the devotees of the circulating libraries, I dare not compliment their *pass-time*, or rather *kill-time*, with the name of *reading*. Call it rather a sort of beggarly day-dreaming, during which the mind of the dreamer

believed it all and was delighted to have him safely home again. Today the little liar of yesterday was the owner of a famous library and a name no less famous.

Kien abhorred falsehood; from his earliest childhood he had held fast to the truth. He could remember no other falsehood except this. And even this one was hateful to him. Only the conversation with the schoolboy, who had seemed to him the image of his own childhood, had recalled it to him. Forget it, he thought, it is nearly eight o'clock. Punctually at eight his work began, his service for truth. Knowledge and truth were for him identical terms. You draw closer to truth by shutting yourself off from mankind. Daily life was a superficial clatter of lies. Every passer-by was a liar. For that reason he never looked at them. Who among all these bad actors, who made up the mob, had a face to arrest his attention. They changed their faces with every moment; not for one single day did they stick to the same part. He had always known this, experience was superfluous. *His* ambition was to persist stubbornly in the same manner of existence. Not for a mere month, not for a year, but for the whole of his life, he would be true to himself. Character, if you had a character, determined your outward appearance. Ever since he had been able to think, he had been tall and too thin. He knew his face only casually, from its reflection in bookshop windows. He had no mirror in his house, there was no room for it among the books. But he knew that his face was narrow, stern and bony; that was enough.

Since he felt not the slightest desire to notice anyone, he kept his eyes lowered or raised above their heads. He sensed where the bookshops were without looking. He simply relied on instinct. The same force which guides a horse home to the stable, served as well for him. He went out walking to breathe the air of alien books, they aroused his antagonism, they stimulated him. In his library everything went by clockwork. But between seven and eight he allowed himself a few of those liberties which constitute the entire life of other beings.

Although he savoured this hour to the full, he did all by rote. Before crossing a busy street, he hesitated a little. He preferred to walk at a regular pace; so as not to hasten his steps, he waited for a favourable moment to cross. Suddenly he heard someone shouting loudly at someone else: 'Can you tell me where Mut Strasse is?' There was no reply. Kien was surprised; so there were other silent people besides himself to be found in the busy streets. Without looking up he listened for more. How would the questioner

---

furnishes for itself nothing but laziness and a little mawkish sensibility . . .
    Samuel Taylor Coleridge, *Biographia Literaria* (1817)

behave in the face of this silence? 'Excuse me please, could you perhaps tell me where Mut Strasse is?' So; he grew more polite; he had no better luck. The other man still made no reply. 'I don't think you heard me. I'm asking you the way. Will you be so kind as to tell me how I get to Mut Strasse?' Kien's appetite for knowledge was whetted; idle curiosity he did not know. He decided to observe this silent man, on condition of course that he still remained silent. Not a doubt of it, the man was deep in thought and determined to avoid interruption. Still he said nothing. Kien applauded him. Here was one among thousands, a man whose character was proof against all chances. 'Here, are you deaf?' shouted the first man. Now he will have to answer back, thought Kien, and began to lose his pleasure in his protégé. Who can control his tongue when he is insulted? He turned towards the street; the favourable moment for crossing it had come. Astonished at the continued silence, he hesitated. Still the second man said nothing. All the more violent would be the outburst of anger to come. Kien hoped for a fight. If the second man appeared after all to be a mere vulgarian, Kien would be confirmed in his own estimation of himself as the sole and only person of character walking in this street. He was already considering whether he should look round. The incident was taking place on his right hand. The first man was now yelling: 'You've no manners! I spoke to you civil. Who do you think you are? You lout. Are you dumb?' The second man was still silent. 'I demand an apology! Do you hear?' The other did not hear. He rose even higher in the estimation of the listener. 'I'll fetch the police! What do you take me for! You rag and bone man! Call yourself a gentleman! Where did you get those clothes? Out of the rag bag? That's what they look like! What have you got under your arm! I'll show you! Go and boil your head! Who do you think you are?'

Then Kien felt a nasty jolt. Someone had grabbed his brief-case and was pulling at it. With a movement far exceeding his usual effort, he liberated the books from the alien clutch and turned sharply to the right. His glance was directed to his brief-case, but it fell instead on a small fat man who was bawling up at him. 'You lout! You lout! You lout!' The other man, the silent one, the man of character, who controlled his tongue even in anger, was Kien himself. Calmly he turned his back on the gesticulating illiterate. With this small knife, he sliced his clamour in two. A loutish creature whose courtesy changed in so many seconds to insolence had no power to hurt him. Nevertheless he walked along the

---

What a place to be in is an old library! It seems as though the souls of all the writers, that had bequeathed their labours to those Bodleians, were reposing here, as in some dormitory, or middle state. I do not want to handle, to profane the leaves, their winding-sheets. I could as soon dislodge a shade. I seem to inhale learning, walking amid

streets a little faster than was his usual custom. A man who carries books with him must seek to avoid physical violence. He always had books with him.

There is after all no obligation to answer every passing fool according to his folly. The greatest danger which threatens a man of learning, is to lose himself in talk. Kien preferred to express himself in the written rather than the spoken word. He knew more than a dozen oriental languages. A few of the western ones did not even need to be learnt. No branch of human literature was unfamiliar to him. He thought in quotations and wrote in carefully considered sentences. Countless texts owed their restoration to him. When he came to misreadings or imperfections in ancient Chinese, Indian or Japanese manuscripts, as many alternative readings suggested themselves for his selection as he could wish. Other textual critics envied him; he for his part had to guard against a superfluity of ideas. Meticulously cautious, he weighed up the alternatives month after month, was slow to the point of exasperation; applying his severest standards to his own conclusions, he took no decision, on a single letter, a word or an entire sentence, until he was convinced that it was unassailable. The papers which he had hitherto published, few in number, yet each one the starting point for a hundred others, had gained for him the reputation of being the greatest living authority on sinology. They were known in every detail to his colleagues, indeed almost word for word. A sentence once set down by him was decisive and binding. In controversial questions he was the ultimate appeal, the leading authority even in related branches of knowledge. A few only he honoured with his letters. That man, however, whom he chose so to honour would receive in a single letter enough stimuli to set him off on years of study, the results of which – in the view of the mind whence they had sprung – were foregone conclusions. Personally he had no dealings with anyone. He refused all invitations. Whenever any chair of oriental philology fell vacant, it was offered first to him. Polite but contemptuous, he invariably declined.

He had not, he averred, been born to be an orator. Payment for his work would give him a distaste for it. In his own humble opinion, those unproductive populisers to whom instruction in the grammar schools was entrusted, should occupy the university chairs also; then genuine, creative research workers would be able to devote themselves exclusively to their own work. As it was there was no shortage of mediocre intelligences. Should he give

---

their foliage; and the odour of their old moth-scented coverings is fragrant as the first bloom of those sciential apples which grew amid the happy orchard.

Charles Lamb, 'Oxford in the Vacation',
Essays of Elia (1823)

lectures, the high demands which he would necessarily make upon an audience would naturally very much reduce its numbers. As for examinations, not a single candidate, as far as he could see, would be able to pass them. He would make it a point of honour to fail these young immature students at least until their thirtieth year, by which time, either through boredom or through a dawning of real seriousness, they must have learnt something, if only a very little. He regarded the acceptance of candidates whose memories had not been most carefully tested in the lecture halls of the faculty as a totally useless, if not indeed a questionable, practice. Ten students, selected by the most strenuous preliminary tests, would, provided they remained together, achieve far more than they could do when permitted to mingle with a hundred beer-swilling dullards, the general run of university students. His doubts were therefore of the most serious and fundamental nature. He could only request the faculty to withdraw an offer which, although intended no doubt to show the high esteem in which they held him, was not one which he could accept in that spirit . . .

Kien took a private vow that if he should ever be threatened by blindness, he would die of his own free will. Whenever he met a blind man this cruel fear clutched at him. Mutes he loved: the deaf, the lame and other kinds of cripples meant nothing to him; the blind disturbed him. He could not understand why they did not make an end of themselves. Even if they could read braille, their opportunities for reading were limited. Eratosthenes, the great librarian of Alexandria, a scholar of universal significance who flourished in the third century of the pre-Christian era and held sway over more than half a million manuscript scrolls, made in his eightieth year a terrible discovery. His eyes began to refuse their office. He could still see but he could not read. Another man might have waited until he was completely blind. He felt that to take leave of his books was blindness enough. Friends and pupils implored him to stay with them. He smiled wisely, thanked them, and in a few days starved himself to death.

Should the time come this great example could easily be followed even by the lesser Kien, whose library comprised a mere twenty-five thousand volumes.

The remaining distance to his own house he completed at a quickened pace. It must be past eight o'clock. At eight o'clock his work began; unpunctuality caused him acute irritation. Now and again, surreptitiously he felt his eyes. They focused correctly; they felt comfortable and unthreatened.

[Our] libraries have improved the general conversation of the Americans, made the common tradesmen and farmers as intelligent as most gentlemen from other countries, and perhaps have contributed in some degree to the stand so

His library was situated on the fourth and topmost floor of No. 24 Ehrlich Strasse. The door of the flat was secured by three highly complicated locks. He unlocked them, strode across the hall, which contained nothing except an umbrella and coat-stand, and entered his study. Carefully he set down the brief-case on an armchair. Then once and again he paced the entire length of the four lofty, spacious communicating rooms which formed his library. The entire wall-space up to the ceiling was clothed with books. Slowly he lifted his eyes towards them. Skylights had been let into the ceiling. He was proud of his roof-lighting. The windows had been walled up several years before after a determined struggle with his landlord. In this way he had gained in every room a fourth wall-space: accommodation for more books. Moreover illumination from above, which lit up all the shelves equally, seemed to him more just and more suited to his relations with his books. The temptation to watch what went on in the street – an immoral and time-wasting habit – disappeared with the side windows. Daily, before he sat down to his writing desk, he blessed both the idea and its results, since he owed to them the fulfilment of his dearest wish: the possession of a well-stocked library, in perfect order and enclosed on all sides, in which no single superfluous article of furniture, no single superfluous person could lure him from his serious thought.

The first of the four rooms served for his study. A huge old writing desk, an armchair in front of it, a second armchair in the opposite corner were its only furniture. There crouched besides an unobtrusive divan, willingly overlooked by its master: he only slept on it. A movable pair of steps was propped against the wall. It was more important than the divan, and travelled in the course of a day from room to room. The emptiness of the three remaining rooms was not disturbed by so much as a chair. Nowhere did a table, a cupboard, a fireplace interrupt the multi-coloured monotony of the bookshelves. Handsome deep-pile carpets, the uniform covering of the floor, softened the harsh twilight which, mingling through wide-open communicating doors, made of the four separate rooms one single lofty hall.

Kien walked with a stiff and deliberate step. He set his feet down with particular firmness on the carpets; it pleased him that even a footfall such as his waked not the faintest echo. In his library it would have been beyond the power even of an elephant to pound the slightest noise out of that floor. For this reason he set great store by his carpets. He satisfied himself that the books were still in

---

generally made throughout the colonies in defence of their privileges.

Benjamin Franklin, *Autobiography* (1793)

the order in which he had been forced to leave them an hour before. Then he began to relieve his brief-case of its contents. When he came in, it was his habit to lay it down on the chair in front of the writing desk. Otherwise he might perhaps have forgotten it and have sat down to his work before he had tidied away its contents; for at eight o'clock he felt a very strong compulsion to begin his work. With the help of the ladder he distributed the volumes to their appointed places. In spite of all his care – since it was already late, he was hurrying rather more than usual – the last of the books fell from the third bookshelf, a shelf for which he did not even have to use the ladder. It was no other than Mencius beloved above all the rest. 'Idiot!' he shrieked at himself. 'Barbarian! Illiterate!' tenderly lifted the book and went quickly to the door. Before he had reached it an important thought struck him. He turned back and pushed the ladder as softly as he could to the site of the accident. Mencius he laid gently down with both hands on the carpet at the foot of the ladder. Now he could go to the door. He opened it and called into the hall:

'Your best duster, please!'

Almost at once the housekeeper knocked at the door which he had lightly pushed to. He made no answer. She inserted her head modestly through the crack and asked:

'Has something happened?'

'No, give it to me.'

She thought she could detect a complaint in this answer. He had not intended her to. She was too curious to leave the matter where it was. 'Excuse me, Professor!' she said reproachfully, stepped into the room and saw at once what had happened. She glided over to the book. Below her blue starched skirt, which reached to the floor, her feet were invisible. Her head was askew. Her ears were large, flabby and prominent. Since her right ear touched her shoulder and was partly concealed by it, the left looked all the bigger. When she talked or walked her head waggled to and fro. Her shoulders waggled too, in accompaniment. She stooped, lifted up the book and passed the duster over it carefully at least a dozen times. Kien did not attempt to forestall her. Courtesy was abhorrent to him. He stood by and observed whether she performed her work seriously.

'Excuse me, a thing like that can happen, standing up on a ladder.'

Then she handed the book to him, like a plate newly polished. She would very gladly have began a conversation with him. But

---

And now, TWOPENNY TRASH, dear little twopenny trash, go thy ways! Thou hast acted thy part in this great drama. Ten thousand wagon loads of the volumes that fill the libraries and booksellers' shops have never caused a thousandth part of the thinking nor a millionth part of the stir

she did not succeed. He said briefly, 'Thank you' and turned his back on her. She understood and went. She had already placed her hand on the door knob when he turned round suddenly and asked with simulated friendliness:

'Then this has often happened to you?'

She saw through him and was genuinely indignant: 'Excuse me, Professor.' Her 'Excuse me' struck through her unctuous tones, sharp as a thorn. She will give notice, he thought; and to appease her explained himself:

'I only meant to impress on you what these books represent in terms of money.'

She had not been prepared for so affable a speech. She did not know how to reply and left the room pacified. As soon as she had gone, he reproached himself. He had spoken about books like the vilest tradesman. Yet in what other way could he enforce the respectful handling of books on a person of her kind? Their real value would have no meaning for her. She must believe the library was a speculation of his. What people! What people!

He bowed involuntarily in the direction of three Japanese manuscripts, and, at last, sat down at his writing desk.

Auto da Fé (Jonathan Cape, 1946)

that thou hast caused. Thou hast frightened more and greater villains than ever were frightened by the jail and the gibbet. And thou hast created more pleasure and more hope in the breasts of honest men than ever were created by tongue or pen since England was England. When thy stupid,

FLANN O'BRIEN

Buchhandlung

A visit that I paid to the house of a newly-married friend the other day set me thinking. My friend is a man of great wealth and vulgarity. When he had set about buying bedsteads, tables, chairs and what-not, it occurred to him also to buy a library. Whether he can read or not, I do not know, but some savage facility for observation told him that most respectable and estimable people usually had a lot of books in their houses. So he bought several bookcases and paid some rascally middleman to stuff them with all manner of new books, some of them very costly volumes on the subject of French landscape painting.

I noticed on my visit that not one of them had ever been opened or touched, and remarked the fact.

'When I get settled down properly,' said the fool, 'I'll have to catch up on my reading.'

This set me thinking. Why should a wealthy person like this be put to the trouble of pretending to read at all? Why not get a professional book-handler to go in and suitably maul his library for so much per shelf? Such a person, if suitably qualified, could make a fortune.

DOG EARS FOUR-A-PENNY

Let me explain exactly what I mean. The wares in a bookshop look completely unread. On the other hand, a schoolboy's Latin dictionary looks read to the point of tatters. You know that the dictionary has been opened and scanned perhaps a million times, and if you did not know that there was such a thing as a box on the ear, you would conclude that the boy is crazy about Latin and cannot bear to be away from his dictionary. Similarly with our non-brow who wants his friends to infer from glancing around his house that he is a high-brow. He buys an enormous book on the Russian ballet, written possibly in the language of that distant but

---

corrupt, malignant, and cowardly enemies shall be rotten and forgotten, thou wilt live, be loved, admired and renowned.
William Cobbett, *Cobbett's Weekly Political Register* (1820)

beautiful land. Our problem is to alter the book in a reasonably short time so that anybody looking at it will conclude its owner has practically lived, supped and slept with it for many months. You can, if you like, talk about designing a machine driven by a small but efficient petrol motor that would 'read' any book in five minutes, the equivalent of five years' or ten years' reading being obtained by merely turning a knob. This, however, is the cheap soulless approach to the times we live in. No machine can do the same work as the soft human fingers. The trained and experienced book-handler is the only real solution to this contemporary social problem. What does he do? How does he work? What would he charge? How many types of handling would there be?

These questions and many more I will answer the day after tomorrow.

THE WORLD OF BOOKS

Yes, this question of book-handling. The other day I had a word to say about the necessity for the professional book-handler, a person who will maul the books of illiterate, but wealthy, upstarts so that the books will look as if they have been read and re-read by their owners. How many uses of mauling would there be? Without giving the matter much thought, I should say four. Suppose an experienced book-handler is asked to quote for the handling of one shelf four feet in length. He would quote thus under four heads:

'Popular Handling – Each volume to be well and truly handled, four leaves in each to be dog-eared, and a tram ticket, cloak-room docket or other comparable article in each as a forgotten book-mark. Say, £1 7s 6d. Five per cent discount for civil servants.'

'Premier Handling – Each volume to be thoroughly handled, eight leaves in each to be dog-eared, a suitable passage in not less than 25 volumes to be underlined in red pencil, and a leaflet in French on the works of Victor Hugo to be inserted as a forgotten bookmark in each. Say, £2 17s 6d. Five per cent discount for literary university students, civil servants and lady social workers.'

A RATE TO SUIT ALL PURSES

The great thing about the graduated scale is that no person need appear ignorant or unlettered merely because he or she is poor.

Meek men grow up in libraries, believing it is their duty to accept the views which Cicero, which Locke, which Bacon, have given; forgetful that Cicero, Locke and Bacon were only young men in libraries when they wrote these books.
Ralph Waldo Emerson, *The American Scholar* (1837)

Not every vulgar person, remember, is wealthy, although I could name . . .

But no matter. Let us get on to the more expensive grades of handling. The next is well worth the extra money.

'De Luxe Handling – Each volume to be mauled savagely, the spines of the smaller volumes to be damaged in a manner that will give the impression that they have been carried around in pockets, a passage in every volume to be underlined in red pencil with an exclamation or interrogation mark inserted in the margin opposite, an old Gate Theatre programme to be inserted in each volume as a forgotten bookmark (3 per cent discount if old Abbey program-mes are accepted), not less than 30 volumes to be treated with old coffee, tea, porter or whisky stains, and not less than five volumes to be inscribed with forged signatures of the authors. Five per cent discount for bank managers, county surveyors and the heads of business houses employing not less than 35 hands. Dog-ears extra and inserted according to instructions, twopence per half dozen per volume. Quotations for alternative old Paris theatre programmes on demand. This service available for a limited time only, net, £7 18s 3d.'

ORDER YOUR COPY NOW

The fourth class is the Handling Superb, although it is not called that – *Le Traitement Superbe* being the more usual title. It is so superb that I have no space for it today. It will appear here on Monday next, and, in honour of the occasion, the *Irish Times* on that day will be printed on hand-scutched antique interwoven demidevilled superfine Dutch paper, each copy to be signed by myself and to be accompanied by an exquisite picture in tri-colour lithograph of the Old House in College Green. The least you can do is order your copy in advance.

And one more word. It is not sufficient just to order your copy. Order it *in advance*.

It will be remembered (how, in Heaven's name, could it be forgotten) that I was discoursing on Friday last on the subject of book-handling, my new service, which enables ignorant people who want to be suspected of reading books to have their books handled and mauled in a manner that will give the impression that their owner is very devoted to them. I described three grades of

---

What a sad want I am in of libraries, of books to gather facts from! Why is there not a Majesty's library in every country town? There is a Majesty's gaol and gallows in every one.
Thomas Carlyle (1795–1881)

handling and promised to explain what you get under Class Four –
the Superb Handling, or the *Traitement Superbe*, as we lads who
spent our honeymoon in Paris prefer to call it. It is the dearest of
them all, of course, but far cheaper than dirt when you consider the
amount of prestige it will gain you in the eyes of your ridiculous
friends. Here are the details:

'Le Traitement Superbe'. Every volume will be well and truly
handled, first by a qualified handler and subsequently by a master-
handler who shall have to his credit not less than 550 handling
hours; suitable passages in not less than fifty per cent of the books
to be underlined in good-quality red ink and an appropriate phrase
from the following list inserted in the margin, viz:

Rubbish!
Yes, indeed!
How true, how true!
I don't agree at all.
Why?
Yes, but cf. Homer, Od., iii, 151.
Well, well, well.
Quite, but Boussuet in his *Discours sur l'histoire Universelle* has
already established the same point and given much more forceful
explanations.
Nonsense! nonsense!
A point well taken!
But *why* in Heaven's name?
I remember poor Joyce saying the very same thing to me.

Need I say that a special quotation may be obtained at any time for
the supply of Special and Exclusive Phrases? The extra charge is
not very much really.

FURTHERMORE

That, of course, is not all. Listen to this.

'Not less than six volumes to be inscribed with forged messages
of affection and gratitude from the author of each work, e.g.,

'To my old friend and fellow-writer, A.B., in affectionate
remembrance, from George Moore.'

'In grateful recognition of your great kindness to me, dear A.B.,
I send you this copy of *The Crock of Gold*. Your old friend, James
Stephens.'

My notion of the librarian's function does not imply that he
shall be king over us; nay, that he shall ever quit the address
and manner of a *servant* to the [London] Library; but he will
be a *wise* servant, watchful and diligent, discerning what is
what, incessantly endeavouring, *rough-hewing* all things for

'Well, A.B., both of us are getting on. I am supposed to be a good writer now, but I am not old enough to forget the infinite patience you displayed in the old days when guiding my young feet on the path of literature. Accept this further book, poor as it may be, and please believe that I remain, as ever, your friend and admirer, G. Bernard Shaw.'

'From your devoted friend and follower, K. Marx.'

'Dear A.B. – Your invaluable suggestions and assistance, not to mention your kindness, in entirely re-writing chapter 3, entitles you, surely, to this first copy of *Tess*. From your old friend T. Hardy.'

'Short of the great pleasure of seeing you personally, I can only send you, dear A.B., this copy of *The Nigger*. I miss your company more than I can say . . . (signature indecipherable).'

Under the last inscription, the moron who owns the book will be asked to write (and shown how if necessary) the phrase 'Poor Conrad was not the worst.'

All this has taken me longer to say than I thought. There is far more than this to be had for the paltry £32 7s 6d that the Superb Handling will cost you. In a day or two I hope to explain about the old letters which are inserted in some of the books by way of forgotten bookmarks, every one of them an exquisite piece of forgery. Order your copy now!

BOOK HANDLING

I promised to say a little more about the fourth, or Superb, grade of book handling.

The price I quote includes the insertion in not less than ten volumes of certain old letters, apparently used at one time as bookmarks, and forgotten. Each letter will bear the purported signature of some well-known humbug who is associated with the ballet, verse-mouthing, folk-dancing, wood-cutting, or some other such activity that is sufficiently free from rules to attract the non-brow in their swarms. Each of the letters will be a flawless forgery and will thank A.B., the owner of the book, for his 'very kind interest in our work', refer to his 'invaluable advice and guidance', his 'unrivalled knowledge' of the lep-as-lep-can game, his 'patient and skilful direction of the corps on Monday night', thank him for his generous – too generous – subscription of two hundred guineas, 'which is appreciated more than I can say'. As an

---

us; and, under the guise of a wise servant, *ruling* actually while he serves. He should be like a nobleman's steward.
                                          Thomas Carlyle (1840)

up-to-the-minute inducement, an extra letter will be included free of charge. It will be signed (or purport to be signed) by one or other of the noisier young non-nationals who are honouring our beautiful land with their presence. This will satisfy the half-ambition of the majority of respectable vulgarians to maintain a second establishment in that somewhat congested thoroughfare, Queer Street.

The gentlemen who are associated with me in the Dublin WAAMA League have realised that this is the off-season for harvesting the cash of simple people through the art-infected begging letter, and have turned their attention to fresh fields and impostures new. The latest racket we have on hands is the Myles na Gopaleen Book Club. You join this and are spared the nerve-racking bother of choosing your own books. We do the choosing for you, and, when you get the book, it is *ready-rubbed*, i.e. subjected free of charge to our expert handlers. You are spared the trouble of soiling and mauling it to give your friends the impression that you can read. An odd banned book will be slipped in for those who like conversation such as:

'I say, did you read this, old man?'

'I'm not terribly certain that I did, really.'

'It's banned, you know, old boy.'

'Ow.'

There is no nonsense about completing a form, asking for a brochure, or any other such irritation. You just send in your guinea and you immediately participate in this great cultural uprising of the Irish people.

The Best of Myles (MacGibbon and Kee, 1968)

I have now a library of nearly nine hundred volumes, over seven hundred of which I wrote myself.

Henry David Thoreau (1817–62)

EDMUND BLUNDEN

In a Library

A curious remedy for present cares,
And yet as near a good one as I know;
It is to scan the cares of long ago,
Which these brown bindings lodge.
                           In black print glares
The Elizabethan preacher, heaping shame
On that iniquitous gay hell, the stage;
And here's another full of scriptural rage
Against high Rome. Fie, parson, be more tame.
The critic gnashes his laborious teeth
And that, whose subtlety seems no such matter;
This merchant bodes our economic death,
This envoy hastens with his hard-won chatter;
Age hacks at youth, youth paints the old town red –
And in the margin Doomsday rears his head.

Shut not your doors to me proud libraries,
For that which was lacking on all your
           well-fill'd shelves,
      yet needed most, I bring
Forth from the war emerging, a book I have
        made.
                   Walt Whitman, 'Shut not your doors'

GARRISON KEILLOR
Your Book Saved My Life, Mister

All of my books, including *Wagons Wesward!!! Hiiiii-YAW* and *Ck-ck Giddup Beauty! C'mon Big Girl, Awaaaaayy!* and *Pa! Look Out! It's Aiiiiieee!*, have been difficult for my readers, I guess, judging from their reactions when they see me shopping at Val–Mar or sitting in the Quad County Library and Media Center. After a rough morning at the keyboard, I sort of like to slip into my black leather vest, big white hat, and red kerchief, same as in the book-jacket photos, and saunter up and down the aisle by the fruit and other perishable items and let my fans have the thrill of running into me, and if nobody does I park myself at the table dead smack in front of the Western-adventure shelf in Quad County's fiction department, lean back, plant my big boots on the table, and prepare to endure the terrible price of celebrity, but it's not uncommon for a reader to come by, glance down, and say, 'Aren't you Dusty Pages, the author of *Ck-ck Giddup Beauty! C'mon Big Girl, Awaaaaayy!*' and when I look down and blush and say, 'Well, yes, ma'am, I reckon I am him,' she says, 'I thought so. You look just like him.' Then an awful silence while she studies the shelf and selects Ray A. James, Jr., or Chuck Young or another of my rivals. It's a painful moment for an author, the reader two feet away and moments passing during which she does not say, 'Your books have meant so much to me,' or 'I can't tell you how much I admire your work.' She just reaches past the author like he was a sack of potatoes and chooses a book by somebody else. Same thing happens with men. They say, 'You're an author, aren'tcha? I read a book of yours once, what was the name of it?'

I try to be helpful. 'Could it have been *Wagons Westward!!! Hiiiii-YAW!*'

'No, it had someone's name in the title.'

'Well. I wrote a book entitled *Pa! Look Out! It's Aiiiiieee!*'

'No, I think it had the name of a horse.'

'Could it have been *Ck-ck Giddup Beauty! C'mon Big Girl, Awaaaaayy!*'

A library is not worth anything without a catalogue – it is Polyphemus without any eye in his head.

Thomas Carlyle (1849)

'That's the one. Did you write that?'

'Yes, sir, I did.'

'Huh. I thought so.'

And right there you brace for him to say, 'Y'know, I never was one for books and then my brother gave me yours for Christmas and I said, "Naw, I don't read books, Craig, you know that," and he said, "But this is different, Jim Earl, read this, this isn't the girls' literature they stuffed down our throats in high school, this is the real potatoes," so I read it for two days and for two nights without a minute of shuteye. Your book changed my life, mister. I'm glad I got a chance to tell you that. You cleared up a bunch of stuff that has bothered me for years – you took something that had been inside me and you put it into words so I could feel, I donno, not so weird, feel sorta like *understood*, y'might say. That was me you put in that book of yours, mister. That was my life you wrote about there, and I want to say thanks. Just remember, any time you're over in Big Junction, Wyoming, you got a friend there name o' Jim Earl Wilcox' – but instead he says, 'You wouldn't know where the little boys' room is, wouldja?' as if I were a library employee and not a book author. So it's clear to me that when people read my books they like me a little less at the end than at the beginning. My fourth book, *Company A, Chaaaaaaarge!*, is evidently the worst. Nobody bought it at all.

I know what it's like to be disappointed by a hero. You think I don't know? Believe me, I know. I met my idol, Smokey W. Kaiser, when I was twelve. I'd read every one of his books twice – the Curly Bob and Lefty Slim series, the Lazy A Gang series, the Powder River Hank series – and I had waited outside the YMCA in Des Moines for three hours while he regaled the Rotary with humorous anecdotes, and when he emerged at the side door, a fat man in tight green pants tucked into silver-studded boots, he looked down and growled, 'I don't sign pieces of paper, kid. I sign books. No paper. You want my autograph, you can buy a book. That's a rule of mine. Don't waste my time and I won't waste yours.'

Smokey's problem was that he was a jerk, but mine is that I get halfway through a story and everything goes to pieces. In *Wagons Westward!!! Hiiiii-YAW!* the pioneers reach Council Bluffs, having endured two hundred solid pages of Indian attacks, smallpox, cattle stampedes, thirst, terror, bitter backbiting, scattered atheism, and adulterous inclinations, and then they sit on the bluffs and have a meeting to decide whether they really want to forge onward

You ask me where I spend my evenings. Where do you suppose, with a free prentice library containing more than four thousand volumes within a quarter of a mile of me and nobody at home to talk to?
Mark Twain, to his sister Emma from New York at 18 (1853)

to Oregon or whether maybe they should head east toward Oak
Park or Evanston instead. Buck Bradley, the tall, taciturn, sandy-
haired, God-fearing man who led them through the rough stuff,
stands up and says, 'Well, it's up to the rest of you. Makes no
nevermind to yours truly, I could go either way and be happy –
west, south, you name it. I don't *need* to go west or anything. You
choose. I'll go along with whatever.' I don't know. I wrote that
scene the way I heard it in my head but now I see it in print, it
looks dumb. I can certainly see why it would throw a reader, same
as in *Giddup Beauty! C'mon Big Girl, Awaaaaayy!*, when Buck rides
two thousand miles across blazing deserts searching for Julie Ann
and finally, after killing twenty men and wearing out three mounts
and surviving two avalanches, a prairie fire, a blizzard, and a passel
of varmints, he finds her held captive by the bloodthirsty Arapaho.
'So, how are you doing?' he asks her. 'Oh, all right, I guess,' she
says, gazing at him, wiping the sweat from her brow. 'You want
to come in for a cup of coffee?' 'Naw, I just wanted to make sure
you were okay. You *look* okay.' 'Yeah, I lost some weight, about
twenty pounds.' 'Oh really. How?' 'Eating toads and grasshop-
pers.' 'Uh-huh. Well, now that I look at you, you *do* look lighter.'
'Sure you won't have coffee?' 'Naw, I gotta ride. Be seein' ya,
now.' 'Okay, bye!' To me it seemed more realistic that way but
maybe to the guy reader it sounded sort of unfocused or
something. I don't know. Guys have always been a tough audience
for me. The other day a guy grabbed my arm in the Quad County
and said, 'Hey, Dusty! Dusty Pages! That right? Am I right or am I
right?'

'Both,' I said.

'Mister,' he said, 'your book saved my life. My brother gave it
to me and said, "Buck, read this sometime when you're sober,"
and I put it into my pocket and didn't think about it until October,
I was elk hunting up in the Big Coulee country, other side of the
Little Crazy River, and suddenly *wham* it felt like somebody
swung a bat and hit me in the left nipple. I fell over and lay
there, and doggone it, I felt around and didn't find blood – I go
"Huh???????" Well, it was your book in my jacket pocket that
saved my life – bullet tore through the first half of it, stopping at
page 143. So, by Jim, I thought, "This is too crazy, I got to *read*
this," and I started to read and I couldn't believe it. That was me in
the book – my life, my thoughts, it was weird. Names, dates,
places – it was my life down to the last detail, except for the beer. I
don't drink Coors. The rest you got right. Here.' And he slipped

---

A man's library is a sort of harem.
                    Ralph Waldo Emerson, 'In Praise of Books',
                                    The Conduct of Life (1860)

an envelope into my hand. 'This is for you,' he said.

It was a subpoena to appear in US District Court the 27th of November to defend myself in a civil suit for wrongful use of another for literary gain. I appeared and tried to defend, but I lost. My attorney, a very, very nice man named Howard Furst, was simply outgunned by three tall ferret-faced bushwhackers in black pinstripes who flew in from Houston and tore him limb from limb in two and a half hours in that cold windy courtroom. They and their client, Buck Bradley, toted away three saddlebags full of my bank account, leaving me nothing except this latest book. It's the first in a new series, the Lonesome Bud series, called *The Case of the Black Mesa*, and it begins with a snake biting Bud in the wrist as he hangs from a cliff while the Navajo shoot flaming arrows at him from below and a torrent of sharp gravel showers down on his bald head. From there to the end, it never lets up, except maybe in Chapter Four, where he and the boys shop for bunk beds. I don't know what I had in mind there at all.

We Are Still Married (Faber and Faber, 1989)

NOT JUST BOOKS

In romantic fiction librarians are girls in tweed skirts and pink cardigans who blush whenever a Donald or a Gordon enters the room; by comparison shrinking violets seem like blooming dahlias. Occasionally someone tries to vamp them up but such efforts are invariably half-hearted. Even if experience gainsays it, librarians are forever condemned to be seen as virginal spinsters or bespectacled, celibate bachelors who would not say 'boo' to a goose, who take unflinchingly the slings and arrows thrown at them (see Saul Bellow's *Him with His Foot in His Mouth*) or toil oblivious to the social intercourse of others (Anthony Burgess's encounter with a seductress in Manchester's central library).

The image is confirmed in Anita Brookner's fine novel *Lewis Percy*, in which a single, agoraphobic girl ('Her clothes were asexual') is pursued by wimpish Lewis who has recently lost his mother, the implication being that this is the best he can hope for. The most telling remark, however, concerns the woman in charge of the library, Miss Clarke, whom Lewis's recently deceased mother could only imagine marrying 'a rotter'. 'Why wouldn't someone like that want to marry her?' asks Lewis. 'Well, he might be a homosexual,' answered Mrs Percy.

This is rather rum on Miss Clarke. But even in this dessicated situation Brookner's prose crackles with sexual electricity. Libraries (it may surprise those who work in them to learn) are like that, generating an unusual heat. If one personally doubted it, this was confirmed in the course of researching this book. A former colleague sent me a clipping from a thriller (*The Midnight Chill* by Marten Claridge) in which a female character studying in the reference library where I was once employed describes a young librarian with 'a tight wee bum encased in jeans tight enough to make her wonder'. Hmmm.

BARBARA PYM

His Nibs

Ianthe always hurried past the vet's house, fearful of seeing or hearing something dreadful. The basement cattery seemed to her a sinister place, though she knew that the animals were most lovingly tended by Miss Pettigrew. They had got into conversation one evening when Ianthe was coming back from the library where she worked, and it had reassured her – coming as a stranger to this rather doubtful neighbourhood – to meet somebody whom her mother would have described as a 'gentlewoman'.

Ianthe was the only child of elderly parents, who seemed to be a whole generation removed from those of her contemporaries. When her father died it had been necessary for her to do some kind of work and the training in librarianship had seemed the most suitable. Working among books was, on the face of it, a ladylike occupation, Mrs Broome had thought, and one that would bring her daughter into contact with a refined, intellectual type of person. She had never seen Ianthe handing out books to the ill-mannered grubby students and cranks of all ages who frequented the library of political and sociological books where she worked.

On the crowded train a man gave up his seat to Ianthe and she accepted it gracefully. She expected courtesy from men and often received it. It was as if they realised that she was not for the rough and tumble of this world, like the aggressive women with shaggy hairstyles who pushed their way through life thrusting their hard shopping baskets at defenceless men. The man who had offered the seat had seen Ianthe as a tall fragile-looking woman in a pretty blue hat that matched her eyes. He might also have noticed that her dark hair was touched with grey and that although she was not exactly smart there was a kind of elegance about her. She saw herself perhaps as an Elizabeth Bowen heroine – for one did not openly identify oneself with Jane Austen's heroines – and *To The North* was her favourite novel. Even her little house was somehow in keeping with this picture, although it was definitely not St John's Wood and there was no delicate wrought-iron balcony with

---

I go into my library, and all history rolls before me. I breathe the morning air of the world while the scent of Eden's roses yet lingered in it . . . I see the pyramids building; I hear the shoutings of the armies of Alexander . . . I sit as in a theatre – the stage is time, the play is the play . . . of the world.
Alexander Smith, 'Books and Gardens', *Dreamthorpe* (1863)

steps leading down to the green garden. Yet her small garden *was* green, if only because of much rain and leaves rather than flowers, and there was a little mossy stone cherub left behind by the previous owner. It was so much more congenial than the flat near Victoria – unsuitably dominated by Westminster Cathedral – where she had lived with her mother. Ianthe arrived at the library five minutes before she need have done. Mervyn Cantrell, the librarian, was unpacking his lunch. He was a tall thin irritable-looking man in his early forties, who had the idea that he could not 'take' restaurant food, at least of the kind served in the restaurants where the rest of the staff had their midday meal – luncheon was hardly the word for it – and therefore always brought a packed meal with him. Today it was a cold fish mayonnaise with lettuce and French dressing in a little bottle, brown rolls, and a special goatsmilk cheese obtainable only at one particular shop in Soho.

'Good morning, Miss Broome,' he said, for they were not always 'Ianthe' and 'Mervyn' to each other and the early morning was usually a very formal time. 'I hope you're getting settled into your new house.'

'Yes, thank you – my furniture seems to fit in very well.'

'You've got some nice things, haven't you.' There was a tinge of envy in his tone, for his humdrum childhood home in Croydon had not provided him with the kind of 'things' his taste now craved.

'Well, family things, you know – but one gets attached to them.' Mervyn had visited the flat once for tea on a Sunday afternoon when her mother was still alive, but the occasion had not been very successful. Mrs Broome had not thought much of Croydon as was evident from her patronising manner.

'I remember you had a lovely Pembroke table – I coveted *that*.' He laughed, not very mirthfully. 'And those dining-room chairs – Hepplewhite, aren't they?'

'Yes, I believe so,' said Ianthe uncertainly. She found the conversation embarrassing and wondered if the time had come when she could no longer avoid asking him to come and see her new house.

'Surely you must know if they are,' he said testily.

'You must come and see for yourself when I've got things a bit tidier,' she said, trying not to be irritated. Poor Mervyn, she knew that she ought to feel sorry for him, living with his disagreeable old mother – at least, this was how she appeared in Ianthe's imagination – disappointed at not having got a job in one of the

---

Keep the modern magazine and novel out of your girl's way: turn her loose into the old library every wet day, and let her alone.

John Ruskin, *Sesame and Lilies* (1865)

University libraries, unable to find staff accurate enough to
appreciate the niceties of setting out a bibliographical entry
correctly, with it seemed few friends of either sex, unable to eat
restaurant food – really, the list seemed endless when one thought
about it.

'I shall be sorting out some of the applications for Miss Grimes's
job this morning,' Mervyn said. 'She's really getting past her work
and it'll be a relief when she goes. What we need is a younger
person.'

Ianthe sighed, perhaps foreseeing the day when both of them
would be replaced by younger persons.

'A young *man*, I think,' he went on, holding up a letter. 'This
one sounds quite promising, but of course I must see him first –
one can't always tell from the application,' he added primly.

'No, he might be *quite* unsuitable,' Ianthe agreed, half hoping
that he would be. She would have preferred a woman of her own
age and background. She did not like men very much, except for
the clergy, and found younger women rather alarming. Miss
Grimes, with whom she had worked for several years, was hardly
the most congenial of companions but at least she was familiar.

This morning she was dusting books in the reading room which
was so far empty of readers.

'And how's his nibs this morning?' she grunted in her slightly
Cockney voice. It was this voice and expressions like 'his nibs'
which jarred on Ianthe. Indeed, Miss Grimes was sometimes
altogether jarring. She was a squat, dusty-looking woman on the
threshold of sixty, who had been taken on in the library during the
war and whom Mervyn had tried unsuccessfully to dislodge ever
since he had become librarian. But now the passage of the years
was doing it for him. 'Time like an ever-rolling stream,' Mervyn
had said, 'bears even Miss Grimes away.' But Ianthe did not like
jokes about hymns.

'I'll help you with the books,' she said.

'It's not your day, is it, dear?'

'No, but they've got to be done, and Shirley's making the tea.'
Ianthe had not told her mother that she sometimes had to dust the
books in the library.

Later when she was drinking her tea Mervyn came into the
room with a card in his hand.

Ianthe realised from his triumphant expression that he had
caught her out in a mistake and waited with resignation to hear
what it was.

A great library contains the diary of the human race.
George Dawson, opening the Birmingham Free Library
(26 October 1866)

'*Government in Zazzau*,' he declared. 'The place of publication is London, *not* Oxford. It was published *by* the Oxford University Press *for* the International African Institute – do you see?' From behind his back he now produced the book itself, open at the title page.

'Of course – how stupid of me. I'm so sorry, I'm afraid I do make mistakes sometimes.'

'But there is no need to make *that* kind of mistake,' he said rather obscurely and left the room with a springy step.

So Ianthe's day passed, punctuated by cups of tea and a lunch of Welsh rarebit and trifle at a café run by gentlewomen. It was not much different from other days. At five minutes to five, Shirley, the typist who had been helping Ianthe to file some cards, covered up her typewriter, put on the black imitation leather coat she had just bought, and hurried away singing. Ianthe herself stayed until nearly six o'clock to avoid the rush-hour crowds. She was still not completely used to the journey northwards to the small empty house, when for so long she had gone southwards to the big flat near Westminster Cathedral, where her mother had waited, eager to hear every detail of her day.

An Unsuitable Attachment (Macmillan, 1982)

Consider what you have in the smallest chosen library. A company of the wittiest men that could be picked out of all the civil countries in a thousand years have set in best order the results of their learning and wisdom. The men themselves were hid and inaccessible, solitary, impatient of

WILLIAM McILVANNEY

In the Library

In the library the first time
I stood in a pool of awe.
Wonder for taking, acres of promise.
The lady with the specs
And the hair-tuft on her cheek
Asking me if I had washed my hands.
The holy ritual of the water – what was this?
Superstitious as a Goth, I grabbed and ran.
At the bus-stop I discovered I had looted
A book about a girls' school. It was good.

Ridiculous, small moment but it stays.
Seed of an anger perennially mine.
The hope I lugged to that place
Back and forth and afterwards
Brought to how many books . . .
Raising my eyes
For several million pages I have seen
The small boy standing there.

The time it took
The fields there were to cut, the loads to carry,
Hutches to be filled
The roads to lay
The tired nights in narrow beds, the rage
To bring him to his patch of floor,
His eyes like begging bowls.

---

interruption, fenced by etiquette; but the thought which
they did not uncover to their bosom friend is here written
out in transparent words to us, the strangers of another age.
  Ralph Waldo Emerson, 'Books', *Society and Solitude* (1870)

I forgive
The determined absence of himself he was to find.
The self-perpetuating silliness, the cliques
Of convoluted silence, the lies,
The long articulate anathema
Against him and his pals.
They were nowhere to be seen unless those bits
Between the lines and down the edges
Were for them.

No wonder they drew graffiti in the margins.

Library. Before the invention of paper the thin rind between
the solid wood and the outside bark of certain trees was
used for writing on; this was in Lat. called *liber*, which came
in time to signify also a 'book'. Hence our *library*, the place

ANITA BROOKNER

Something of a Day-Care Centre

Another library, he thought. He felt doomed, irritated, yet at the same time submissive. Here was destiny staring him in the face. Not exactly here but somewhere very like, up imposing steps, through swing doors, into the arched and silent room, where a timid sun sent coloured refractions through the lozenge shapes of art deco fanlights, where children sat at one of the two long tables composing essays for their English homework, and where old men, cloth capped and mufflered, read the *Express* and the *Telegraph* and sometimes dozed until it was time to go home. This was a kindly place, something of a day care centre for the lonely, the naturally silent, the elderly and the reclusive. The lighting and the heating were generous, even if the rules were strict: there was to be no talking, not one word, emphasised Miss Clarke, the librarian, and although she was well disposed she would not countenance outright sleep, however frail the sleeper. Tapping across the parquet floor on her military-sounding high heels, she would shake the offender by the shoulder. 'This is a library, Mr Baker, not a dormitory! And you were beginning to snore.' This admonition had to be repeated rather frequently. Mr Baker, white stubble nestling in the folds of a very ancient, once handsome silk scarf, damp of nostril but calm of presence, his former bearing resurrected for the occasion, had once, in Lewis's hearing, replied, 'You make more noise than I do, you silly bitch,' and had been ordered to leave. 'Poor old thing,' Mrs Percy had said. 'He probably has nowhere else to go.' 'Oh, he'll be back tomorrow,' said Miss Clarke, with a laugh that was tolerant but a little too hearty. 'I like to do my best for everyone but I can't have the atmosphere disturbed. I feel sorry for him really. But old people can be very tiresome, can't they?' She was perhaps forty-three to Grace Percy's sixty-two. 'Yes,' Grace Percy had smiled in return. 'Yes, I dare say they can.'

'There is something very sad about that woman,' she had said to her son on their journey home. 'I somehow doubt that she will

for books; *librarian*, the keeper of books; and the French *livre*, a book.

Brewer's Dictionary of Phrase and Fable (1870)

marry. And she knows this. It has probably broken her heart but she is too good a woman to show her feelings. What comes out is a terrible cheerfulness, with no cheer in it.'

Lewis had laughed and pressed his mother's arm. He loved her in this mood. 'Go on,' he said. 'What happened to her? Did some rotter let her down?'

'Oh no,' said Mrs Percy, surprised. 'There never was a rotter, that's the trouble. She's the sort of great-hearted woman who would be magnificent with a rotter. That deep bosom, that high colour. The sacrifices she would have made! The faith in his untested abilities she would have maintained! She would have taken on his parents, his friends, even his lovers. I can just see her keeping open house for all his hangers-on, being decent to the women who ring up, lending him money.'

'Why wouldn't someone like that want to marry her?' Lewis had asked in his innocence.

'Well, he might be a homosexual,' his mother had replied. She thought it her duty, for which she braced herself, to introduce her son to these complexities. 'At any event someone who couldn't tolerate the intimacy of women. And I have to say, although I shouldn't, that Miss Clarke gives the impression of someone whose intimacy might be a little tiring.'

She said no more, thinking to spare Lewis the spectacle, which she had quite clearly in front of her, of Miss Clarke, full-throated, wild-eyed, in the throes of some spectacular but unrequited ardour. It was the sort of thing for which actresses became famous in the theatre. Jacobean tragedy would have suited her, she reflected.

'The sad thing is that many women of Miss Clarke's type never marry,' she said mildly. 'And yet they would make excellent wives. Miss Clarke probably has a chest of drawers full of expensive linen' (nightdresses, she thought, but kept the thought to herself). 'She probably still adds to it. And she always looks well turned out, have you noticed? Those very pretty blouses, those high heels. And nice discreet scent. And always well made up. And her hair always immaculate.'

'I suppose she's all right for her age,' said Lewis. 'But I think she's pretty unattractive.'

'She was possibly always heavy in the bust, even as a girl,' said his mother. 'Now, of course, her waist is bigger than it was before. That happens to women in their forties,' she said, giving Lewis's arm a tap. 'You should know that. So that you're not

---

I believe there are several persons in a state of imbecility who come to read in the British Museum. I have been informed that there are several in that state who are sent there by their friends to pass away their time.

Thomas Carlyle (1795-1881)

disappointed when your wife gets a little older. The figure loses definition,' she added, although her own had long disappeared into a kind of Gothic sparseness. Contemplation of Miss Clarke's misplaced and unsought abundance always brought her a tiny spasm of personal gratitude for her own good fortune. Although Lewis did not know this, Mrs Percy always reflected at this point, 'After all, I had darling Jack.' But such thoughts were not to be spoken, and after thinking them Mrs Percy felt a little ashamed.

'Remember, Lewis,' she had said. 'Good women are better than bad women. Bad women are merely tiresome. Learn to appreciate goodness of heart. Learn to look beyond the outer covering. Would you like some of those crumpets for tea?'

They had been passing one of the mild small shops that did duty for a bakery in this unworldly district. Two girls in overalls carelessly swathed uncut loaves in tissue paper and swung bags round by corners, varying this activity with sorties to the window to pick out yellow Bath buns and virulent jam tarts with fingers arched daintily for the purpose.

'Remember, Lewis,' his mother had said. 'Never buy cakes unwrapped.'

'I wouldn't buy this stuff anyway,' said Lewis, whose standards in these matters remained haughtily and unrealistically Parisian. 'I could just fancy a strawberry tart,' he added. 'Freshly made.'

'Nevertheless,' said his mother, 'I'm sure you won't say no to the crumpets. Fortunately, they come in packets.'

'Good afternoon, Hazel,' she had said to one of the two girls behind the counter. 'Father feeling better?'

For she had been the genius of the place, he thought, and had somehow made her peace with its lack of pretension, loving its modesty, its uneventfulness, its quiet afternoons. Like ceremonies – the planting of the hyacinth bulbs in the blue china bowls, the drawing of the curtains in the evenings, the bars of soap slipped between the clean sheets in the linen cupboard – all these had kept her happy, kept her attentive, so that with the help of her reading, and with her pride in her son, she had lived a peaceful widowhood, maintained a dignity for which he was grateful. He had had time to reflect on her life, which he now saw as excellent, and which he hoped would always remain with him, and even, when some time had elapsed, cancel out the memory of her death. He would always see her here, against the background of the Common, or else stepping on her narrow beautifully shod feet into the little bakery, the little grocery, exchanging remarks with the

Good as it is to inherit a library, it is better to collect one.
Augustine Birrell, 'Book-Buying', *Obiter Dicta* (1884)

shopkeeper, or the girl assistant. Going home to put on the kettle, to build up the fire for the evening, to water the plants. This was a life, thought Lewis, that would always be part of him, although in his mind he longed impatiently to be somewhere else, to be off to a wider, more sophisticated metropolitan setting, one more in keeping with the adult he hoped he had it in him to be, although adulthood still seemed to him to be a long way away. His boyhood, the last days of which he was sorrowfully living, would remain imprinted with his mother's quiet habits, whose decency he would always defend.

His mother's presence was particularly strong on this day when he returned the library books she would never exchange for others. He mounted the steps, pushed through the swing doors, obediently straightened his tie. Once again he succumbed to suburban peace, aware of a rawness round his heart which responded gratefully to the books, to the readers, to the sunlight through the windows, to the smell of polish. Mr Baker was there he noticed, doing the crossword in *The Times*, although this was forbidden; at least he was not asleep. Miss Clarke was on duty, in a red dress that brought out her high colour; even the lobes of her ears, tightly clasped by the large pearl studs, looked suffused. The other girl, the pale one, was searching through the tickets that went back into the books being returned by a very old lady, who drew each one, trembling, from the depths of a woven brown leather bag. Miss Clarke flashed him her famous smile, the one she used to enslave men and reprimand wrongdoers.

'Mother not with you today?' she asked. It was the question he had been dreading.

'My mother has died,' he said. 'I've brought her books back.'

There was a shocked silence. The pale girl turned round, even paler. Miss Clarke, her hand on her heart, paused in her task.

'Well, this has been quite a shock,' she said, after a second or two lowering the hand to pluck a dazzling white handkerchief from her sleeve. 'This is a sad day for the library, Mr Percy. We've known your mother for ages. Always so kind. Always took an interest. I had noticed she was looking a bit tired, mark you. But I never dreamed . . .'

'It was her heart,' said Lewis miserably, feeling once again the full weight of his misfortune.

'And then, of course, she missed you,' Miss Clarke went on inexorably, 'She once said to me, "I'm counting the days, Madeleine". But she didn't want you to know that.'

A man should keep his little brain attic stocked with all the furniture that he is likely to use, and the rest he can put away in the lumber room of his library, where he can get it if he wants it.

Sir Arthur Conan Doyle, 'Five Orange Pips',
The Adventures of Sherlock Holmes (1892)

And now I do, thought Lewis. In order not to prolong the
conversation he went over to the shelves to try to find a book that
his mother might have liked, hoping to maintain contact in that
way if in no other. He found a couple of Edith Whartons, and
feeling lonely and self-conscious, took them to the desk. The pale
girl came forward, two spots of red in her cheeks.

'She was awfully proud of you, Mr Percy,' the girl said. 'And
she was quite all right on her own, you know. Not weak, or
anything. She never complained, never said there was anything
wrong. Please don't blame yourself.' She ducked her head in
embarrassment at having said so much and busied herself with the
date stamp.

'Thank you,' said Lewis.

'I was very fond of your mother,' said the girl. Lewis saw that
despite her pallor, or because of it, she had an air of delicacy, or
narrowness, that pleased him. Her clothes were asexual: a pale blue
sweater and a grey flannel skirt, school-girl's clothes, which made
her seem younger than her age. He reckoned she was about
twenty-five. What he noticed mostly were her long unmarked
slightly upcurling fingers, white as if they had never been engaged
in a common or unseemly task. The face, momentarily enlivened
by her emotion and the forwardness she obviously thought she
was exhibiting, was equally long and pale, and could, he thought,
look mournful. The face was framed by thick hair, in a colour
midway between blonde and beige, and held back by a black velvet
band. Susan had had one of those, he remembered: they must be
the fashion. She had large, rather beautiful dark blue eyes, shadowed
by long colourless lashes. The skin was fine, the teeth unexpectedly strong, slightly protruding. The chin, he noticed, was a
little weak. He wondered why she was not pretty. His mother
would have known why the face was so withdrawn, so unmarked.
That pose of the head, held slightly on one side, as if listening to an
inner voice, those narrow, slightly hunched shoulders, those
prayerful hands, set him thinking of pale virgins in stone, the kind
he had seen in the Victoria and Albert Museum. Perhaps all virgins
had something in common, he thought, revising her age slightly
upward. And yet, outside the V and A, he had never seen one so
spectacularly virginal. Everything about her looked untouched.
Beneath the pale blue jersey, the breasts were scarcely noticeable.
He felt drawn to her on account of her little speech, which, he
supposed, given her shyness, must have cost her an effort. He was
grateful to her for telling him what he had wanted to be told. She

---

I keep my books at the British Museum and Mudie's.
                    Samuel Butler, 'Ramblings in Cheapside',
                              The Humour of Homer (1892)

was the agent of his deliverance.

'Tissy, your mother's here,' called Miss Clarke.

'Tissy?' said Lewis quickly, intrigued by this name, which he had never heard.

'My name's Patricia, really. Patricia Harper. When I was little I couldn't say Patricia, so I called myself Tissy, and the name's stuck. I get called it all the time now. Would you excuse me, Mr Percy? My mother's come to take me out to lunch. I just want you to know I was fond of Mrs Percy, and I'm sorry for your trouble.'

Again she blushed, seemed almost weakened by the effort of speaking. In the face of her alarming fragility he held out his hand, partly in gratitude, partly to reassure himself that she was all right. She clasped his hand lightly with very cold fingers, then turned and disappeared.

'A tragedy, that girl,' said Miss Clarke, leaning her bosom on the counter. Mr Baker, looking up, put his finger ostentatiously to his lips. Miss Clarke took no notice.

'Agoraphobia,' she said, with melancholy satisfaction. 'Says she can't go out alone. Her mother brings her in the mornings, collects her for lunch, brings her back at two, and collects her again in the evening. I've tried to talk to her, but to no avail. Apparently it came on with adolescence, although I believe there was some family trouble as well. The father,' she said, lowering her voice to imply discretion, but also comprehension. 'Another woman, I suppose. That's usually the way of it, isn't it? A good little worker, mind you: I've no complaints. But who else would have her?'

'Doesn't she ever go out then?' asked Lewis.

'Well, I've encouraged her, of course, I've told her she can't stay with her mother all her life. But she turns faint if you go on at her. Frightened to death, you see. And it ties the mother down too, now that there's just the two of them. Still, she seems quite happy. And we can't always have things the way we want them, can we? Into each life a little rain must fall. Anyway you don't want to hear about all this, what with your recent tragedy.' She pressed her handkerchief to a ready tear. 'Taking those, are you? Ah, *The Age of Innocence*, my favourite book.' Lewis was ashamed of himself for thinking patronisingly of Miss Clarke. She was a romantic, and therefore an ideal reader, someone like himself. Nevertheless, walking home with the books under his arm, it was Miss Harper, Tissy, whose image stayed in his mind, tiny, chill, eternally distant, like something seen through the wrong end of a telescope. He had thought her quite plain.

For myself, public libraries possess a special horror, as of lonely wastes and dragon haunted fens. The stillness and the heavy air, the feeling of restriction and surveillance, the mute presence of other readers, 'all silent and damned',

She might be somebody he could marry, he thought, quailing at the prospect of his mother's empty house. The thought, though idle, was sudden yet not surprising. And then he could cure her, and she would be able to go out again. Or else she could stay indoors, waiting for him to come home. It would be nice to be expected again.

He raced through *The Age of Innocence* and *Ethan Frome* and was back at the library two days later. This time he was disappointed: no sign of Tissy Harper, or even of Miss Clarke. No sign of anyone, and only a large indolent girl he had never seen before at the desk. He took out an Elizabeth Bowen and a Margaret Kennedy. He found himself drawn to the books his mother had loved, as if in reading them he could get in touch with her in a way of which she would have approved. In any event such reading seemed to him salutary. He began to think that his official reading, which involved him in grown-up theories about heroism, and nineteenth-century heroism at that, might have led him, not exactly astray, but perhaps a little too far from normal concerns. He whiled away several evenings with what he thought of as his mother's type of book, and for a time he was soothed and charmed, although the moment at which he was forced to emerge from these tender fictional worlds was always harsh and painful. He began to long for a female presence, something shadowy, beneficent, something that would bring health and peace back into his life, which he perceived as threatened. The desire for such a presence was infinite, although he saw little possibility of its being satisfied. He thought how sad it was for a man of his age to be reduced to loneliness, with only his books for company. At the same time he began to realise that he could not spend his life reading. The British Museum was his refuge, but it was also his prison. He felt mildly distressed when the library closed, but once that moment had passed he strode out down the steps with a feeling of liberation. As the year stretched once more into spring the days perversely got both longer and chillier. Walking home, he could hear sad bird song under a darkening sky. In the gardens crocuses were already splayed and untidy, past their best. Timid buds showed on bushes; even the cheerless privet seemed brighter. In a moment of depression he turned out again one evening after his supper and took the Elizabeth Bowen back to the library. He had left it late and arrived just as the lights were being clicked on and off to signify closing time. But he was rewarded by the sight of Tissy Harper, this time in a pale pink twinset, one arm already

---

combine to set up a nervous irritation fatal to quiet study.
                    Kennedy Grahame, *Pagan Papers* (1893)

inserted into the sleeve of a grey jacket.

'Take your time,' she whispered. 'I won't put the lights out until you go.'

'I just wanted to return this,' he said, placing the book on the counter, near her hand. 'I'll come back another day.' He hesitated, and then asked, 'Can I walk you home?'

'Thank you,' she said, 'but my mother's here.'

Her mother was in fact looking at him rather insistently from the vantage point of a seat opposite the one Mr Baker would have been occupying had he not been turned out earlier by Miss Clarke. Ah, but the mother was a surprise, the mother, thought Lewis, was a beauty, a bold strenuous-looking woman, with a curiously out-of-date sexual appeal. She was heavily made up, her mouth a dark red, her eyebrows arched in permanent astonishment, an artificial streak of white inserted into her upswept dark hair. She had exactly the same look of disdain that he remembered from the screen goddesses of his childhood. For all its apparent and carefully nurtured perfection the face was discontented, with an incipient puffiness round the mouth and chin. Lewis could see no resemblance at all between the mother and the daughter, but, then he remembered Miss Clarke hinting that the father had gone off with another woman, and he supposed this renegade, this ingrate, to have had the same fair looks that his daughter now possessed.

But why had the father gone off? What sort of a woman did a man go off to, when he had this red-lipped smouldering creature at home? For she was still in the prime of life, not much more than fifty, he supposed. She looked tricky, hard to please, and also capricious, exigent, the last person to be the guardian of a pristine semi-invalid daughter. A fur coat was flung back from a plumpish compact little body; her skirt was short enough to show fine legs in fine stockings. He could see no sign of conjugal or maternal disillusionment in her face, but simply impatience. Mrs Harper looked like a woman whose husband had left only a minute before, to perform some necessary but unimportant duty, and who would return immediately once the duty were out of the way. Mrs Harper, in fact, looked like a woman invisibly accompanied by a man. Yet there she was, tied to her daughter, clocking in at the library four times a day, without any possibility of release from this obligation until the daughter resumed her autonomy.

Lewis felt a pang of pity for them both. He felt too that if he could wean Tissy away from her mother he might effect the

---

Having had some time at my disposal when in London, I had visited the British Museum, and made search among the books and maps in the library regarding Transylvania; it had struck me that some foreknowledge of that country could

happiness of three people. He still retained a sense of chivalry towards women. He was aware of his lack of experience, and ashamed of it, but he was even more ashamed of certain publications bought in Paris and hidden beneath his sweaters until they could be safely deposited in public rubbish bins. These texts had left him with a sense of surprise and disappointment, and he hated the idea that the getting of wisdom involved both. For himself he envisaged something more chaste, if that could be managed: it could be brief, but it must be perfect, heroic. He would be prepared to lose all, but only if at some point he had gained all. Although Tissy Harper, with her prayerful hands and her downcast eyes, might not provide the promised sins of the flesh, she still represented a quest and a safeguard. She would be kind, would not mock or disregard him, would care for him studiously and with gratitude. And her mother could go back to whatever society she had been forced to abandon – he imagined hotel terraces, bridge games, cocktails – when the girl, her so unsuitable daughter, had become her only occupation.

The problem now was how to divide the mother and daughter for as long as it might take him to pursue his plan. For he had to emancipate her from her tutelage before he could do anything else. The project appealed to him: it had the requisite altruism. He had an obscure feeling that a man must perform an act of nobility before claiming his prize. This, he knew, was ridiculous. But he had never felt comfortable when he had been merely lewd and selfish. He supposed that in later life, in remote middle age, perhaps, these attributes might be sufficient to motivate him, but by then he would have sunk far from grace, as old people did, his mother excepted. For the time being he knew himself to be not only young but powerless. His powerlessness was reinforced by his virginity, which he felt to be tardy and shameful. In Paris nothing had happened to change his hopeful self. With his abundant hair, his short-sighted smile, and his respectful expression, he had attracted no predatory gaze. And he suspected that he would not have been equal to such a situation. The prospect before him now promised a certain equality, if only of inexperience, and vouchsafed him, at the same time, a quota of generosity, of honour, even. He needed these feelings not only because they were pleasurable in themselves but because they were required to offset certain censorable images that crept back to him from his unofficial Parisian readings. He had no sensation of being attracted to Tissy Harper. What he felt was a mixture of respect and charity. He would rescue her and take his

hardly fail to have some importance in dealing with a noble of that country.

Bram Stoker, *Dracula* (1897)

reward first and leave her with a legacy of freedom, waking her,
like the Sleeping Beauty, from the strange enchantment that had
kept her a prisoner for so long. For how long? Since the father had
left home, Miss Clarke had implied. When would that have been?
There was no clue to this. The key to the whole enigma was the
mother, he thought. And if he could free them both they could
thank him by performing various domestic duties about the place.
These were becoming urgent. No matter how many times he
changed the sheets he habitually forgot the day on which the
laundry was collected and delivered. He was, as always, extremely
hungry. If they would look after him, he thought, he would take
them both on. He would marry them both.

Yet initially they must be separated. This looked to him to be a
virtual impossibility. Stealthily he followed them out of the
library, studied their backs, as they walked, arm in arm, down the
lighted street. The mother walked elaborately, in the manner of
one throwing out physical hints to passers-by, hips in movement,
leg thrust forward, small feet turned outward, like a dancer's.
Beside her her daughter appeared awkward, apologetic, large of
foot, meek of gesture, head dipping in obedience or in fear,
beautiful indigo eyes cast downwards. Lewis saw that they walked
on decisively, disdaining the bus stop, and he did the same,
thinking that at least he could find out where they lived. This did
not seem to him underhand; he was in any event going in the same
direction. Having no strategy at his disposal he merely said,
'Hello, again, Miss Harper. Or perhaps I should say good evening.
Good evening,' he added, in the direction of Tissy's mother.

'Oh, Mr Percy.' Miss Harper was not unduly surprised. 'I don't
think you've met my mother. Mr Percy, mother. You may have
seen him before. In the library, I mean.'

'No, I don't think so,' said Mrs Harper, tonelessly, in a voice
that contained chest notes but was harshened by cigarette smoke.
'How do you do?'

'We seem to be walking in the same direction,' Lewis hazarded.

'We live in Britannia Road,' said Miss Harper. 'And you?'

'Further on. Opposite the Common,' he replied. 'May I walk
along with you?'

So the meeting was effected. But it was only to be a meeting,
that was clear. He sensed a powerful indifference emanating from
the mother; he felt her deliberately withholding her interest in him.
And why should she be interested, he thought humbly. She was
obviously a woman of the world, a woman of some experience.

I recall a tragic-comical incident of life at the British
Museum. Once, on going down to the lavatory to wash my
hands, I became aware of a notice newly set above a row of
basins. It ran somehow thus: 'Readers are requested to
bear in mind that these basins are to be used only for casual

The daughter must take after the absent father, the father who had
so inexplicably left home. He imagined the mother trapped,
baffled, chafing at the legacy of that useless husband, inwardly
raging at the chore that fell to her lot four times a day. Lewis, in his
mind's eye, saw Mrs Harper raising a cigarette to her lipsticked
mouth, stroking her hair up from the nape of her neck, appraising
herself in a glass. He did not see how there could be any room for a
Miss Harper in Mrs Harper's life. Mrs Harper, he thought, gave
out all the signals of a woman accustomed to playing for high
stakes, rather than of merely being a pawn in the game. And Tissy,
poor Tissy, must represent to her both burden and sacrifice. In the
light of Mrs Harper's dead-eye acknowledgement of his presence,
Lewis crept nearer to Tissy, wondering if he dared take her hand.

He saw them to their door. Their house looked trim, immaculate, at least from the outside. Clearly he was not to be invited in.
He watched the mother extract the key from a powerful handbag,
while the daughter stood politely to one side, like a guest.
Desperately he sought to prolong the encounter. Ask me in, he
thought, ask me in. Ask me to share your meal: be pleasant, be
merciful. He felt all the desolation of one who goes home to an
empty house. Above all he was a little shocked by their exclusivity.
Surely it was in the bounds of normal politeness to express an
interest in a new acquaintance? Yet he could hardly go on asking
questions, with their own attention to him so minimal. They were
too used to each other's company, he supposed, and the routine of
their days was so deadening that they had lost their manners. For a
moment he felt intensely sorry for himself, could hardly face the
short distance that separated him from his own house. But I know
no one else, he thought sadly. This will have to do.

'Miss Harper, ' he called. She turned back from the door. 'I
could walk you home, if you like,' he said, feeling himself blush. 'I
mean it would give your mother a break. And we live so near each
other.'

It was to be concluded that he knew all about her disability; he
thought it better to make no reference of it. And she seemed quite
tranquil in the knowledge that she had no explanations, no excuses
to offer. Looking back on this later Lewis wondered whether he
should have challenged her at this point, brought matters out into
the open. He could see, past her, through the open front door, a
hallway papered in brilliant red. This shocked him; such colours
were unknown in his milieu. All his mother's rooms were white.
He saw the dark blushing cave into which Miss Harper was about

---

ablutions.' Oh, the significance of that description? Had I not
more than once been glad to use this soap and water more
largely than the sense of the authorities contemplated? And
there were poor fellows working under the great dome,
whose need in this respect was greater than mine. I laughed

to be subsumed in womb-like terms: this was to be a birth in reverse. Every night, when the lights were on and the walls glowed red, Miss Harper would become the property of her mother all over again. The creature of her mother. He promised himself he would examine this thought when he got home. For the time being, whatever reservations he felt about their hospitality, he had to have an answer to his offer, his request, his plea.

'Well, I'm not sure,' was her reply. But she lingered; that was a good sign.

'Do you always walk home?' he went on. 'I do every evening. The evenings are so long now that my mother's gone.' He felt a charlatan, introducing the subject of his mother into the simulcrum of a flirtation. But it is time, he told himself. I am lonely and why shouldn't she know it? Why shouldn't she take account of me for a while? After all, I'm not going to frighten her. She has nothing to fear.

'We only walk the whole way in the evening,' she said conscientiously. 'We usually catch the bus in the morning. And we have lunch out, near the library. I really don't think . . .'

'Tissy,' came her mother's voice, to be followed by her mother's outline, solid black against the brilliant red hallway. She was smoking a cigarette.

'Mother, Mr Percy has very kindly offered to see me home one evening. But I've told him . . .'

'Tell Mr Percy that you're very grateful for his kind offer,' she said. Lewis detected a certain sarcasm in the remark. 'I don't mind the walk. But you could ask him if he'd like to come to tea one day. Saturday would do. He can walk home with us then.'

Lewis blushed again, and thanked her, and promised to meet them at five o'clock on the following Saturday. Having accomplished his mission he was anxious to be gone. It seemed to him that he had worked too hard for the minimal concession she had made, and he disliked the feeling. He could not quite make out this couple, he thought; he would need his mother to decipher them. A great wave of misery broke over him. He trudged along the street, away from the false promise of that lighted hallway, back to the dark house that it was now difficult to think of as home. He stood for a long time at the window, staring into the empty street. Then he let the curtain fall and went upstairs to his room. On the landing he opened his mother's door and watched the moon stream in over her bed. This, strangely, comforted him. If his mother was present, in however dematerialised a form, he could proceed. And

heartily at the notice, but it meant so much.
George Gissing, *The Private Papers of Henry Ryecroft*
(1902)

the future was there, after all; it simply had to be filled in. He went thoughtfully to bed, thankful, at least, to have so many new reflections to keep him company.

Lewis Percy (Jonathan Cape, 1989)

I have a wife, a son, a home, six good hunters and a library of Romance literature. I mean to enjoy them. If I am wanted, I can be found.

George Wyndham, letter to Charles Boyd (1908)

ANTHONY BURGESS

A French Lesson

Everybody talked about sex, but I kept quiet about my pre-mature experience of it: one should not kiss and tell. Peter O'Brien [a fellow student] only talked of it negatively, in the sense that he did not believe it existed, or, if it did exist, it was not necessary, since doctors and nurses were responsible for babies. I knew it existed, more than ever before, since I was being instructed in it by a very mature woman. Br Andrew, our teacher of English, had taught us a poem by James Elroy Flecker – the 'War Song of the Saracens', from *Hassan*, in anapaestic hexameters – and he ordered me to fill one of our free Wednesday afternoons by going to the Central Library [in Manchester], finding me such information on Flecker as I could, and afterwards delivering a lecture on that minor poet. I went to the Central Library, at that time in Piccadilly, and had difficulty with the index system. It was all numbers and I was looking for names. A woman of about forty put me right, a charming woman running acceptably to fat, dressed in a green skirt and a blue sweater, her hair prettily mousy, before getting down to her study of Engels. When I had gained enough information about Flecker (he had married a Greek girl named Miss Skidaresse), she apparently had gained enough information about Engels, whoever he was. On the steps of the library she said I looked cold and asked if I would like tea. I thought she was proposing the Kardomah cafe, but she put myself and herself on a tram and took me to Ardwick, where she had a small flat over a confectioner's shop. It was a bookish flat, warmed by a gas fire, with bright rugs and pictures on the walls that were nothing like the anecdotal post-Millais horrors we had at home. These pictures were like what I had painted in the elementary school before my daltonianism was painfully and hilariously discovered. But she told me they were by great artists, only reproductions of course: I needed, she said, to be educated.

She meant more than instruction in the visual arts. She was a widow whose husband had drowned at Southport (this seemed

---

The first thing to have in a library is a shelf.
Fr'm time to time this can be decorated with lithrachure. But th' shelf is th' main thing.
    Finley Peter Dunne, 'Books', *Mr Dooley Says* (1910)

improbable: I had been to Southport and had never even seen the sea), and she was earning a living by lecturing for the Workers' Educational Association. Marx and Engels, whoever they were, were among the subjects of her lectures. But she was not disposed to talk about them after our strong tea and ginger snaps. She took from a drawer under her shelves of economic history a packet of condoms. I had heard of these but had never yet seen them. They were commonly called French letters, presumably because they let or hindered pregnancy. I knew that this term had a vulgarity unacceptable to, and perhaps unknown by, educated people, since I had seen one of Br Andrew's literary magazines, which had a section headed 'Our American Letter' and another headed 'Our French Letter', and this latter had been about people writing poems in Paris. She now gave me detailed instruction about love-making on the rug before the gas fire. She had fine big bouncing breasts, ripe not ripening, and her skin had an acrid smell as of woodsmoke. Now, protected by latex, I did the deed. It was a totally anonymous undertaking, since she did not ask me my name or divulge hers. It did not seem to be sin, because the tone was educative, as for a serious session of the Workers' Educational Association, and the moans of fulfilment had an appropriate decorum. She seemed a healthy woman, Protestant of course, who had certain physical needs which needed to be regularly gratified. She gave me a little postcoital instruction in the materialistic philosophy on which Marxist economic theory was based. God was a fable designed to uphold the capitalist exploiters, and sin was a fabrication intended to make the workers feel guilty about demanding their rights. Then, as tumescence renewed itself, that aspect of my education was intermitted. I got home late and weary. My stepmother, not normally given to commiseration, remarked on my tired eyes and said they were making me study too 'ard. She gave me two fried eggs with my bacon.

Little Wilson and Big God, Being the First Part of the Confessions of Anthony Burgess (Heinemann, 1987)

THE BRITISH MUSEUM

'At the present rapid rate of accumulation', wrote W.N.P. Barbellion at the turn of the century, 'the time must come when the British Museum, thousands of years hence, will occupy an area as large as London and the *Encyclopaedia Britannica* will be housed in a building as big as the Crystal Palace.' The biologist and some-time sclerotic was not right about the Britannica which today can be contained in a compact disc, but viewing the latest manifestation of the BM as it sprawls over King's Cross he could yet be right about that.

The Museum's origins were in Montagu House in Great Russell Street while the growth of its collections can be dated back to an Act of 1753. The library owes much to the collection of Sir Robert Cotton, the sixteenth-century antiquary, and the Licensing Act of 1663. What gives it its romance is the domed reading-room and the seats arranged as spokes in a wheel.

For generations it has been a scholar's club. The attendants are notoriously laconic and unimpressed with reputation. Karl Marx wrote *Das Kapital* there and when a biographer asked a member of the staff what he remembered about him he could recall nothing. He asked for a description. 'Ah, Mr Marx', he said, 'whatever became of him?'

Apocryphal as this anecdote may be, it does convey something about the attitude of the old place which will be hard to replace in the new building, which has the allure of a monstrous supermarket. All the grandees used it at one time or other, some, such as the three-decker novelist Rearden in George Gissing's *New Grub Street*, as a home from home. It is what gives Bloomsbury its tone. Fingering the cards in the ancient catalogue, it is not hard to imagine Dickens or Shaw doing the same thing a century before, filling in slip after slip and falling into a reverie until the books appear. It is somehow comforting to know that after the Second World War the underrated novelist Angus Wilson was among the staff prominent in the rebuilding of the collection. Almost alone among scholars, Carlyle did not take to the place but that may have been more to do with his antipathy towards Sir Anthony Panizzi, the Museum's Italian-born librarian, than to the place itself. That commands nothing surely but affection, which is why it is the most written-about library in the world. David Lodge named a novel after it. When he wrote *The British Museum Is Falling Down* the title stated the unthinkable. Will we ever feel the same about its successor?

NIGEL WILLIAMS

Getting In

'And what,' said the young man behind the desk, 'is your interest in the seventeenth century?'

He asked this question in the tone of a hotel desk clerk, checking in a couple who have just announced they have no luggage, no means of identification, and that their married name is Smith. It was as if the British Museum was bombarded with requests from suspicious individuals eager to try any excuse or stratagem just as long as they could get in out of the cold and wrap their fingers round a juicy slice of pornography.

'I am a writer,' I said, pausing as I always do after this description of myself.

The young man sneered visibly. 'They all say that,' his expression seemed to say.

'And an honours graduate in history from the University of Oxford,' I went on.

This had absolutely no effect on him whatsoever.

'Yes?' he said.

From the pocket of my anorak I got out the crumpled letter which Gottlieb had written on my behalf.

'This is a letter telling you who I am,' I said.

TO WHOM IT MAY CONCERN

Jamie Matheson is one of the most astonishingly talented young novelists and screenwriters to have emerged in Britain during the last five years. Witty, ferocious and intellectually rigorous, he has been translated into both Finnish and Norwegian.

He is at present working on a project for this company that requires historical research and I would ask that you give him access to the facilities of the British Library.

Yours sincerely
Nat Gottlieb
Executive Producer – *Cavaliers*

She [Q.D. Leavis in *Fiction and Reading Public*, 1932] shows that, though fiction of the bestseller type has been turned out for over the last two hundred years, it has only lately realised its power, and that the popular novelist of today tends to be venomous and aggressive towards his more

The young man looked up quizzically.

'*Cavaliers* eh?' he said.

'It's a working title.'

'Mmm.'

He pouted again and glanced over my left shoulder like an orchestral player wearily registering the eccentricities of yet another conductor. I marvelled once again at Gottlieb's ability to splash about adverbs of degree such as 'astonishingly' or 'uniquely', especially when yoked to adjectives such as 'brilliant', 'talented' or 'powerful', on occasions when these adjectives were to be applied to writers to whom Gottlieb had paid money. Words mean nothing to Gottlieb, except as a way of getting what he wants.

I didn't like the Finnish and Norwegian bit either. Just because my books aren't of world import, i.e. long. Finns are very discriminating. I don't want to be of world import anyway. It's too late. I no longer have the urge to write sentences that wind gloriously upward like a mountain road, snaking through mists, along the edge of ravines, skirting pine forests, vertical clumps of rock and dizzying drops to dried out riverbeds, to come out on level ground, nothing below them, nothing, in fact, in view, but a magnificent prospect of absolutely fuck all. On my passport it says 'Screenwriter'. I'm proud of that.

'And how long,' said the young man, 'will . . . this . . .' (here he tapped Gottlieb's letter contemptuously) '. . . take?'

This was obviously a trick question.

'Clearly,' I said, 'it's not a question of years.'

I should bleeding well cocoa said the expression on the young man's face.

'But,' I went on, 'it's not something I could do in . . . weeks.'

Christ, there were several million books in there. What did the guy want? For me to break down and admit that I lacked the intellectual equipment to know which were the right ones for me to read? The young man squirmed forward in his seat and sighed elaborately. On the other side of the room a young woman was talking her way quietly, earnestly into possession of a reader's ticket. What was she offering? Money? Sexual favours? A combination of the two?

'Six months?' I said, trying to keep the pleading tone out of my voice. But he was ready for this show of reasonableness.

'Do you have any identification?'

'I'm sorry?'

---

artistic brethren – an attitude in which he is supported by most of the press, and by the cheap libraries.

E.M. Forster, *Does Culture Matter?*

'A driving licence?'

I looked blank. He became patient.

'You see I have no proof that you are . . .' he tapped the letter again – 'Jamie Matheson.'

He said this in a tone of rank disbelief, as if to suggest that not only was it unlikely that I bore the names in question but that 'Jamie Matheson' itself was such an improbable construct that the chances were against anyone anywhere actually being him.

To reassure myself as much as anyone else, I groped in the saddle-bag that lay at my feet. The young man peered over at me as my hands scrabbled blindly for that rare thing, a copy of my last novel. As I fished it out and thrust the back of the jacket at him, I felt, once again, a stab of doubt about the title. *Say Goodnight to Alfie Barnacle*. No. No no no no no.

'There,' I said, pointing at the black and white photograph on the back.

'That's me. Author. Picture of me. OK?'

He pursed his lips. Even the studio portrait made me look like something that had crawled out from under a stone in a Scandinavian fairy story. Meg always said that I looked like a troll. Jake Bolewski's picture just made me look like a carefully lit troll.

'Jamie Matheson,' said the young man, in tones that hovered just on the edge of a giggle, 'is already widely known as a screenwriter, author of the thirteen part series *Dust Ashes* . . .' He widened his eyes and drew his chin into his neck like a chicken on the move. I suppressed the urge to discuss the work in question.

'Me,' I said thickly, 'I wrote it.'

Even as I said it I wished, once again, that it were not true. The young man did a lot of squinting between studio portrait and subject. He reminded me of an East German customs official, or the keen young Cuban who kept me for three hours at Havana Airport. Finally, he said, wearily:

'Do you know which papers you'll be looking at?'

'If I knew that,' I said between clenched teeth, 'I wouldn't need to go in in the fucking first place would I?'

'Will you need to go into the North Library?'

'I will need,' I said, 'to go to the South Hall, the West wing, the North Transept, the East Tower and the South East Corridor. I want to go all over the British Library. Please.'

'Very well,' said the young man, 'we can probably issue you with a ticket for six months.'

He started to recite the rules governing the conduct of those

---

Coffined thoughts around me, in mummycases, embalmed in spice of words. Thoth, god of libraries, a birdgod, moonycrowned. And I heard the voice of that Egypt highpriest.

lucky enough to get into the British Library but the life had gone out of him. I could tell he was already gearing up for the next encounter – some charlatan calling himself Graham Greene perhaps, or a Nobel prizewinner in search of a quiet kip. I was photographed, presented with a plastic ID card and sent on my way.

I was in. I was a historian again. A serious person.

Witchcraft (Faber and Faber, 1987)

In painted chambers loaded with tilebooks.
James Joyce, Stephen Dedalus on the reading room in the National Library, Dublin, *Ulysses* (1922)

JEROME K. JEROME

A Severe Case of Hypochondria

I remember going to the British Museum one day to read up the treatment for some slight ailment of which I had a touch – hay fever, I fancy it was. I got down the book, and read all I came to read; and then, in an unthinking moment, I idly turned the leaves, and began to indolently study diseases, generally. I forget which was the first distemper I plunged into – some fearful, devastating scourge, I know – and, before I had glanced down the list of 'premonitory symptoms', it was borne in upon me that I had fairly got it.

I sat for a while frozen with horror; and then in the listlessness of despair, I turned over the pages. I came to typhoid fever – read the symptoms – discovered that I had typhoid fever, must have had it for months without knowing about it – wondered what else I had got; turned up St Vitus's Dance – found, as I expected, that I had that too – began to get interested in my case, and determined to sift it to the bottom, and so started alphabetically – read up ague, and learnt that I was sickening for it, and that the acute stage would commence in about another fortnight. Bright's disease, I was relieved to find, I had only in a modified form, and, so far as that was concerned, I might live for years. Cholera I had, with severe complications; and diphtheria I seemed to have been born with. I plodded conscientiously through the twenty-six letters, and the only malady I could conclude that I had not got was housemaid's knee.

I felt rather hurt about this at first; it seemed somehow to be a sort of slight. Why hadn't I got housemaid's knee: was this invidious reservation? After a while, however, less grasping feelings prevailed. I reflected that I had every other malady in the pharmacology, and I grew less selfish, and determined to do without housemaid's knee. Gout, in its most malignant stage, it would appear, had seized me without my being aware of it; and zymosis I had evidently been suffering with since boyhood. There were no more diseases after zymosis, so I concluded there was

---

During the autumn and winter the delivery of books is not infrequently hindered by darkness or fog.
A Guide to the Use of the [British Museum] Reading Room
(1924)

nothing else the matter with me.

I sat and pondered. I thought what an interesting case I would be from a medical point of view, what an acquisition I should be to a class! Students would have no need 'to walk the hospitals', if they had me. I was a hospital in myself. All they needed to do was walk round me, and, after that, take their diploma.

Then I wondered how long I had to live. I tried to examine myself. I felt my pulse. I could not at first feel any pulse at all. Then, all of a sudden, it seemed to start off. I pulled out my watch and timed it. I made it a hundred and forty-seven to the minute. I tried to feel my heart. I could not feel my heart. It had stopped beating. I have since been induced to come to the opinion that it must have been there all the time, and must have been beating, but I cannot account for it. I patted myself all over my front, from what I call my waist up to my head, and I went a bit round each side, and a little way up the back. But I could not feel or hear anything. I tried to look at my tongue. I stuck it out as far as ever it would go. I could only see the tip, and the only thing that I could gain from that was to feel more certain than before that I had scarlet fever.

I walked into that reading room a happy healthy man. I crawled out a decrepit wreck.

Three Men in a Boat (1889)

William B. McIntosh, the librarian of the *Aquitania*, has retired. He crossed the Atlantic 1300 times.
                              Scots Observer (4 February 1932)

LOUIS MacNEICE

The British Museum Reading-Room

Under the hive-like dome the stooping haunted readers
Go up and down the alleys, tap the cells of knowledge –
   Honey and wax, the accumulation of years –
Some on commission, some for the love of learning,
Some because they have nothing better to do
Or because they hope these walls of books will deaden
   The drumming of the demon in their ears.

Cranks, hacks, poverty-stricken scholars,
In pince-nez, period hats or romantic beards
   And cherishing their hobby or their doom
Some are too much alive and some are asleep
Hanging like bats in a world of inverted values,
Folded up in themselves in a world which is safe and silent:
   This is the British Museum Reading Room.

Out on the steps in the sun the pigeons are courting,
Puffing their ruffs and sweeping their tails or taking
   A sun-bath at their ease
And under the totem poles – the ancient terror –
Between the enormous fluted Ionic columns
There seeps from heavily jowled or hawk-like foreign faces
   The guttural sorrow of the refugees.

On our way from Rompton to Edbury I went into the public
library, and, though Paddy did not want to read, I suggested
he should come in and rest his legs. But he preferred to wait
on the pavement. 'No,' he said, 'de sight of all dat bloody
print makes me sick.'
   George Orwell, *Down and Out in Paris and London* (1933)

DAVID LODGE

An Aquarium for Tropical Fish

He passed through the narrow vaginal passage, and entered the huge womb of the Reading Room. Across the floor, dispersed along the radiating desks, scholars curled, foetus-like, over their books, little buds of intellectual life thrown off by some gigantic act of generation performed upon that nest of knowledge, those inexhaustible ovaries of learning, the concentric inner rings of the catalogue shelves.

The circular wall of the Reading Room wrapped the scholars in a protective layer of books, while above them arched the vast, distended belly of the dome. Little daylight entered through the grimy glass at the top. No sounds of traffic or other human business penetrated to that warm, airless space. The dome looked down on the scholars, and the scholars looked down on their books; and the scholars loved their books, stroking the pages with soft pale fingers. The pages responded to the fingers' touch, and yielded their knowledge gladly to the scholars, who collected it in little boxes of filecards. When the scholars raised their eyes from their desks they saw nothing to distract them, nothing out of harmony with their books, only the smooth, curved lining of the womb. Wherever the eye travelled, it met no arrest, no angle, no parallel lines receding into infinity, no pointed arch striving towards the unattainable: all was curved, rounded, self-sufficient, complete. And the scholars dropped their eyes to their books again, fortified and consoled. They curled themselves more tightly over their books, for they did not want to leave the warm womb, where they fed upon electric light and inhaled the musty odour of yellowing pages.

But the women who waited outside felt differently. From their dingy flats in Islington and cramped semis in Bexleyheath, they looked out through the windows at the life of the world, at the motor-cars and the advertisements and the clothes in the shops, and they found them good. And they resented the warm womb of the Museum which made them poor and lonely, which swallowed

---

Gordon [Comstock] knew her type at a glance, but he was too preoccupied to care.

'Have you any books on gynaecology?' he said.

'Any *what*?' demanded the young woman with a pince-nez flash of unmistakable triumph. As usual! Another male in search of dirt!

up their men every day and sapped them of their vital spirits and made them silent and abstracted mates even when they were at home. And the women sighed for the day when their men would be expelled from the womb for the last time, and they looked at their children whimpering at their feet, and they clasped their hands, coarsened with detergent, and vowed that these children would never be scholars.

Lawrence, thought Adam [Appleby]. It's time I got on to Lawrence.

He weaved his way to the row of desks where he and Camel usually worked, and noted the familiar figures at whose sides he had worked for two years, without ever exchanging a word with any of them: earnest, efficient Americans, humming away like dynamos, powered by Guggenheim grants; turbanned Sikhs, all called Mr Singh, and all studying Indian influences on English literature; pimply, bespectacled women smiling cruelly to themselves as they noted an error in somebody's footnote; and then the Museum characters – the gentleman whose beard reached to his feet, the lady in shorts, the man wearing odd shoes and a yachting-cap reading a Gaelic newspaper with a one-stringed lute propped up on his desk, the woman who sniffed. Adam recognised Camel's coat and briefcase at one of the desks, but the seat was unoccupied.

Eventually he discovered Camel in the North Library. They did not usually work there: it was overheated, and its low rectangular shape and green furnishings gave one the sense of being in an aquarium for tropical fish. The North Library was used especially for consulting rare and valuable books, and there were also a number of seats reserved for the exclusive use of eminent scholars, who enjoyed the privilege of leaving their books on their desks for indefinite periods. These desks were rarely occupied except by piles of books and cards bearing distinguished names, and they reminded Adam of a waxworks from which all the exhibits had been withdrawn for renovation.

'What are you doing here?' he whispered to Camel.

'I'm reading an allegedly pornographic book,' Camel explained. 'You have to fill out a special application and read it here under the Superintendent's nose. To make sure you don't masturbate, I suppose.'

'Good Lord. D'you think they'll make me do that for *Lady Chatterley's Lover*?'

'Shouldn't think so, now you can buy it and masturbate at home.'

'Well, any books on midwifery? About babies being born, and so forth.'

'We don't issue books of that description to the general public,' said the young woman frostily.

'I'm sorry – there's a point I particularly want to look up.'

'What seat did you save for me in the Reading Room?'

'Next to mine. Number thirteen, I think.'

'You seem to have an attachment to the number thirteen where I'm concerned,' said Adam, petulantly. 'I'm not superstitious, but there's no point in taking chances.'

'What kind of chances?'

'Never mind,' said Adam.

He returned to the Reading Room and, wielding the huge volumes of the catalogue with practised ease, filled in application slips for *The Rainbow* and several critical studies of Lawrence. Then he returned to the seat Camel had saved for him, to wait. One of the Museum's many throwbacks to a more leisured and gracious age was that books were delivered to one's desk. So vast was the library, however – Adam understood it amounted to six million volumes – and so understaffed, that it was normal for more than an hour to elapse between the lodging of an application and the arrival of a book. He sat down on the large padded seat, ignoring the envious and accusing glances of the readers in his vicinity. For some reason only about one in ten of the Reading Room seats was padded, and there was fierce competition for the possession of them.

The padded seats were magnificently comfortable. Adam wondered whether they were made by Brownlong and Co. If so, he felt he could address himself to the competition with real enthusiasm.

> *I always choose a Brownlong chair*
> *Because I wrote my thesis there.*

The manufacturer's name was usually found on the underside of chairs, wasn't it? Adam wondered whether he might turn his chair upside down for inspection, but decided that it would attract too much attention. He looked round: no one was watching. He deliberately dropped a pencil on the floor, and bent down to recover it, peering under his seat the while. He dimly discerned a small nameplate but could not read the inscription. He put his head right under the seat, lost his balance and fell heavily to the floor. Startled, annoyed or amused faces were turned upon him from the neighbouring desks. Red with embarrassment and from the blood that had rushed to his head while he hung upside down, Adam recovered his seat and rubbed his head.

Adam was filled with self-pity. It was the second time that

'Are you a medical student?'

'No.'

'Then I don't *quite* see what you want with books on midwifery.'

George Orwell, *Keep the Aspidistra Flying* (1936)

morning that he had fallen down. Then there were the hallucina-
tions. Clearly, something was seriously the matter with him. He
was approaching a nervous breakdown. He repeated the words to
himself with a certain pleasure. Nervous. Breakdown. They
evoked a prospect of peace and passivity, of helpless withdrawal
from the world, of a huge burden of worry shifted on to someone
else's shoulders. He saw himself lying mildly in a darkened room
while anxious friends and doctors held whispered conferences
round his bed. Perhaps they would make a petition to the Pope and
get him and Barbara a special dispensation to practise artificial
contraception. Or perhaps he would die, his tragic case be brought
to the attention of the Vatican Council, and the doctrine of Natural
Law revised as a result. A fat lot of good that would do *him*. Adam
decided not to have a nervous breakdown after all.

To work, to work. He began briskly to unpack his bulging
holdalls. Soon the broad, blue leather-topped desk was heaped
with books, files, folders, index-cards and odd scraps of paper
with notes and references scribbled on them. Adam's energy and
determination subsided like the mercury of a thermometer
plunged in cold water. How would he ever succeed in organising
all this into anything coherent?

The subject of Adam's thesis had originally been 'Language and
Ideology in Modern Fiction' but had been whittled down by the
Board of Studies until it now stood as 'The Structure of Long
Sentences in Three Modern English Novels'. The whittling down
didn't seem to have made his task any easier. He still hadn't
decided which three novels he was going to analyse, nor had he
decided how long a long sentence was. Lawrence, he thought
hopefully, would produce lots of sentences where the issue would
not be in doubt.

Adam listlessly turned over pages of notes on minor novelists
who were now excluded from his thesis. There was this great wad,
for instance, on Egbert Merrymarsh, the Catholic belletrist,
younger contemporary of Chesterton and Belloc. Adam had
written a whole chapter, tentatively entitled 'The Divine Wisecrack' on Merrymarsh's use of paradox and antithesis to prop up
his facile Christian apologetics. All wasted labour.

Adam yawned, and looked at the clock above the entrance to the
North Library. There was still a long time to go before his books
would arrive. Everyone but himself seemed to be working with
quiet concentration: you could almost hear a faint hum of cerebral
flywheels and sprockets busily turning. Adam was seized by

My grandfather, however, John Jay Smith, left Burlington as
a boy, and sailing down the Delaware to Philadelphia,
establishing himself there first as a chemist's assistant,
soon began to engage in other activities. Among the
stipulations which James Logan had made on bequeathing
his books to the Philadelphia Library was one to the effect

conflicting emotions of guilt, envy, frustration and revolt. Revolt
won: this still repose, this physical restraint, was unnatural.

He fiddled idly with his pencil, trying to make it stand on end.
He failed, and the pencil fell to the floor. He stooped cautiously to
recover it, meeting, as he straightened up, the frown of a distracted
reader. Adam frowned back. Why shouldn't he be distracted? Dis-
traction was as necessary to mental health as exercise to physical.
It would be a good idea, in fact, if the Reading Room were cleared
twice a day, and all the scholars marched out to do physical jerks in
the forecourt. No, that wouldn't do – he hated physical jerks
himself. Suppose, instead, the circular floor of the Reading Room
were like the revolve on a stage, and that every hour, on the hour,
the Superintendent would throw a lever to set the whole thing in
motion, sweeping the spokes of the desks round for a few
exhilarating revolutions. Yes, and the desks would be mounted so
as to go gently up and down like horses on a carousel. It wouldn't
necessarily interrupt work – just give relief to the body cramped in
the same position. Tone up the system. Encourage the circulation.
Yes, he must remember to mention it to Camel. The British
Museum Act. He closed his eyes and indulged in a pleasing vision
of the gay scene, as the floor rotated, and the scholars smiled with
quiet pleasure at each other as their seats rose above the partitions,
and gently sank again. Perhaps there might be tinkling music . . .

Adam felt a tap on his shoulder. It was Camel.

'Why are you humming "La Ronde"? You're getting some black
looks.'

'I'll tell you later,' said Adam, in some confusion. He fled from
the Reading Room to avoid the hostile glances directed at him
from all sides.

In the foyer, he decided to ring Barbara again. To his surprise,
the booth was still occupied by the fat man. Adam was beginning
to make awed calculations of the cost of a thirty-minute call to
Colorado, when his attention was caught by various signs of
distress the fat man was making. He had somehow managed to
close the door of the booth, which folded inwards, but his girth
rendered him incapable of opening it again. After some moments
of strenuous exertion, Adam was able to extricate him.

'Well,' said the fat man. 'You seem to be my private boy scout
today.'

'Did you make your phone call all right?' Adam inquired.

'I experienced some linguistic difficulties.'

'Don't they speak English in Colorado?'

that his eldest son should be the librarian, and his eldest
grandson in the male line should succeed; and should the
male line fail, the position should be offered to the eldest of
the female line. To my grandfather this appointment was
given; he occupied it many years, and was succeeded in it
by one of my uncles. James Logan's will was, I believe,

'Sure they do. But your operator kept saying, "You're through" before I'd even started . . . do you smoke cigars?' he suddenly demanded.

'My father-in-law usually gives me one on Christmas Day,' said Adam.

'Well, save these and astonish him in December,' said the fat man, thrusting a fistful of huge cigars into Adam's breast pocket.

'Thank you,' murmured Adam faintly, as the fat man trundled off.

'Thank *you!*'

Adam entered the phone booth, which smelled suspiciously of rich cigar smoke, and made his call. There was a clatter as the receiver was lifted at the other end, and a childish voice intoned:

'Battersea Double Two One – O.'

'Oh hallo, Clare darling. What are you doing at the phone?'

'Mummy said I could practise answering.'

'Is Mummy there?'

'She's just coming down the stairs.'

'And how are you, Clare? Have you been a good girl this morning?'

'No.'

'Oh. Why's that?'

'I cut a hole in Dominic's tummy.'

'You *what*?'

'Cut a hole in Dominic's tummy. With the kitchen scissors.'

'But Clare, *why*?' Adam wailed.

'We were playing maternity hospitals and I was giving him a Caesarian.'

'But Clare, you mustn't do that.'

'You mean boys can't have babies? I know.'

'No, I mean cut people with scissors. Look, is Mummy there?'

'Here she is.'

'Hallo, Adam?'

'Darling, what's all this about Clare cutting a hole in Dominic's stomach?'

'It's only a nick. It didn't even bleed.'

'Only a nick. But what was she doing with the scissors in the first place?'

'Are you trying to blame me, Adam?'

'No, darling. I'm just trying to get at the facts.'

'As long as you're not trying to blame me. You've no idea what it's like having to look after Clare all day.'

---

invalid; the position thus dubiously bequeathed was a modest one; but since it was held for more than fifty years by members of our family, our claim to this humble librarianship came to be regarded, at least by ourselves, as conferring a kind of dim distinction; and it was originally intended that I should succeed my uncle (who had no son) in

'I know, I know. But if you could just keep the scissors out of her reach . . .'

'I do. She got the step-ladder out.'

'Did you smack her?'

'You know smacking doesn't have any effect on Clare. She just says, "I hope this is doing *you* good, Mummy." She's heard us discussing Doctor Spock.'

'God help us when she learns to read,' sighed Adam. He decided to drop the subject. 'Have you looked up the 13th in your diary?'

'You'll wish you hadn't asked.'

'Why?' said Adam, his heart sinking.

'According to the chart, ovulation should have taken place about then.'

Adam groaned.

'. . . And the 13th was a Friday,' continued Barbara.

'This is no time for joking,' said Adam, suspiciously.

'Who's joking?'

'I'm certainly not. Can't you remember anything about that night?'

'I remember you were a bit . . . you know.'

'A bit what?'

'You know what you're like when you've had a few drinks.'

'You're just the same,' said Adam defensively.

'I'm not blaming you.'

'D'you think we could have . . .?'

'No. But I wish my period would start.'

'How do you feel now?'

'About the same.'

'What was that? I've forgotten.'

'Never mind. I'm getting bored with the subject. Shouldn't you be working.'

'I can't while I'm trying to think what we did that night.'

'Well, I can't help you, Adam. I can't stay any longer. Mary Flynn is bringing her brood round for lunch.'

'How many has she got now?'

'Four.'

'Well, there's always someone else worse off than yourself.'

'Good-bye then, darling. And try not to worry.'

'Good-bye, darling.'

On his way back to the Reading Room, Adam had a thought. He returned to the phone booth and rang Barbara again.

'Hallo, darling.'

---

this; as we imaginatively designated it, the only hereditary office in America.

Logan Pearsall Smith, *Unforgotten Years* (1938)

'Adam, for heaven's sake –'

'Look, I've had a thought. About that night. Did you happen to notice the sheets the next day . . .?'

Barbara rang off. This is denaturing me, he thought.

He was getting tired with trekking backwards and forwards to the telephone. After the coolness of the foyer, the atmosphere of the Reading Room, when he re-entered it, struck him as oppressively hot. The dome seemed screwed down tightly on the stale air, sealing it in. It hung over the scene like a tropical sky before a storm; and the faint, sour smell of mouldering books and bindings was like the reek of rotting vegetation in some foetid oriental backwater. Appleby cast a gloomy eye on the Indians and Africans working busily in their striped suits and starched collars.

There comes a moment in the life of even the most unimaginative man – and Appleby was not that – when Destiny confronts him with the unexpected and the inexplicable, when the basis of his universe, like a chair which has so habitually offered its comforting support to his limbs that he no longer troubles to assure himself of its presence before entrusting his weight to it, is silently and swiftly withdrawn, and the victim feels himself falling with dismaying velocity into an infinite space of doubt. This was the sensation of Appleby as, mopping away with a soiled handkerchief the perspiration which beaded his forehead like the drops of moisture on the interior of a ship's hull that warn the knowledgeable mariner that he is approaching the equatorial line, he came in sight of the desk where he had left his books and papers. He staggered to a halt.

That *was* his desk, surely? Yes, he recognised on the one next to it his comrade's raincoat and broad-brimmed trilby. His own belongings, however, had vanished: his books, papers, index-cards – all had disappeared. But it was not this fact which made Appleby lean against a bookcase for support, and pass his right hand several times across his eyes. Grouped round his desk, and gazing at it with rapt attention, were three Chinese: not the Westernised, Hong Kong Chinese he was familiar with, draped in American-style suits and wielding sophisticated cameras, but authentic Chinese Chinese, dressed in loose, belted uniforms of some drab, coarse-grained material.

It was their attitude, above all, which made the hair on Appleby's nape prickle as at the brush of a passing ghost – an attitude which suggested prayer rather than conspiracy, and was

---

I spent my days at the British Museum, and must, I think, have been very delicate, for I remember putting off hour after hour consulting some necessary book because I shrank from lifting the heavy volumes of the catalogue.

William Butler Yeats (1865–1939)

the more frightening because the more unaccountable. If they were waiting for him, why were their backs turned, why were they poring, with bowed heads and hands clasped behind their backs, upon the bare expanse of his desk? It was as if they were engaged in some hypocritical act of mourning for a crime they had already committed.

Appleby perceived that the strangers' presence had not gone unnoticed by the other readers in the vicinity, but it seemed almost as if the latter were trying to pretend otherwise. Without lifting their heads from their books, they were stealing glances, first at the Chinese, and then at himself. An African law student, sitting near him, rolled a white eye and seemed about to speak, but thought the better of it and turned back to his books. If only, Adam felt, he could see the faces of his visitors, he would know what they had come for. He shrank from the encounter, but anything was preferable to the mystery. Or was it . . .? If he were to walk away, go home and think about it, and come back later, tomorrow say, perhaps they would have gone away, and his books would be back on the desk, and he could forget all about it. As he stood wavering at this fork in the road of his moral self-exploration, he was suddenly relieved of the choice by a light tap on his shoulder and a voice which murmured, 'Mr Appleby?'

'So it appeared,' said Adam, biting into a Scotch egg, 'that these Chinese were some cultural delegation or something from Communist China, and that they'd asked if they could look at Karl Marx's desk – you know, the one he worked at when he was researching *Das Kapital*. Did you know that, Camel? That you saved me Karl Marx's seat?'

Camel, whose face was buried in a pint tankard, tried to shake his head and spilled a few drops of beer on his trousers.

'I should have thought it would have singed your good Catholic arse,' said Pond.

'It makes you think, doesn't it?' Adam mused. 'All the famous backsides who have polished those seats: Marx, Ruskin, Carlyle . . .?'

'Colin Wilson,' suggested Pond.

'Who?' Adam asked.

'Before your time, old boy,' said Camel. 'The good old days of the Museum, when everyone was writing books on the Human Condition and publishers were fighting under the desks for the options.'

In the library [at Hillside, a preparatory school at Godalming] I could read the papers. I would rush through my breakfast and dash there to snatch the *Daily Sketch* on the morning following the Theatrical Garden Party, when the centre page would be filled with photographs of the stars – (I can see

'You'd think you only had to sit at any of those desks,' Adam went on, 'and the wisdom would just seep up through your spinal cord. It just seems to seep out of mine. Look at today, for instance; lunchtime and I haven't done a thing.'

They were in the Museum Tavern, Adam, Camel and Pond. Pond was a full-time teacher at the School of English where Camel taught a few evening classes. It was run by a crook, and Pond was worked very hard, but Adam and Camel found it difficult to commiserate with him because he earned so very much money. He and his pretty wife, Sally, had a Mini-Minor and a centrally-heated semi in Norwood with a four-poster bed draped in pink satin. Pond usually lunched with Adam and Camel one day a week, among other things in order to rid himself of the xenophobia which, as he explained, was both an occupational state of mind and a professional crime. According to Camel, he was the soul of kindness to his foreign pupils while on the job.

'That's because Karl Marx was a Jew,' he now said in reply to Adam's complaint. 'All you have to do is change your seat.'

'That's right,' said Camel, 'find yourself the seat Chesterton used. Or Belloc.'

'Or Egbert Merrymarsh,' said Adam.

'Who?'

'Who?'

'Before your time,' said Adam. 'The good old days of the Museum, when there was a crucifix on every desk. The trouble is,' he went on, 'that Merrymarsh probably chose an unpadded seat, just to mortify himself.'

'So what about the Chinese?' said Camel. 'What did you say to them?'

'Well, I was just summing up courage to go up to them and say . . . say . . . well, say something, I don't know, like, this is my seat, or, what have you done with my books, when this superintendent came up and explained. He'd been looking for me, but I was telephoning Barbara.'

'He's always telephoning his wife,' explained Camel to Pond.

'Well, that's all right; I like to phone Sally myself occasionally,' said Pond.

'Ah, that's just uxoriousness. Appleby is a neurotic case.'

'I'm not neurotic,' said Adam. 'I toyed with the idea this morning, but I decided against it. Though, I must admit, those Chinese had me worried for a minute.'

'Chinks', said Pond. 'Don't be afraid of good old prejudiced

---

one now – Nelson Keys as Katharine of Aragon and Arthur Playfair as Henry VIII in a skit on the [Sir Herbert Beerbohm] Tree production in *The Grand Giggle*). On these I would gaze enraptured. The library was a favourite retreat of mine. The

English usage.'

'I must say, whoever it was had a nerve removing your books,' said Camel.

'Oh, I could see their point. Like tidying up a grave or something.'

Pond shuddered, as he always did at the mention of death, and swigged some beer.

'What exactly did the Superintendent say to you?' Camel asked. 'I want to know exactly what he said. Did he say, "I hope you won't mind, but three Chinese gentlemen are looking at your desk"?'

'Yes, he did, actually,' said Adam, surprised. 'That's exactly what he did say.'

'And what did you say?'

'I didn't say anything at first. I tell you, I felt pretty queer.'

'So what happened then?'

'Well, he looked a bit embarrassed, and said, "It was Karl Marx's desk, you see. We often get visitors wanting to see it."'

'So what did you say then?'

'Well, that's what I was going to tell you. I *think* I said: *Mr Marx, he dead!*'

Camel and Pond looked meaningfully at each other. 'I told you,' said Camel. 'Appleby is cracking up.'

'I can see,' said Pond. 'He's going to become one of the Museum eccentrics. Before we know it, he'll be shuffling around in slippers and muttering into a beard.'

'It's a special form of scholarly neurosis,' said Camel. 'He's no longer able to distinguish between life and literature.'

'Oh yes I can,' said Adam. 'Literature is mostly about having sex and not much about having children. Life is the other way round.'

The British Museum is Falling Down
(MacGibbon and Kee, 1965; Secker, 1981)

---

only alarming feature was the window seat, which had cupboards running all round it underneath, making a sort of tunnel in which I was sometimes imprisoned by my enemies. Here I would lie, bent double, and half suffocated,

WILLIAM PLOMER

A Ticket for the Reading-Room

With a smile of secret triumph
   Seedy old untidy scholar,
Inkstains on his finger-nails,
   Cobwebs on his Gladstone collar,

Down at heel and out at elbows
   Off he goes on gouty feet
(Where he goes his foxy smell goes),
   Off towards Great Russell Street.

Unaware of other people,
   Peace and war and politics,
Down the pavement see him totter
   Following his *idée fixe*.

Past the rowdy corner café
   Full of Cypriots and flies
Where the customers see daggers
   Looking from each other's eyes,

Past the sad but so-called Fun Fair
   Where a few immortal souls
Occupy their leisure hours
   Shooting little balls at holes,

Past the window full of booklets,
   Rubber goods and cures for piles,
Past the pub, the natty milk-bar
   Crowded with galactophiles,

Through the traffic, down the side-street
   Where an unfrocked parson thrives
('Palmist and Psychologist')
   Cutting short unwanted lives,

---

while my captors sat on the window seat above me,
drumming with their boots on the cupboard doors which
barred all chance of escape.

John Gielgud, *Early Stages* (1939)

Through the shady residential
　　Square in which a widow runs
A quiet gambling-shell, or 'bridge club',
　　Fleecing other women's sons,

On he shuffles, quietly mumbling
　　Figures, facts and formulae –
Bats are busy in the belfry,
　　In the bonnet hums a bee.

At the Reading Room he settles
　　Pince-nez on his bottle nose,
Reads and scribbles, reads and scribbles,
　　Till the day draws to a close.

Then returns to oh, what squalor!
　　Kippers, cake and dark brown tea,
Filthy sheets and filthier blankets,
　　Sleep disturbed by mouse and flea.

What has the old man been doing?
　　What's his game? Another book?
He is out to pour contempt on
　　Esperanto, Vōlapük,

To fake a universal language
　　Full of deft abbreviation
For the day when all mankind
　　Join and form one happy nation.

In this the poor old chap resembles
　　Prosperous idealists
Who talk as if men reached for concord
　　With their clenched or grasping fists.

Keepers of books, keepers of print and paper on the
shelves, librarians are keepers also of the records of the
human spirit – the records of men's watch upon the world
and on themselves. In such a time as ours, when wars are
made against the spirit and its works, the keeping of these

KATE MORRIS

A Very Brief Encounter

According to Ms Bradley, who wrote to *The Daily Telegraph* last week, 'the British Library is the easiest place in London to associate with the opposite sex' – the queue at Advance Reservations is apparently 'the steamiest part of the room'.

Could it be true? What exactly is going on behind those decorous walls? Determined to 'exchange a glance, slightly too long, over the indexes', as she had done, I set off to try to find romance with a Byronic stranger. I wanted to be approached by a short man, blond or dark, in an unlikely location.

Inspired by the Italians, who *'fare una passeggiata'* – take a walk – on balmy evenings for the very purpose of finding someone to share a cappuccino and a kiss with, I stopped off at the Accademia Italiana, where a small exhibition of Giorgio Morandi is on display. Maybe a sexy, sensitive man would be contemplating a painting. Perhaps he would use the highly original pick-up line commonly used in art galleries: 'Are you a painter?' Unfortunately I was the only person at the exhibition, apart from a middle-aged woman who had brought her own fold-up chair.

Getting into the British Library cannot be achieved on a whim. Passes and photographs and letters are required. Once past the platoon of guards there is a sense of belonging to an exclusive club, which perhaps explains why it feels safe to exchange smouldering glances with other members.

The Reading Room is large and round. I walked around the outskirts in my brown dogtooth suit, hoping to spot a likely candidate. As far as I could see, everybody had their heads bent down over a great and large book.

One man walked back and forth. He had a reddish face and reddish hair, he wore a floppy hat, and he glanced at me. But did he glance at me because I glanced at him, or had he glanced at me first? By the time I looked again he had disappeared.

'Advance Reservations' – there it was, the sign to 'the steamiest part of the room'. Advance Reservations is a desk at the end of a

---

records is itself a kind of warfare. The keepers, whether they wish so or not, cannot be neutral.
Archibald MacLeish, 'Of the Librarian's Profession',
A Time to Speak (1941)

long, airless corridor. A handful of middle-aged, grey-faced men waited in an orderly silent queue while a large Indian man who was working behind the desk muttered: 'There's not enough staff in here, too much bloody work.'

The North Library is smaller, and the light is more flattering. I wandered upstairs with the book I had grabbed, *The Quotable Woman*, and sat next to a large bearded man wearing a short-sleeved shirt. 'I don't want to make money. I just want to be wonderful,' I read: Marilyn Monroe. There was an inaudible announcement on the loudspeaker. The bearded man spoke to me: 'I didn't hear a thing, did you?' This was it, I was being picked up. 'No,' I smiled at him. 'I hope it wasn't important,' he said, going back to his book. Was that it? He wasn't exactly sexy but this was ridiculous. 'Do you know where to go for coffee?' I asked, wondering if he would offer to show me.

'I go outside for coffee,' he drawled and turned to his notebook. I took my glasses off and walked back to the main Reading Room where I exchanged a smouldering glance with a tall, dark man, at least I think I did. I couldn't really see if he smouldered back.

If I had time to spend a few more days there, I'm sure I would eventually have a coffee with someone. In the suppressed, soporific atmosphere of the British Library there is a desperate need to break out and lose your head for a while. Back in Advance Reservations a woman behind the desk was saying: 'I am so tired now, I can't bear anything.'

The Evening Standard (22 June 1993)

She'll always be high on nerves and low on animal emotion. She'll always breathe thin air and smell snow. She'd have made a perfect nun. The religious dream, with its narrow-ness, its stylised emotions and its grim purity, would have been a perfect release for her. As it is she will probably turn

ANDREW BARR

Off the Shelf

I was very interested in Kate Morris's article about looking for love in the British Library ('A very brief encounter', 22 June) because I have acquired two girlfriends there.

Advance reservations is a good place to start talking to people.

The standard opening gambit is to mention the length of time you have to wait, or how the book you want seems to have been lost or destroyed in the war. Otherwise, try chatting in the photocopying room or make eye contact over the catalogues. Going out for a fag under the colonnade is not as effective as it used to be since fewer readers smoke.

But Museum Street is blessed with an excellent coffee bar which takes half an hour to serve you – giving a much better chance of getting well acquainted.

The British Library is not the place for a quick pick-up, however; people are there to work, after all. But at least you can be sure that anyone you meet will be literate.

The Evening Standard (23 June 1993)

---

out to be one of those acid-faced virgins that sit behind little desks in public libraries and stamp dates in books.
Raymond Chandler, *The High Window* (1943)

STAMPING OUT

The routine of libraries is not much covered in the annals of the profession. As in other professions, some chores are deemed professional, others the preserve of the 'unqualified'. Though it's less obvious today, libraries are as hierarchical as the Indian caste system and woe betide those who stray into an area where trespassers are not welcome.

Every Tuesday in the branch library where I first worked, new books were delivered from the Central Library. There they had been logged in and catalogued but there were still myriad things to be done to the pristine volumes before the public would be allowed at them. Rubber stamps were a major feature of this routine; half a dozen was about the minimum required to get a book ready for circulation. Then there was the jacketing, labelling and card writing; it is easier to prepare a five-year-old for his first day at school.

Once books are on the shelf they are liable to be borrowed. This many librarians regard as unfortunate. 'Difficulties only arise in libraries,' a senior librarian once said, 'when the readers are admitted.' One book was no big deal. You inked the stamp, opened the book and stamped the date it was due back on the label. Readers were supposed to have books ready opened at the proper place to speed up the process. When there were queues the librarian himself would bustle out of his office and take charge of the date stamp, flashing it with the dexterity of a true professional, and race through the queue like a ticket tout at Covent Garden.

Since the issue counter is the sharp end of the library, many library readers think this is all there is to libraries. This irritates librarians no end, especially those who believe in higher things, like conferences, seminars and mission statements. If only the public could understand the many attributes one needs to be a librarian, just how complicated and demanding a job it is. A survey suggested that the average librarian needed a lawyer's tact, a diplomat's charm, a nurse's solicitude, a baker's patience . . . It was manna to the ears of many. Then the *Sunday Times* said that in the stress league table librarians were on a par with Tibetan monks. We were back to square one.

KINGSLEY AMIS

The Bevan Ticket

'The Bevan ticket,' I said, 'has expired, and will have to be renewed.' The middle-aged woman put her hand to her mitre-like hat and frowned across the counter at me. After some time, she said: 'Mrs Bevan said she just wanted one like the one she had out last time.'

I was used to this sort of thing, as indeed to every sort of thing that could go on here. 'The Bevan ticket,' I repeated in the same tone, or lack of one, 'has expired and will have to be renewed.'

My gaze, slightly filmed by afternoon drowsiness, swam round the square, high room, fixing idly on the etching, or daguerrotype, or whatever it was, of Lord Beaconsfield's face which hung over the Hobbies and Handicrafts Section. Lord Beaconsfield had had some connection with the founding of the library, which took place a long time ago. At the moment his likeness was glowing in a cloudy beam of late spring sunshine, and looked as if it wanted to be sick but knew that this would be wrong. I nodded imperceptibly to it.

'She couldn't get in herself this afternoon, you see, Mr Lewis,' the woman was saying; 'she's had to go down the Food Office because of her boy, so I said I'd take her book and change it while I was changing mine, like. Quite often I do it for her.'

I allowed a pause to elapse. From the dozen or so other borrowers present came sounds that had grown familiar to me; the squeaking of shoe-leather, a fairly loud grumble of voices, the thud of a book replaced on the wrong shelf or dropped. Quite a long way away to my left a date-stamp thumped intermittently. I wetted the ring finger of my right hand and smoothed the place next to the parting where my hair was just beginning to go. Then I swayed my long thin body over the rows of tickets, taking time about bringing my face nearer the woman's. My face is a round and rubicund one, and a girl I once knew used to say it looked cheerful, but that was before I got this job. Anyway, I now moved it forward, making an effort not to blink my eyes, which are grey.

I have never felt anything but *degraded* as the librarian in this hole of toad's turds.

Philip Larkin, on his stint as librarian of Wellington, Shropshire (1946)

They began to smart a little, but I've often thought that not blinking makes me look more formidable, and I could do with that. It doesn't seem to work when I try it in the mirror, but you couldn't expect it to, I suppose. I stood facing the woman, keeping absolutely still, as if I were waiting for her to scream or faint. Nothing happened apart from the collapse of a loaded shelf in the Geography Section, which one of the other assistants was rearranging that day. Weighing my words, I said: 'The Bevan ticket has expired and will have to be renewed.'

'But you've always let me do it in the past, Mr Lewis. I've never had any difficulty about it before. And Mr Jenkins, is it? – he always let me do it too.'

'Mrs Edwards,' I said compassionately, 'have you been listening to what I've been saying?'

She looked timidly down at her shopping-basket, which was stuffed with goodies for her luckless family. 'No,' she said.

That Uncertain Feeling (Victor Gollancz, 1955)

The only thing the State could usefully do is to divert more of the public money into buying books for the public libraries . . . Unfortunately the British public won't at present spend money on books, although it reads more and more and its average taste, I should say, has risen greatly in the last

BERNARD MacLAVERTY

Merderer

Cal stood at the back of the queue in the post office. He wondered why Mrs Doyle, who owned the place, didn't worry about security. In the next town the post office had been modernised and the wire grille replaced with bullet-proof glass. This would be an easy place to do and there was plenty of money lying around. His stomach tightened at the thought and he looked instead at a poster on the wall urging him to prevent warble-fly. When he got his money he bought a packet of cigarettes and fumbled to find the red tab that would open the cellophane. On the street he lit up and stood at the corner, his hands in his trouser pockets. Arty McGlynn, smiling because he too had just got his Giro money, joined him. They had been at school together.

'Hiya, Cal.'

'Hi.' Cal took out one hand to hold his cigarette and measured a long spit into the roadway.

'What are you doing with yourself this weather?' Cal considered this.

'Fondling,' he said. He spat again and walked away up Main Street to the library. It was a converted shop with a shop-front displaying books. Inside a couple of old men browsed through the papers and a couple more were down among the shelves. It was warm and quiet and Cal had found it a good place to pass some of the time. He had tickets which he used occasionally to borrow some cassette tapes but rarely, if ever, did he borrow books. He sat on a chair and flicked through *Time* magazine. There were pictures and an article about Northern Ireland and he felt proud that the place where he lived was given so much room in such an important magazine. When he was at school it was an occasion if anything from Northern Ireland got a mention on the news. He looked up from his magazine and noticed that there was a new woman behind the counter. She was small and dark-haired with very brown eyes. She seemed to match the wood colours of the place. She was going through the index file, pulling out the small drawers and riffling

twenty years. At present, I believe, the average British citizen spends round about £1 a year on books, whereas he spends getting on for £25 on tobacco and alcohol combined. Via the rates he could easily be made to spend more without even knowing it – as, during the war years, he spent far

through the cards. Over the top of the cabinet she briefly raised her eyes and solemnly looked at Cal. He stared back at her but she turned away to a customer, smiling at him and stamping his books with amazing speed. She looked foreign, had that sallowness of skin which he associated with France. He tried to guess her age but couldn't. She wasn't young, perhaps somewhere in her late twenties.

The tapes were on a revolving stand near the desk and Cal went up to take a closer look at this woman. He turned the stand and watched her file the tickets in a rank of them. Another old man came up with an armful of detective stories. He set his books down and hung his walking stick on the counter, and Cal watched it swing slowly to and fro. The old man leaned forward, resting his elbows on the desk-top, and the woman smiled and talked to him as if she knew him. Cal turned the rack of tapes squeakily but continued to stare at her through them, willing her to look at him again. She had a lovely mouth as well as eyes. It moved beautifully when she talked. She stamped the old man's books and took his tickets, slotting the books' cards inside them. When the transaction was complete he unhooked his walking stick and seemed embarrassed by the number of books he was borrowing.

'The best of luck anyway, Marcella,' he said.

Marcella.

'Oh, Jesus,' said Cal into himself. Marcella. He put out his hand to move the rack again. It gave a faint screech as it turned and he saw his hand frozen in mid-air. At that moment she looked at him and smiled. He moved his mouth to smile back but the muscles on his face would not respond properly. Marcella.

He left the library, stumbling on the old man's heels, and in the street he said it out loud.

'Oh, Jesus.' He shook his head as if there were an insect crawling in the porch of his ear.

It took him three matches to light another cigarette. He started for home but stopped for a moment at the post office counter. There couldn't be many Marcellas around. He closed his eyes and leaned his head against a brick wall. Then he half ran, half walked to his house. He stood in the middle of the bedroom floor, not knowing what to do. It must be her. He tried to recall the woman's face but could not. He sat on the bed, stood up to look out of the window but ended pacing the floor. Yet it might not be her. The more he thought of her, the more his fascination and curiosity grew. He felt a great need to recall her face. He could only summon up a bland set of features he knew were not hers. He

more than usual on radio, owing to the subsidising of the BBC by the Treasury. If the Government could be induced simply to earmark larger sums for the purchase of books, without in the process taking over the whole book trade and turning it into a propaganda machine, I think the writer's

rooted in his drawer, rattling among useless lighters and Biros that no longer worked, and produced two buff tickets. He walked quickly back to the library.

Once inside, he heard his loud breathing in the silence. The Marcella woman was having a cup of coffee. He studied her face, trying to read into it whether or not she was like *the* Marcella. He could not take his eyes off her, not because of what she was but because of what he might have done to her. Her gesture, the way she raised and rested the rim of the cup on her lip before sipping, every movement of her face hypnotised him. He chose a Blues tape of Muddy Waters and went up to the counter and waited. She took a quick sip, set the cup down and came to him.

'Yes?'

He stared at her, moving his eyes over what he could see of her above the counter. He had come to a library to borrow time. He indicated the cassette and the ticket. Her nails were white and unpainted and she wore a gold ring on her wedding finger. She saw what she was looking for and moved lightly to it.

'Thank you, Mr McCrystal,' she said and Cal looked up, startled. Then he remembered that his name was on the ticket. She set the cassette box on the counter and Cal watched the warm prints of her fingers evaporate from the Perspex. *Merde. Crotte de chien.* Merderer.

When Cal's father came home for his tea he smelt of the abattoir. Cal tried not to breathe through his nose as they both moved about the small kitchen. His father washed his huge hands and as far up as his elbows with carbolic soap. Then he washed his face, making loud spluttering noises, stooped over the sink.

'Towel,' he said, his eyes clenched tightly.

Cal gave it to him. The son was making a fry – eggs, bacon, black puddings and some fried bread. When Shamie had dried his face it looked shiny and red – as if he had sandpapered it rather than washed it. He said, 'There's some yahoos outside.'

Cal left the pan to look between the slats of the venetian blind in the front room. Four youths in denim were lounging against the garden wall at the far side of the street. One of them, wearing a red, white and blue scarf knotted at his neck, was looking over at the McCrystals' house. He saw the slats move and pointed. The others turned to look. The big one with clown-like black boots and scarlet braces swung up his hand, giving Cal's eyes the two fingers.

---

position would be eased and literature might also benefit.
George Orwell, in reply to being asked what more he
thought the State or any other institution should do for
writers, *Horizon* (1946)

'Let them be,' shouted his father. 'These eggs are getting black lace edges.'

Cal rushed back to the pan and with a fish slice served the eggs on to plates. He put all the black puddings on his father's plate. He loathed them, made from blood, like cross-sections of large warts bound in black Sellotape.

They sat at the table and watched the news on television. The Army had shot a deaf mute, saying that he had been seen carrying a weapon, but by the time they had reached the dead man an accomplice had removed the gun. A Catholic father of three had been stabbed to death in a Belfast entry. The police said that there was no known motive for the killing. Gerry Fitt had had a steel door put on his house.

'Any jobs in the paper today?' asked his father.

Cal shook his head, his mouth full. When he had swallowed he said, 'A couple in Belfast.'

'You're safer away from the city.'

When they had finished, Cal cleared the table and washed the dishes while his father sat reading the paper. Cal spoke from the kitchen.

'There's a new woman in the library.'

'Hm-hm?'

'Called Marcella something.'

'That'll be Marcella Morton. I heard some of the lads saying that she'd taken a job to get away from the house.'

Cal closed his eyes. It *was* her. In the hot dishwater his nails had become soft and he trailed them across the metal bottom of the basin to find the last spoon. Oh Jesus. He dried it and put it in the drawer. In some way, he didn't know how, he would have to make it up to her. He cleared the tapes of the black puddings from the hole in the sink. They were limp and slimy and he shuddered as he threw them in the bucket. The water was like grey soup with tiny yellow grease circles. He poured it with a rush down the sink. A last teaspoon rattled out.

'There's always a sneaky bastard.'

He dried his hands and took three cigarettes from his packet and rolled them on to the mantelpiece for his father. Then he went to his bedroom to eat again the ashes of what he had done.

Cal (Jonathan Cape, 1983)

A library is thought in cold storage.
Viscount Samuel, *A Book of Quotations*, 1947

TONY HANCOCK

The Missing Page

SCENE 1 *East Cheam Public Library. There are a few people searching the shelves, which are plainly labelled 'FICTION', 'NON-FICTION', 'CRIME', etc. Tony enters. He is carrying a pile of books. He goes up to the librarian's desk and puts the books down in front of him.*

Tony Good morrow, good curator.

Librarian Oh it's you. Overdue again. Seven reminders I've sent out to you.

Tony My dear good fellow one cannot rush one's savouring of the classics of world literature. Rome wasn't built in a day, and its decline and fall can't be read in one.

Librarian You haven't got Gibbon's *Decline and Fall* there.

Tony That's got nothing to do with it. I've got the love lives of the Caesars here, that tells me everything . . . and between you and me, I'm not surprised it declined and fell after that lot. Kindly shove the cards back in the sockets and give me the tickets.

The librarian goes through the books and looks inside the covers.

Librarian How have you got all these books? How many tickets have you got?

Tony Two fiction and two non-fiction.

Librarian That's four tickets. There's ten books here.

Tony Yes, well, Dolly was on last time.

In periods where Colonel Stingo is what he describes as 'non-holding', or financially straitened, he spends a large part of his time in the reading-room of New York Public Library, seeding the clouds of printed erudition above his already overflowing reservoir of odd information. Such

Librarian Do you mean Miss Hargreaves?

Tony She may be Miss Hargreaves to you, but to people who she reckons she is Dolly. And to me she is Dolly. And she always lets me have a few over the odds.

Librarian That's three and eight to pay on this lot.

Tony Three and eight? I don't want to buy 'em.

Librarian Well don't take so many out if you can't read them all in time. There are other people who want to borrow these books you know.

Tony I can't think why. A bigger load of old rubbish I haven't clapped my reading glasses on in years.

Librarian Then why did you take them out?

Tony Well there's not much choice in here, is there? I suppose *Lolita*'s still out.

Librarian Yes.

Tony I thought so.

Librarian There's twenty-five thousand other books to choose from.

Tony I've read them all. I've been coming in here since I was six years old and I've read *Biggles Flies East* twenty-seven times . . . I'm not wading through that again.

Librarian *(handing him a leaflet)* There's a list of our latest additions. And one book one ticket. I'm not Dolly.

Tony All right then. Come on, give me my tickets.

Librarian Not till you've paid your fine. Three and eight.

Tony Disgusting . . . they're even taxing learning these days.

---

information he refers to verbally as 'esatorid', although he can spell the word all right. When he ceases to be non-holding, and has an adequate amount of what he refers to as 'Tease', he makes his *rentrée*, usually telling his favourite bartenders in detail about conditions in some place he has

He gets the money out. The librarian is examining a book, and points to a page in it.

Librarian Did you do this?

Tony No I didn't. I don't like eggs. And you needn't examine the corners of the pages, I don't bend them over. I use bookmarks. I use a piece of ribbon off my chocolate box.

Librarian Yes, well take it out.

He hands him a book with a piece of ribbon sticking out. Tony takes the book, opens it, and all the pages fall out all over the floor. The librarian watches all this in silence.

Tony It's nothing to do with me.

Librarian You've been bending the books round backwards, haven't you? That's going to cost you another seven and six.

Tony I'm not paying for bad workmanship.

Librarian Do you know how to read a book?

Tony Yes of course I do.

Librarian You hold it like this.

He opens a book and holds it in a reading position.

Librarian You rest it in your hand like that. You don't bend it back like this . . .

He bends it back and all the pages fall out.

Tony Touché. Stand by with your date stamping machine. I shall return.

He goes over to the bookshelves. There are some people looking for books, others sitting down at the reference table. All is quiet. Big notices reading 'SILENCE' are hanging up. As he passes the reference table . . .

---

been reading up on in the Public Library. 'Glad to be back,' he says. 'There's no place like New York.'
                              A.J. Liebling, *The Honest Rainmaker:
                    The Life and Times of Colonel John R. Stingo* (1952)

Tony Morning.

The readers look up and angrily shush him.

Tony Charming. I was only passing the . . .

They shush him again.

Tony Oh come now, after all . . .

Renewed 'sshhhs' from the readers.

Tony Yes but . . .

They all shush him. A little man who hasn't been joining in now looks up from his book and shushes all the people who have been shushing Tony.

Tony Quite right too. If you must sshhh don't sshhh so loud.

Little Man *(to Tony)* Ssshhh!

Tony Oh shut up.

A man standing by the bookshelves turns round.

Man *(very loudly)* Quiet please.

Everybody turns and shushes him. Tony goes over to the shelves. A woman is choosing a book from the Crime section. Tony stops and looks at the title. He shakes his head, pulls out another book, and hands it to her. Gives her the thumbs up and carries on. He stops a little further on and starts examining the titles on the Crime shelves. He apparently can't find what he's looking for so he moves on to the next section which is marked 'Greek Philosophy'. He starts searching for some books, then snaps his fingers and beckons. The librarian comes up.

Librarian Can I help you?

Tony Yes, I'm looking for Sir Charles Bestead's complete history of the Holy Byzantine Empire.

Librarian *(impressed)* Oh, you want to borrow it?

He left Fifth Avenue and walked west towards the movie houses. Here on 42nd Street it was less elegant but no less strange. He loved this street, not for the people or the shops but for the stone lions that guarded the great main building of the Public Library, a building filled with books and

Tony Yes please.

Librarian I'm so pleased. We don't get much call for it. I'm so pleased there are still men of culture left. It's a magnificent edition.

Tony Oh yes, yes, most useful.

Librarian I do hate to see it neglected.

Tony Oh I often borrow it, I find it most helpful.

Librarian I think I've misjudged you, haven't I? Is there anything else I can get for you?

Tony Yes er . . . Plato's *Republic*, the complete translation of Homer's *Iliad*, and Ulbricht's *Roman Law* . . . The Wilkinson edition, of course.

Librarian Of course. A very wise choice. You've chosen probably the four best books in the library.

Tony I agree . . . have you got them?

Librarian Of course, I'll get them.

Librarian (*going off*) The first time in four years there's been any call for these.

He finds the four volumes, all great big books, about six inches thick. He goes back to Tony.

Librarian There we are. It's times like this that make my job worth while.

Tony Thank you very much, they're the ones.

Librarian You can have all these on one ticket.

Tony Oh, that's most kind of you.

He puts them on the floor at the Crime section, then stands on them, stretches up, and takes down a book from a higher shelf.

---

unimaginably vast, and which he had never yet dared to enter. He might, he knew, for he was a member of the branch in Harlem and was entitled to take books from any library in the city. But he had never gone in because the building was so big that it must be full of corridors and

Tony Ah, that's the little beauty I'm after. *Lady Don't Fall Backwards. (He steps off the books)* Thank you very much. I won't need those any more for now. Keep them handy though, they're just the right height.

The librarian picks up the books lovingly.

Librarian *(with passion)* You barbarian! You're illiterate you are, ignorant and illiterate.

The readers turn on them and shush them loudly.

Tony You see what you've done now, you've set them off again. Go on – be about your business, you highly strung fool.

The librarian goes off in a huff.

Tony Really, these beatniks are becoming impossible.

He turns back to the bookshelves and studies the titles, then takes another couple of books. He moves a pile along and we see Sid's face looking through from the other side.

Sid Hallo.

Tony Oh cor . . . *(Has a turn)* What are you doing there? Oh dear, you frightened the life out of me.

Sid I thought I'd come and see what it was all about. All this book business. So I've come to get some books out.

Tony You've never read a book in your life. Don't give me that. You've run one yes, but you've never read one.

Sid No, straight up. I joined today. I thought I'd see what it's all about, so I've come round here.

Tony And straight to the Crime section. I expect you're looking for some new ideas aren't you.

Sid Well you're looking at the Crime section as well.

---

marble steps, in the maze of which he would be lost and never find the books he wanted. And then everyone, all the white people inside, would know that he was not used to great buildings, or to so many books, and they would look at him with pity. He would enter on another day, when he had

Tony That is neither here or there. I read thrillers purely as relaxation between the heavy stuff. I find fifty pages of *Dead Dames Don't Talk* the perfect hors-d'oeuvre to an all night bash at Bertrand Russell.

Sid Bertrand Russell, didn't he write *Kiss the Blood off my Hands?*

Tony *Kiss the Blood off my Hands.* Bertie of all people. Of course he didn't. That's not his style at all. You're thinking of Aldous Huxley.

Sid Well there's nothing round here. Anything round your side?

Tony There's one or two things that might appeal to you.

Sid Hang on.

Sid disappears and then comes round the end of the bookshelf and joins Tony.

Sid Let's have a look then. *(He selects a book)* What about this one? Smashing cover.

He laughs raucously and a reader turns and shushes them.

Sid *(to the reader)* Who are you shushing? Are you looking for a mouthful of signet rings?

Tony Sid please, not in here . . . no punch-ups on municipal property.

Sid Well, I'm not taking that . . . you heard him shushing me, I wasn't doing anything.

Tony *(whispers)* He's entitled to, you're not supposed to make a noise in a public library.

Sid Oh all right then, but he'd better watch it.

Tony Yes all right. Give us your book.

He looks at it. The following dialogue is in loud whispers.

---

read all the books uptown, an achievement that would, he felt, lend him the poise to enter any building in the world.
James Baldwin, *Go Tell It On The Mountain* (1953)

Tony I've read it.

Sid What's it like?

Tony Not very good. I wouldn't bother.

Sid Yeah, but what's it about? What happens?

Tony Well you see, this bird is in the room with this bloke and suddenly the door's flung open and her husband walks in and . . .

The readers turn round and shush them. Tony now mimes the action of the book to Sid, with Sid reacting appropriately. Tony describes the girl's shape, then a man with big shoulders, does the lover kissing her passionately. Jumps back, opens a door and does melodramatic step into the room as the husband with the melodramatic 'Ah ha'. The husband and the lover have a terrific fight, strangling each other, etc. Finally the husband draws a gun and shoots the lover several times. Does the lover doing the death scene, then, as husband, kicks the body and jumps on it. Then does the girl pleading on her knees. The husband throws her on one side. Has a struggle with the gun and the gun gets forced against her and it goes off. Another big death scene from the girl. She dies. The husband is remorseful. He tries to revive her. He jumps up and puts hand to ear. He turns round and puts hands up as the police come in the door. Holds out his hands for handcuffs. Next Tony imitates the judge sitting at the bench. Describes the wig with his hands, bows to three sides of the court, raps gavel three times, then does advocate pleading the case. Puts black cap on and grabs back of collar to indicate being strung up. By now the librarian has come on to the scene and has watched the last half of this pantomime. Tony suddenly realises he is there and, with great embarrassment, busies himself selecting some book.

Librarian What do you think you're doing?

Tony And just what do you mean by that?

Librarian This is a library, not the Royal Academy of Dramatic Art. I've been watching you. You've been creating a disturbance ever since you came in here.

Tony I was merely trying to describe to my friend what this book is about.

Librarianship suits me – I love the feel of libraries – it has just the right blend of academic interest and administration.
                                                      Philip Larkin (1959)

Librarian We get a thousand people a day in here, supposing they all did it? A thousand people, all gesticulating. We can't have that in a public library.

Tony I was not gesticulating.

Librarian You were gesticulating . . . And there have been complaints. It's most distracting. You'd better get your books stamped up and leave.

Sid Just a minute mate, don't you tell me what to do, mate. You're trying it on with the wrong kiddy . . . just don't tell me what to do. I'm not the type.

One of the readers shushes loudly. Sid stalks over to the reading table.

Sid Who did that? Come on, who shushed? Who was it?

Tony *(restraining him)* Sid, come away. Don't start anything. You're always showing me up. *(To the readers)* I do apologise, it's not his fault, he can't stand rules and regulations. It's the gipsy in him. Come on, back to your caravan, I'll buy you a new pair of earrings.

He escorts Sid reluctantly over to the counter, where the librarian stamps the books and hands them to him.

Librarian There's your books. Back in fourteen days, or I shall ask you to turn in your tickets.

Tony *(pointed)* Very well, but I might warn you, the Chairman of the Library Committee is a member of the same lodge as me, if you get what I mean. *(Makes a Mason's sign)* Once a moose always a moose. Just watch it, eh?

Sid and Tony leave the counter.

Tony That's frightened the daylights out of him.

As they go out of the door a woman comes in carrying a book. Tony has a quick look at the title, then yells into the library.

If this nation is to be wise as well as strong, if we are to achieve our destiny, then we need more new ideas for more wise men reading more good books in more public libraries. These libraries should be open to all – except the censor. We must know all the facts and hear all the alternatives and

Tony *Lolita*'s back!

All the people round the reading table jump up and make a dignified rush to the counter for the book.

Man I believe you'll find I'm top of the list . . .

Woman No, no I had my name down before it was published.

SCENE 2 *Tony's living-room. He is engrossed in* Lady Don't Fall Backwards. *He reacts to what he is reading – it is obviously something horrific and very tense. He stops and has a drink of water, then carries on reading. Meanwhile, Sidney finishes his book and closes it.*

Sid Well . . . if that's reading books, I'm going back to the telly. What a lot of old codswallop. *The Stranglers of Bolton*. They should have strangled the bloke who wrote it. *(Looks at the cover)* Grant Peabody. How can you write books with a name like that?

Tony Do you mind? I'm trying to read. Don't interrupt. I'm on the edge of my seat here.

Sid Good is it?

Tony Good? It's red hot, mate. I hate to think of this sort of book getting in the wrong hands. As soon as I've finished this, I shall recommend they ban it.

Sid As good as that is it? What's it about then?

Tony It's a murder mystery. With loads of girls in it, and they've all fallen for the private eye, you see, and they're all rich and they're all beautiful and he's got a big white American car. Oh dear, it's the sort of life you dream about. He's good looking, quick repartee, judo, marvellous apartment, all the birds. Well I'm finished with The Saint after this. I'm a Johnny Oxford man from now on. This is marvellous, twenty-five murders so far, the New York Police don't know what's going on at all, the DA's been in to see the Governor, cause it's political as well, you see, anyway this Jocelyn Knockersbury, a typist at UNO, has been done in and the plans stolen, along with the seating arrangements at the peace

listen to all the criticisms. Let us welcome controversial books and controversial authors. For the Bill of Rights is the guardian of our security as well as our liberty.

John F. Kennedy

conference. Since which time another twenty-four have been done in . . .

Sid What, all UNO typists?

Tony Yes, twenty-five of them . . . *(Reads a bit more)* Hallo . . . another one's gone. Ooh what a nasty way to go. Someone poured water over her electric typewriter. Well this is a mystery. Who's behind it all? Who's the murderer? Now the bloke I suspected is in Salt Lake City, it can't be him. Do you know I've been wrong on every page so far. Every time I suspect someone, they get killed. I can't wait to get to the end of this . . . it's going to be a complicated ending, this one.

Sid Yeah, well hurry up and finish it, it's getting late. Have a look at the last page.

Tony You can't do that. It makes the whole thing pointless, you might as well not read it. It's like looking at the next card when you're playing snap. Please do be quiet, I've read the same sentence three times. Hallo, he's found something. It's all right, Johnny knows who did it. He's found a ginger hair on her skirt. He's solved it! He's narrowed his eyes and a little smile has flickered across his face. He always does that when he knows something.

Sid Well come on then, who done it?

Tony It'll be on the last page. He always keeps you in suspense till the last page this bloke. *(Reads on, getting more excited)* Yes I thought so, he's invited everybody into his flat. He always does that. He lashes them up with drinks, lights a cigarette and explains who did it. Then the murderer rushes to the window, slips and falls, hits the pavement, and Johnny Oxford turns round to the guests, finishes his Manhattan and says, 'New York is now a cleaner place to live in'. The End. Turn over, a list of new books and an advert for skinny blokes.

Sid If you always know what's going to happen, why bother to read it?

Tony Because I don't know who it is who's going to hit the pavement. Now please keep quiet, Johnny's just started his

---

There is no colliery town in South Wales which could hold the candle to Tredegar for its library and institute; more money is spent on books here than in any institution of its size in Wales. But two institutions have grown up in the train of industrialisation of the valleys which are more responsible

summing up, prior to unmasking the murderer. *(He concentrates on the book, making odd noises as he notes the points being made)* Oh so she was in on it, the one I told you about. She said she'd never been to the Mocambo Club, but she had a book of matches in her handbag. Oh so that's what put him on to it. That's clever you know, very clever . . . Of course, the trail of footprints in the snow. All made with a size 10 left-footed shoe. So it had to be someone who could walk comfortably in two left shoes. That told him it was a small man who had put a big man's shoe on to lay the suspicion on somebody else. But he didn't realise that in his hurry he'd put two left shoes on. Well I never thought of that. I've been waiting for two one-legged twins to turn up.

Sid Come on, come on, so who done it then?

Tony He's coming to it, it's on the last page, I told you that. Here we are . . . *(Reads)* ' "So, Inspector, you can see that the only person who could have done all these murders is the man sitting over there." So saying, Johnny Oxford pointed his finger at . . .' *(He turns the page over to look at the last page. It isn't there)* 'Men, are you skinny, do you have sand kicked in your face, if so' . . . wait a minute, that's not right. *(Feverishly examines the pages)* There's a page missing. The last page is missing! *(He looks on the floor, then on the chair where he has been sitting)* Where's the last page? *(To Sid)* What have you done with the last page?

Sid I haven't touched it.

Tony *(looks again at the book)* Well, where is it? It's gone. The solution's on the last page. Oh, this is ridiculous. Here I am, a bag of tensed-up nerves waiting to see who did it, and this happens. It's enough to drive a man round the twist. I must find that last page.

Sid Show me the book. *(He examines it)* There you are.

Tony What?

Sid See that jagged edge along there . . . it's been torn out.

Tony Torn out?

Sid Yeah. They probably lit a fag with it or something.

---

for moulding the character of the miners than anything else and these were the Sunday Schools which cultivated the gift of expression and the Workmen's Institutes which provided the reading facilities.

Aneurin Bevan (1897–1960)

Tony Lit a fag with it? The last page? They can't do that. There's plenty of other pages. This skinny bloke for a start, he could have gone without any hardship whatsoever. But the last page of a murder mystery. This is sheer unmitigated sadism.

Sid All right, what's done's done now. That's a mystery in itself, isn't it? Who tore the last page out? I know who done it.

Tony Who? Who?

Sid The murderer, so nobody'll know who it was. *(Laughs.)*

Tony Very very funny. I must know who did it. I've got to find that last page.

Sid Forget about it. It's only a book. Read another one.

Tony Don't be such a fool. How can I read another one with that one still haunting me? *(He begins to pace up and down)* The last page of all pages. What a terrible nerve-wracking thing to do to a chap. The last page.

SCENE 3 *The Bedroom. Tony is now pacing up and down in pyjamas and dressing-gown. Sidney is in his bed asleep. Tony carries on pacing up and down.*

Tony The last page . . . fancy tearing out the last page. How could anybody do a thing like that.

Sid appears from under the bedclothes.

Sid Oi! Why don't you turn the light out and go to sleep.

Tony I want to know who did the murder.

Sid And I want to get some sleep. And if you don't turn out the light and stop pacing up and down, there'll be another murder they'll be trying to find out who did it. Now go to sleep.

Tony reluctantly gets into his bed and turns the light out. The room is now in darkness.

I can tell you . . . that since my time as a student – all my life, in fact – libraries have been a formidable idea to me. I don't know whether it is so elsewhere, but there was always an air of discipline about the places, and later the laws against

Tony *(after a pause)* You were the same when you couldn't think of the name of that bit player in 'Wagon Train' yesterday. You were up all night pacing up and down trying to think of it.

Sid *(muffled)* Go to sleep.

Tony I wonder who did it? *(Pause)* I know!

The light goes on and he is sitting upright in bed.

Tony I'll work it out for myself. I'll deduce it! I'll be Johnny Oxford. All the salient points are in the book, it's like a jigsaw puzzle . . . just fit it together and you've got the solution. You don't need the last page. *(Takes the book)* Let's see now . . .

Sid turns over and covers his head. He is furious. Tony takes paper and a pencil and a notepad from the table next to his bed.

Tony Now – list of characters in order of appearance. This is where my theatrical training comes in. Jocelyn Knockersbury . . . no, she was the first one who was done in. We'll cross her out. Johnny Oxford . . . no, he couldn't have done it. Let's see, how was Jocelyn done in? *(Refers to book)* Ah yes. Strangled with one of her own nylons. That means whoever did it had access to her stockings. Oh dear, I don't think I'd better pursue that line of enquiry. Freda Wolkinski was asleep in her pull-down bed, when somebody pressed the button, and she flew up into the wall and suffocated. That must have been somebody who knew her bed was a pull-down one . . . therefore they must have been familiar with the topography of her boudoir. Therefore . . . Hmmm. I don't think I'll pursue that line of enquiry either. Still, no, no when you're a sleuth, you've got to be prepared to be confronted with the seamy side of life. After all, New York is probably a lot racier that East Cheam. I mustn't let my natural prudery detract me from the work in hand. Now . . . people associated with her – three girl friends, all murdered . . . two boy friends, one in the Navy in Japan, and one in California with an alibi. Now . . .

Sid's patience is exhausted. He jumps up in bed, and snatches the book from Tony's hand.

Sid Will you turn it in and go to sleep.

---

smoking . . . How long can you sit up straight and read without a smoke?

Arthur Miller (1917–)

Tony Give me my book back. I want to find out who did it.

Sid Go to sleep.

Tony I refuse to go to sleep until I have solved the mystery.

Sid Well, I'm not laying here all night listening to you rabbiting away to yourself. I'll tell you who done it.

Tony How?

Sid I'll skip through it and work it out. I know how they go about it. Don't forget, I've been involved in many a smart bit of detection. It shouldn't take very long to work out a load of rubbish like this. Then perhaps we can all get some kip.

Sid settles back to read the book . . . Time passes. Dawn breaks outside the window. Sidney is near the end of his book. He reads the last page and puts it down.

Tony *(still awake)* Well, who did it?

Sid *(annoyed)* How do I know who did it? The last page is missing.

Tony Well I know the last page is missing. You said you'd tell me who did it.

Sid Well how did I know it was going to be so involved? I thought it was going to be a straightforward bash on the nut up a dark alley.

Sid lights up a cigarette and starts smoking.

Tony Oh well, we'll just have to go to sleep.

Sid How can I go to sleep when I don't know who done it?

Tony No I know . . . it's so frustrating isn't it.

Sid Let's try and sort it out between us.

My good opinion for a town or village was based largely on the existence of two facilities for its inhabitants and visitors: public libraries and public conveniences.
Emmanuel Shinwell, *Conflict Without Malice* (1955)

They both get out of bed and start pacing up and down.

Sid Now then, who was the bird who drunk the carbolic milk shake?

Tony You mean the fat one.

Sid That's her. Now she's the key. Because she knew about all the others. So whoever did her in must be the murderer, and she must have known him and his relationship with the others.

Tony Yes, so if we can sort out who was nearest to her, we've got him.

Sid And that was the personal manager.

Tony Yes, of course. It was him. Harry . . . er . . . Harry . . .

Sid Belafonte.

Tony Not now Sid, no jokes. Harry . . . Zimmerman!

Sid That's him. Well that's that solved. Harry Zimmerman.

Tony Dear oh dear, thank goodness that's solved. I wouldn't have been able to think about anything else if we hadn't found it. *(Satisfied)* Yes, Harry Zimmerman.

They climb back into bed.

Sid Yes, perfect, he knew all their backgrounds, he knew where they were all living . . . he knew all their habits . . .

Tony Of course he did, and he had opportunities to do it, he could call round on the pretext of business . . . they wouldn't have suspected him. Oh yes, he's the only one who could have done it.

Sid Well that's a relief. He was little too, that explains the shoe theory . . .

Tony Yes, it all fits in. Well, well, Harry Zimmerman. Thank goodness for that. Now we can get some sleep. *(He pulls the*

Graduating in 1918, shortly after his mother's death, Mao did not return home but went to Peiping, where he helped to organise a 'work and learn' programme for students who wished to study in France. Subsequently he took a menial

curtains) Thanks very much Sid. I don't know what I would have done if I hadn't found out. Harry Zimmerman . . . of course, it's obvious now, you've explained it. Oh well. *(Yawns)* Goodnight.

Sid Morning.

Tony Oh yes. *(Yawns again)* Good morning. Harry Zimmerman eh?

They sink beneath the bedclothes. Pause. Suddenly Tony sits bolt upright and throws the bedclothes off.

Tony Harry Zimmerman, he was killed in chapter three, you great buffoon! Why don't you read the book properly . . .

SCENE 4 *The Library. The librarian is at the counter. Tony and Sid stride in and up to the counter.*

Tony I demand an explanation.

Librarian Now what?

Tony Where is the last page of *Lady Don't Fall Backwards?*

Librarian At the end of the book, surely.

Tony Oh well that's more like it I . . . it's not at the end of the book. Look. *(Shows him the book)* It has been torn out.

Librarian *(examining the book)* Did you do that?

Tony Oh for crying out . . . if I'd done it, would I have come in here and asked you where it was?

Librarian Well you did some very strange things in here yesterday.

Tony Have a care, good man. You can go too far you know.

Sid Let me deal with him. *(Threateningly)* Now listen mate . . . if you place any value on your teeth, you won't be so saucy. *(Shows him his fist)* Twenty-three knockouts in that. I could make it twenty-four – no trouble.

---

position as an assistant at the Peiping University library, while studying in his spare time.

Current Biography (1962)

Tony You want to take notice, one wallop from that, you'll go right through the autobiographies.

Sid Where's the last page?

Librarian I don't know.

Tony Well who did the murder then?

Librarian I don't know, I haven't read it.

Tony It's your book, you should know what they're all about. What sort of a librarian are you?

Librarian I can't read them all.

Tony *(inspired)* Wait a minute . . . another copy. Have you got another copy?

Librarian No, we only buy one of each.

Tony Oh this is ridiculous.

Sid goes over to the reading table. It is the same lot who were there the day before, in the same positions.

Sid Oi! . . . has anybody here read *Lady Don't Fall Backwards*?

Woman I beg your pardon?

Sid Have you read *Lady Don't Fall Backwards?*

Woman I . . . I'm afraid I don't read books like that.

Sid Don't give me that jazz. You like a bit of spice the same as everybody else. Come on now . . . who done it?

Woman Who done . . . who did what?

Sid Who did the murders in *Lady Don't Fall Backwards?* You must have read it.

The book in the pre-literate world appears as a magical form of miraculously repeated symbols. To the literate world the book serves a myriad of roles, ornamental and recreative and utilitarian. What is to be the new nature and form of the book against the new electronic surround? What will be the

Woman I don't know what you're talking about. Please go away before I call the police.

She gets her smelling salts out and has a sniff.

Sid All right, all right, forget it. Go back to sleep.

Sid returns to the counter where Tony and the librarian are still arguing.

Tony Are you sure you haven't got another copy?

Librarian I'm positive.

Tony Well what could have happened to the last page? You must see the book when it comes in.

Librarian Perhaps the previous reader knows something about it.

Tony Of course! That's it! Who had it out last?

Librarian I don't know.

Tony Well have a look then. Really, you're not being very helpful.

The librarian looks in the book.

Librarian Er . . . here we are . . . last taken out, June 21st 1951.

Tony 1951. Must have been a best-seller, that one.

The librarian refers to his file.

Librarian There was a threepenny fine, so we might have a record of the person who took it out.

Tony That's more like it. We're cooking with gas now, man.

Librarian Pardon?

Tony Johnny Oxford – in the book – that's what he says. I believe it's a phrase employed when one is being favourably impressed

___

effect of the micro-dot library on books past, present and future? When millions of books can be compressed in a match-box space, it is not the book merely, but the library that becomes portable.
Marshall McLuhan, *The Gutenberg Galaxy* (1962)

with the prowess of another chap.

Librarian I see. *(He gets a card out of his file)* Yes here we are – Proctor, W., Mr, The Larches, Old Drum Lane.

Tony Oh yes, very salubrious. Thank you very much. I only hope he's still there.

Sid Oh do me a favour . . . it's nine years ago. He's forgotten all about it by now.

Tony It's a chance we've got to take.

They walk away, then Tony comes back.

Tony *(secretive)* I suppose *Lolita*'s still out?

Librarian Yes.

Tony Oh.

He goes off again with Sid. Fade.

SCENE 5 *Outside the Larches, a broken down Victorian house. Tony and Sid go up to the door. Tony knocks. The door is opened by a wild-eyed man.*

Man What do you want?

Tony Mr Proctor, W.?

Man Yes.

Tony Oh good. We've come to see you about a book.

Man Book? What book?

Tony *Lady Don't Fall Backwards.*

The man's face lights up.

Man *Lady Don't Fall Backwards* by Darcy Sarto?

I want to be wise with white hair in a tall library in a deep chair by a fireplace.
Gregory Corso, 'Writ on the Eve of my 32nd Birthday' (1963)

Tony That's the one. You remember it?

Man Of course I remember it. Have you read it?

Tony Yes, and . . .

Man *(grabs him)* Who did it? Who did it? I must know who did it. Who did it?

Tony Have you gone raving mad? I don't know who did it, that's why I'm here, I thought you might know.

Man How should I know, the last page was torn out.

Tony Oh cor. *(To Sid)* Come on, there's no point in staying here.

They turn to go.

Man *(frantic)* You can't just go like that. I spent six years trying to find out who did it . . . it's only these last three years I've managed to forget about it, now you come along and start it all up again.

Tony Yes well I'm very sorry, if we find out who did it, we'll come round and let you know.

Man *(grabbing Tony's coat)* No, no, you can't leave me like this. Where are you going?

Tony We're going to find the one who had it before you.

Man I tried him. He got fed up with it halfway through and never finished it.

Sid We'll go to the publishers then.

Man I went there six years ago. It's out of print, and they haven't got a single copy left.

Tony Well there must be a copy in a shop somewhere.

Man No, all the unsold copies went back to the publishers. They've been repulped. We'll never find out. *(Nearly breaks down)*

There can be few more unrewarding tasks for the educated man of curiosity than the routine duties of librarianship.
Angus Wilson, *The Wild Garden* (1963)

Never . . . never.

Tony There, there, don't take on. Don't break now . . . not after all these years. Johnny Oxford wouldn't, would he? He wouldn't give up and break down.

Man No, no, that's true. He'd keep going wouldn't he? He'd find a copy wouldn't he?

Tony Of course he would. And so will we.

Sid Here . . . what about the original manuscript?

Man I never thought of that.

Sid Who'd have that then?

Man The author.

Tony Darcy Sarto. Of course! And even if he hasn't got the manuscript, he'd remember who did it. Come on, let's find out where he lives. *(To man)* Chin up, I think we're nearly at journey's end. *(He puts his hand on the man's shoulder)* As Johnny would tell you if he were here today . . . stay with it man.

Sid and Tony leave.

SCENE 6 *Outside a Georgian terraced house. Tony and Sid go up to the door.*

Tony Here we are, 44. This is it Sid, at last we'll know. Straight from the horse's mouth. The author himself.

Tony rings the doorbell once, and then again.

Tony *(impatient)* Come on, come on.

He bends down and calls through the letter-box.

Tony Come on, put that pen down. I know you're in there. Come along now please.

The home library cannot be brought under the direction of an interior decorator. The only interior to be decorated is your own mind.

Frank G. Jennings, *This is Reading* (1964)

Sid *(taps him on the shoulder)* Hancock.

Tony brushes him off.

Tony I'm not giving up now. *(Into letter box)* Come on. This is disgusting. Come on. *(Bangs on door)* Open this door.

Sid *(taps him on the shoulder again)* You'll have a long wait.

Tony What?

Sid Look.

Sid indicates an LCC plaque on the wall, which reads as follows: 'Darcy Sarto, novelist lived here. Born 1884 died 1949.' Tony is completely floored.

Tony Dead. The fool. He can't do that to me. No consideration some people. How am I going to find out who did it now?

Sid Let's face it, we're not going to find out. Let's turn it in, I've got other things to do than go chasing round the country after dead authors.

Tony Never, I'm going to find out if it's the last thing I do. *(He has a sudden idea)* Wait a minute, of course.

Sid Now what?

Tony The British Museum!

Sid He won't be there, they've buried him I expect . . .

Tony No, no, not him, the book. The British Museum keeps a copy of every book that's published in this country. Why didn't I think of it before. All we've got to do is to go to the British Museum, borrow the copy, turn to the last page, and there. Cab . . .

They walk off, Tony waving his walking stick.

SCENE 7 *The British Museum Library. Tony and Sid are waiting.*

My alma mater was books, a good library . . . I could spend the rest of my life reading, just satisfying my curiosity.
                                    Malcolm X, *Autobiography* (1964)

Tony You see, I told you so, they've got it. There's not a book published they haven't got.

The British Museum librarian comes in holding a book.

Librarian I've found it. I think this is the one you're looking for.

He blows the dust off, and shows it to Tony.

Tony That's it. That's the one. *(Laughs triumphantly.)*

Librarian Not a very good copy I'm afraid. A very interesting binding though, they're using a new process of gluing the sheets to the . . .

Tony snatches it from him.

Tony Give us it here. I'm not interested in how they glue it. Oh these civil servants. It's not mutilated in any way?

Librarian No, no.

Tony It's all here?

Librarian Oh yes, yes of course.

Tony I can hardly look. *(Opens the book, then quickly shuts it)* It's there! Page 201, it's there!

Sid Well come on, open it, read it out.

Tony Yes, of course. *(Opens the book at the penultimate page)* I'll give you three sentences in. So, Inspector, you can see that the only person who could have done these murders is the man sitting over there. So saying Johnny Oxford pointed his finger at . . . *(He turns the page over)* Men, are you skinny, do you have sand kicked in your face, if so . . . where is it? *(Shakes the old man)* Where's the end? Where's the last page? What have you done with it?

Sid has picked up the book as Tony dropped it on the desk.

Sid The last page is here.

If one knows one's way about the Library of Congress, particularly the area of congressional hearings and reports, the record rooms of the various government agency libraries and similar collections of dust-gathering, ephemeral official literature, presided over by custodians, usually female, who

Tony *(Lets go of the old man)* Where? Where?

Sid There it is . . . there's a publisher's note on it. *(Reads)* At this point Mr Darcy Sarto's manuscript ends. He died before he could finish the story. We decided to publish it because we thought the countless Johnny Oxford fans throughout the world would like the opportunity of reading what there was of Mr Sarto's last work.

Tony is shattered.

Tony *(sits down weakly)* So nobody knows.

Librarian Is there any other book you would like to look at?

Tony No thank you. I've finished with books. I'll never read another book as long as I live. There ought to be a law against selling books with no ending. The Chinese had the right idea, start from the back and work your way forward, you wouldn't catch them like that.

Librarian It's not unusual. Edward Drew, Franz Kafka, they all had unfinished works published.

Tony Exactly. You never know what you're buying. Well I'm not going through all that again. No more books for me. I shall take up some other art form. The gramophone perhaps. Yes, the gramophone. I'll go and buy one.

SCENE 8 *Tony is just putting the finishing touches to placing one loudspeaker. There is another loudspeaker and a gramophone.*

Tony Now, the chair must be eight feet from the loudspeaker. You've got to be just right with this stereophonic lark.

He lines up where the chair should be by pacing out eight feet, one foot in front of the other. He sits down.

Tony That's it. I mustn't break the triangle. Two hundred and fifty pounds worth of equipment here. All set up ready to blast myself out of my chair. *(Sings a bit)* Boom boom boom boom de-boom de-boom de-boom . . . Ha ha, that's it. This is better than who-dunnits. No messing about. You know where you are with

---

are eager to help the rare visitor, then the amount of information available is overwhelming. There is no need for secret or private files. Our government is a continuous and

this stuff. Two hundred and fifty quid. All I need now is a gramophone record. Where's Sid got to? It doesn't take this long to buy a record. If he's been down the Hand and Racquet with my last two pounds . . . I'll . . . I'll . . .

Sid comes in with a gramophone record wrapped up in a paper bag.

Sid Yeah, I couldn't get you Beethoven's Fifth. I thought you might like this instead.

Sid hands him the record. Tony takes it out of the cover, puts the cover on the table. He looks at the label on the record.

Tony Very funny. Very, very funny. *Schubert's Unfinished Symphony.*

Tony quite deliberately breaks the record over Sid's head and walks off.

Ray Galton and Alan Simpson: *The Best of Hancock*
(Robson Books, 1986)

---

compulsive reporter of every aspect of every action. All one needs is the key or keys and out it pours.

Dean Acheson, *Morning and Noon* (1965)

SILENCE © Charles Addams

VICTORIA WOOD

The Library

Inside an Edwardian library in a large-ish town. It is open-plan, with Fiction, Children's and a Reference section, study tables, video machine etc. Pinned up with other local posters is one – 'Tape Your Memories', showing some old dear jabbering away into a tape recorder. Victoria is browsing round the shelves.

Victoria *(to us)* This is the dreariest library in the whole world. They haven't got anything new. I think they're waiting for the Domesday Book to come out in paperback. It's run by this terrible woman called Madge, awfully narrow-minded, makes Mary Whitehouse look like a topless waitress. Never mind Salman Rushdie – she'd have the Swan Vestas to a Catherine Cookson given half a chance. She thinks book-burning is a sensible alternative to oil-fired central heating. Of course they have to order all the newspapers but if it was up to her it would just be *Nursing Mirror* and *Slimming for Nuns*. She can't bear Page Three – in fact she cuts the girls out and replaces them with a knitting pattern. Quite sad seeing all those old blokes sitting around trying to ogle a sleeveless pully.

She encounters Ted, a dirty old man, round a corner. He winks and she retreats.

Madge's taste in fiction; half of these are hospital romances – 'their eyes met over a diseased kidney' – and everything else is in large print. You try reading one with good eyesight. It's like being shouted at for three and a half hours.

She moves into Children's.

And it smells. That typical library aroma of damp gabardine and luncheon meat. And every book's got something scribbled in the margin – things like 'Oh I agree', and 'We washed everything by

This is the lamp where he first read Whitman
   Out of the library large and free.
Every quarter the bus to Kirkstall
   Stopped and waited, but on read he.
            John Betjeman, *Monody on the Death of a Platonist Bank Clerk*, 1966

hand too'. I mean it's a bit disconcerting to flick through a copy of *Hamlet* to find 'This happened to me' scrawled all over Act Four.

Madge appears from nowhere, a large frightening woman.

Madge You know this is Children's?

Victoria I know.

Madge Very well. *(She leaves disapprovingly.)*

Victoria *(crossing to Reference)* She's put me off now. I was just going to squander my ticket on a nice career book: *Wendy Carstairs – Receptionist* or *Petra – Forecourt Attendant*.

She sees Sheila, a thin anxious woman fortyish but dressed older, being shown how to work the video by John the nondescript fortyish assistant librarian.

Victoria Hiya. What are you doing?

Sheila waves her over.

John And when you've finished, press 'Eject' and your tape comes out, and Bob's your Uncle.

Sheila Yes he is. Thank you. I know it's a saying. But he is my uncle. Thank you.

John goes away.

Victoria What are you doing?

Sheila This is the new video machine.

Victoria You can watch videos in the library? Where are they? Have they got *Petra, Forecourt Attendant – The Movie?*

Sheila *(glancing around)* I've joined an agency.

Victoria Have you?

Our libraries are getting bigger, which makes it difficult to find a good book. The shelves are groaning under the pressure of clothbound nothingness.
                    Dagobert D. Runes, *Treasury of Thought* (1966)

Sheila And they've sent me these videos to watch.

Victoria What? Blue videos?

Madge is now hanging around Ted, seated at a table, snatching up papers and folding them with a lot of noise.

Victoria You'd better not watch them there. You know what Madge is like. I've seen her go through a breastfeeding manual crayonning bras on the women.

Sheila I've made a decision, Victoria. I'm coming out of the wardrobe.

Victoria Are you?

Sheila Since Mother died – oh, and thank you for the flowers, we had tributes from everywhere, even the optician – I've taken stock – what do they call it? – stocktaking?

Victoria Yeah?

Sheila And I saw this advertisement in the post office – because I'm trying to sell my stairlift – it's in very good condition, and as I said on the postcard even if you're not disabled, it's FUN! It's called video dating. You've heard of computer dating?

Victoria Yeah?

Sheila Well that's gone by the roof, it's completely blasé now; so the upshot is, they send you six men on a tape and John, the assistant librarian – he used to pick me out something historical for mother – 'Bring me something where nobody dies, Sheila,' she used to say – well, that's the point of history – they're all dead – he's been through the mechanicals with me; I view the men and then contact Valerie.

Victoria Valerie?

Sheila She runs the agency. I've only spoken with her briefly – I had a ten pence stuck – but from the sound of her voice I think she was wearing a tie-neck blouse.

He [Karl Marx] would spend hours in the British Museum searching for some small erotic bauble to present to Engels.
Robert Payne, *Marx: A Biography* (1968)

Victoria So you pick a man?

Sheila That's right. Well, I'm free now, it's about time I turned over a new leaf.

Victoria Put it in then, let's have a look.

Sheila Arrow pointing this way, and press 'PLAY'. *(Nothing happens.)* It's broken, I knew it, it's me *(pressing all buttons)*. I was the same with the spin drier – wet underskirts all over my next-door neighbour, and she's Nigerian – not much of a welcome.

The picture comes up.

The museum tea bar. It is a small, dreary, slightly wholefoody place. Victoria and Sheila are finishing tea.

Victoria I thought you said they did a good date and apple flapjack.

Sheila You just need to work it round your mouth a bit first. *(She roots in her bag.)* Find my notes.

Victoria Nice little book.

Sheila Made by disadvantaged Oriental widows. You can see here where they were too depressed to stick down the edges.

Victoria So who did you fancy?

Sheila Oh I'm no judge of character, Victoria.

Victoria Do you think *I* am? I've had my drive tarmacked eight times.

Sheila Give me your views on Rodney.

Victoria Well, Rodney had white towelling socks, didn't he? Which in my book makes him unreliable, untrustworthy and prone to vaseline jokes. Mark . . .

Sheila The solicitor.

To arrange a library is to practise in a quiet and modest way the art of criticism.

Jorge Luis Borges, (June 1968)

Victoria He was OK – but, as he says himself, he does a lot of conveyancing so that'll be seventeen phone calls just to meet him for a cup of coffee.

Sheila I was rather taken with Simon – the gynaecologist.

Victoria No – too inhibiting. You can't flirt with someone who can visualise your fallopian tubes.

Sheila Now Malcolm – what do you think he meant by 'lively social life'?

Victoria Drink.

Sheila He wants a breezy, uninhibited companion.

Victoria To drink with.

Sheila And what do you think he meant by 'life peppered with personal tragedy'?

Victoria Hangovers.

Sheila I think you're right. He had half an Alka Seltzer stuck in his moustache. Robert.

Victoria Robert?

Sheila In radiators.

Victoria Radiators.

Sheila The blue bri-nylon with the polo collar.

Victoria Oh, the one with the bust! He was creepy. He looked like the sort of man who hangs around outside television shops watching 'Challenge Anneka' with his flies undone.

Sheila Terry was interesting.

Victoria Yes, wasn't he? It's not every nightwatchman who can wear a poncho.

Rock's the best possible of worlds. You get to go on stage, turn up the amplifiers, go wang wang wang and make a fool of yourself. Compare that to being a librarian.

Frank Zappa

Sheila I liked him. He very much put me in mind of someone. Singer – dark curly hair – outgoing . . .

Victoria Tom Jones?

Sheila Alma Cogan. And Kenneth – I've put 'very rushed and jerky'.

Victoria You had him on fast-forward.

Sheila Well I disliked his epaulettes.

Victoria Right.

Sheila So that leaves Keith.

Victoria Well he was all right, wasn't he? What did you put for him?

Sheila Soft, sensitive, a bit woolly.

Victoria Should be all right as long as you don't put him in the washing machine. Where are you going to meet him?

Sheila I thought I'd do him an egg salad at home.

Victoria Are you mad?

Sheila Why?

Victoria Because that's terribly dangerous.

Sheila No. I'd boil them for twenty minutes.

Victoria Inviting a strange man to your home: he could be an axe murderer.

Sheila Oh no – he's got a degree in mechanical engineering.

Victoria Meet him in a restaurant.

I used to be a librarian until I discovered Smirnoff.
Slogan for campaign advertising vodka (c.1970)

Sheila *(panicking)* Oh I'm sending it back. I can't meet him anywhere. I'm no good with men – really. I can't even tackle the milkman face-to-face. I have to bob behind the ironing board and call through. And then he takes advantage. The times I've been saddled with an unrequested bilberry yoghurt.

Victoria Meet him here for a cup of tea.

Sheila I'll clam up. Victoria. I'm no good on my own – I clam up like – what are those things.

Victoria Clams.

Sheila Oysters.

Victoria You won't – you'll be fine.

Sheila After all those years stuck with Mother. I can't just sit down with a man and come up with the bandage. Suppose he chucks in Giscard d'Estaing – how do I respond? I'll be stumped.

Victoria Well – do you want me to come with you?

Sheila Oh if you could just get the ball bowling – that would be marvellous.

Victoria Well I'll just stay and see that you're all right, shall I?

Sheila Mm. Just shush him out.

Victoria And if he looks like being an axe-murderer you keep him talking and I'll immobilise him with the date and apple flapjack. Yep?

The museum tea bar again, on another day. Victoria and Sheila are sitting in readiness with a tray of tea. Sheila is smartly dressed and extremely nervous.

Sheila *(suddenly)* Take off your jacket.

Victoria Eh?

You've never met a librarian like Veronica before – and neither had Henry. Excited by a glimpse of her shapely legs up a library ladder, he draws her close to him and finds she is as excited as he is. As their passion mounts, Henry peels off her sexy garments, to reveal the whole of her luscious

Sheila It's too interesting. Take it off.

Victoria *(taking it off)* What are you worried about?

Sheila Well, as soon as he hears you're in television he's not going to squint my way, is he? He'll be querying left right and centre for insider gossip. He won't want to delve into my doings if he can get the lowdown on Patti Caldwell.

Victoria He's come to meet you.

Sheila What have I ever done? I've never even been mugged.

Victoria You've been burgled.

Sheila And what did they take? Nothing! Two apostle spoons and a bobbing bird. Robbed – I was snubbed.

Victoria Well I'll go then, shall I?

Sheila No don't – he might get the wrong idea: he might think I'm a high class call-girl.

Victoria In a museum tea room?

Sheila He may be a pervert. He may have come here specifically for the purpose of rubbing up against a scale model of Saxon fortifications.

Victoria Well I'll stay for a few minutes.

Sheila Well, dull yourself down a bit. Set me off. Every beautiful painting needs an understated frame.

Victoria Every sizzling casserole needs an oven glove.

Sheila He's here! I recognise his hush puppies. You pour the tea and I'll sparkle.

Keith, early middle-aged in a jacket and sweater, shirt and tie, comes in and looks around vaguely.

---

body to his eager gaze (and yours!). Before you can say 'Silence' they are putting a library table to a use for which it was never intended! An innocent library-user stumbles upon their heated love-making – but they are so carried away they don't even notice him arrive! If you want to know

Victoria He hasn't seen us – wave at him.

Sheila I can't. I've frozen. I'm like this. I was the same with Sacha Distel in Boots. You wave.

Victoria OK.

Sheila Nothing too provocative or sensual.

Victoria *(waves awkwardly.)* Here he comes. Good luck.

Keith Is it Sheila?

Sheila Mmmm.

Keith I wasn't sure if I had the correct museum.

Victoria Would you like to sit down?

Keith Yes I would. *(Sits slowly.)* Well I'm Keith, you're Sheila. Who's the gooseberry.

Victoria I'm Victoria – I have to go in a minute.

Keith Now if you were from Dewsbury, Victoria, you'd be the gooseberry from Dewsbury.

Victoria Ah ha ha.

Keith sits quietly, pleased with this joke. Sheila pours the tea with much rattling.

Keith When I said I was unsure as to whether I'd found the correct museum, the circumstances were these: your note, Sheila, for which many thanks, told me to expect a large building with stone pillars to my left on entering the city centre. *(Pause.)* Now would I be correct in thinking you are not familiar with the workings of the internal combustion engine?

Sheila A with the workings, what, begging?

Victoria You don't drive.

---

what happens next, you'll just HAVE to buy this film.
Advertisement for porn film, *Sex in the Library* (1977)

Sheila Oh no. I've been shown around a tank.

Keith And so, not being cognisant with the traffic lay-out as seen, so to speak, from the steering wheel, it will have escaped your attention that the very first building on the left is not the museum and municipal library, but the Edgar Bentley Treatment Hospital for Tropical Diseases.

Both Ah ah.

Keith Now, having got that off my chest, I will just equip myself with a smallish biscuit to accompany my tea and return forthwith.

Keith leaves. Significant silence.

Sheila *He* nursed an elderly mother.

Victoria I hope she was deaf.

Sheila Well I don't think he's an axe-murderer.

Victoria He doesn't need to be. Hey up.

Keith comes back in.

Keith Well, I'm familiar with Sheila's hobbies and lifestyle as laid out in the video but what's your line of country, Vicky?

Victoria You don't want to hear about me. Sheila's the fascinating one – she writes poems – she's a wonderful cook . . .

Keith No – I'm an orderly fellow. Ask a question, get the reply, that's my handlebar. So, how do you rake in the shekels?

Victoria Oh I've got such a boring job. I can hardly remember what it is.

Keith Well let's not forget three million people in this country would *like* to be bored in that fashion.

Pause.

One day there will be no libraries. Only a global bookshelf.
Brian Redhead (1981)

Victoria I work in an office.

Keith Now, call me a dashingly romantic sentimental old softheart, Vicky . . .

Victoria I haven't got time.

Keith But to me an office is more than a place of work – it's a microcosm of everyday society.

Sheila Goodness.

Keith What do you say to that, Vicky?

Victoria I say – ah ha ha.

Keith I thought so. And what office position do you hold?

Victoria I just answer the phone.

Keith Now therein if I may presume – we've taken tea together so we're halfway to being pals – therein lies the cardinal error of the average telephone receptionist.

Victoria pulls a face at Sheila.

Sheila I see in the paper today Mrs Thatcher's sporting a new brooch.

Keith I'll ignore that, Sheila, for reasons I'll come to in a moment. The telephone receptionist of any company, be it British Telecom or Joe Bloggs of down the road Ltd, holds a unique position in the business framework. Let me clarify myself – this plate is the managing director and this shortbread finger is the retail customer – what comes in between them?

Sheila A doiley?

Keith The telephone receptionist. Now take a typical day in the office . . .

Did you choose librarianship as a career, or was it something you 'lapsed into'?
I think it was something I collapsed into.
        Douglas Dunn, *Viewpoints: Poets in Conversation with*
                                        John Haffenden (1981)

Inside the library, in the video section, a few days later, Victoria and Sheila are checking their notes. Ted is reading the paper at a nearby table.

Victoria Right – so we're going to Richard this time.

Sheila You're sure I shouldn't persevere with Keith?

Victoria He's boring. You've been bored for twenty years. It would be out of the frying pan into the microwave.

Madge *(appears from afar and calls)* You two! This is not a zoo!

Victoria So you can't help me locate the elephant house?

Madge Quiet study or leave, please.

Madge leaves and Ted winks juicily at Victoria.

Ted Heck of a rump on that. By cracky.

Victoria *(more quietly)* What did we put for Richard?

Sheila I've put 'very gentlemanly; interested in fine china and eighteenth-century English furniture. Likes visiting cathedrals, classical music; semi-retired business consultant looking for quiet, refined companion.'

Victoria Well, you're quiet.

Sheila Yes, but I'm not refined. I wouldn't know a Hepplewhite wotnot from a quarter of wine gums.

Victoria It doesn't matter. Just be yourself.

Sheila And we weren't a classical music family. If Joe 'Piano' Henderson couldn't play it we didn't hear it.

Victoria What you want to do – is meet him for a drink and take someone really vulgar and thick with you – then you come out looking erudite and tasteful, he's bowled over and whisks you away in his Rover. What do you say?

Librarianship is in fact an interesting profession, not as dull as I sometimes make it out to be.
Douglas Dunn, *Viewpoints: Poets in Conversation with John Haffenden* (1981)

Sheila Well I can see the reasoning behind it – but I don't know anybody vulgar. Mother wouldn't even have our scissors sharpened because the woman had pierced ears.

Victoria Well – meet him at the wine bar . . .

John comes in.

John Is it working OK now?

Sheila Yes, it wasn't irretrievably jammed, thank you, John. I had it on *pause*.

John *(moving away)* That's good. Now, Ted, come on – no eating your sandwiches here – it's not really fair on the other readers.

Ted pretends to put them away. John leaves.

Victoria What we'll do – you meet him at the wine bar . . .

Madge *(coming in from nowhere)* When will you people appreciate this is an area set aside for silent study – it is not an annexe of the Millwomen and Fishwives' Debating Society.

Victoria Sorry.

Madge *(as she sniffs and wheels round)* You – put those sandwiches away at once. I will not have chutney on my periodicals.

Inside a quiet emptyish wine bar. Richard, a grey-haired, distinguished man in a quiet suit, sits sharing a bottle of wine with Sheila.

Richard Well, here's to a pleasant evening.

Sheila Yes, 'heres'.

She drinks.

Richard I was having a quiet chuckle to myself this morning.

Sheila Oh yes?

More worrying . . . are quite explicit moves to commercialise library services. Tory-controlled Westminster Council, for example, has proposed among other things, to sell space on library walls for commercial advertisements; to sell window space similarly; and even that each book should carry an

Richard Radio 3 – Alicia de Larrocha with the Granados, *Quejas a la maja y el ruisenor* – very amusing interpretation. Did you catch any of it?

Sheila No, I would probably have had on the Ken Bruce programme.

Richard Really? *(Pause.)* I'm pleasantly surprised by the acceptability of this bouquet – are you?

Sheila *(struggling to keep up)* Mm, I'm astounded.

Richard Are you, as they say, 'into' wine?

Sheila We used to make it at one time.

Richard Really – you had a vineyard?

Sheila We had a scullery.

Richard *(recovering)* I should think with homemade wine one would have to be extremely patient – is that so?

Sheila Oh yes – that's the bugbear with it – keeping your hands off the dustbin till the full ten days. *(Pause.)* Van Gogh's a very nice painter, isn't he?

Richard I assume you're using the word in its incorrect sense – interesting.

Sheila I love the Great Painters.

Richard And they are . . .?

Sheila They're a set of table mats.

Pause.

Richard You say a friend of yours is joining us?

Sheila Just breezing through. Here she is now actually.

---

advertisement, 'just like parking meters'. Contraceptive adverts in *Tom Jones* . . . A list of guest-houses in *To the Lighthouse* . . . Fertiliser adverts in *The Waste Land* . . . the mind boggles.

Ken Worpole, *Reading By Numbers* (1984)

Victoria comes in, a vision in skin-tight dress, tormented hair, jewellery, stilettos, the lot.

Victoria Ooh, give us a swig of your vino, crumb-bum; I've been banging like a navvie's drill all affy.

Sheila This is –

Victoria Sapphire. Ciao.

Richard Very pleased to meet you, Sapphire – I'm Richard Casey.

Victoria He looks a bit of a Richard, dunt he, Sheila? Hey, hutch up, I'm sweating cobs. *(She sniffs her armpits.)*

Richard May I pour you a glass, Sapphire?

Victoria Pour us a bin bag – I'm gasping. I tell you, that window cleaner, what a snogger! I've never had such clean tonsils. And never mind a chammy – he certainly buffed up *my* corners.

Richard And what do you do, Sapphire?

Victoria Eh? A bit of this, bit of that, loads of the other! No, to be serious, Richard – I'm an artiste in the entertainment business. *(She fishes in her cleavage.)* Where's my card? *(She gets it out and wipes it.)* 'Miss Sapphire – Poses with a Python'. Now don't get the wrong idea – it's right artistic. Costume-wise, I never wear less than the full three tassels, and between shows I am at that python with the Dettox and a damp cloth even if he haven't been nowhere. *(She slurps her wine.)* God, I needed that – my guts! I don't care what they say on t' adverts – Malibu does not go with piccalilli. The wind I've had, Rich – I won't beat about the bungalow – I've been flatulating – and boy, have I stunk! I mean, I don't mind for t' punters but it's not pleasant for the python. Hey – top us up, Dicky – I've got a big job on tonight. Do you ever get days, Dick when you think, 'I just do not want to thrust my groin in people's faces – I want to go home and have a go at my corns with a potato peeler.' Do you?

Richard Well, I can't say I –

... She decided on her tweed jacket and severe blouse and grey flat-heeled shoes. It was her usual escort outfit, her librarian look. 'I'm naked underneath,' she said, if a man questioned her style.

Paul Theroux, *Doctor Slaughter* (1984)

Victoria So what do you think to our Sheila then? Eh? I mean talk about tasteful. She isn't like me; she wouldn't know a rubberised posing pouch from a sink plunger. Still – if it's a good party, who cares? *(She laughs.)*

Richard Shall I order some more wine?

Victoria No, I'd better push off, Rick – I've got to glue a little novelty toilet into my navel and it takes forever to dry.

Richard Oh, no, have a little champagne before you leave. Waiter!

Victoria All right, just a quick bottle. Now, Sheila – have you told Richard about how you're really into classical music?

Sheila Oh yes. Ravel's 'Bolero', what a pulsing rhythm. Superb for tackling the ironing.

Richard *(patronisingly)* And Sapphire? Any views on Ravel?

Victoria What were he, a juggler?

Richard *(amused)* No, a rather famous composer.

Victoria Oh. Cos jugglers often wear boleros.

Richard You probably know it as the Torville and Dean music.

Victoria Weren't they a lovely couple? And they never did it. Mind you, she spent so much time lying face down on the ice, I'm not surprised.

Richard You're not keen on the classics, then, I take it?

Victoria Never heard of them – what are they?

Richard Beethoven's Fifth.

Victoria No.

Richard Moonlight Sonata.

Invoking the names of education and enlightenment, it has become a system which largely supplies free pulp fiction to those who could well afford to buy it.
                                   Adam Smith Institute, *Ex Libris* (1986)

Victoria Sounds like a hatchback. No.

Richard 1812 Overture.

Victoria That rings a bell.

Richard Daddle addle daddly dat dat dah.

Victoria Oh yeah – my friend Suleema used to do an act to that.

Richard What sort of an act?

Victoria Sort of a contortionist. I won't go into details, but Christmas round her house they never needed a bottle opener, a nut cracker, or somewhere to keep the satsumas.

Richard *(snuggling up)* This is fascinating.

Victoria Sheila, tell Richard about your Elaine Page records.

Richard Elaine Paige?

Victoria You know – blonde, titchy, goes 'Bleuh!' What a Hobsons. How they passed her over for the Royal Wedding beats me. I know she's small, but they could have stood her up on a bucket. Still, that's the Establishment for you.

Richard You're bloody right: we're too damn stuffy about these things. God – you're refreshing.

Victoria *(drinking, pulling a face at Sheila)* Bottoms up.

Sheila *(leaving)* I'll just go and powder my nose.

Victoria Don't forget to flush it!

Richard Crikey – you're funny. So, er, what do you wear on stage exactly? Black leather boots or stilettos? Let's have the full gen.

Victoria Er –

I spent hours, days, in the great Reading Room of the Mitchell Library [in Glasgow]. Young as I was, in my ragged shorts, frayed jersey and ill-fitting jacket, incongruous among the sleek, well-nourished university students, I

The library, a couple of days later; Victoria is hanging around Fiction as before.

Victoria Sheila's given up on this video dating. She says the next time she goes out with a man, she'll be lying down with her eyes shut and he'll be carrying the coffin. What a night with Richard. I mean when a man's on the lookout for quiet refined companionship you don't expect him to try eating pork scratchings out of your cleavage. He was dreadful in the taxi – I haven't been groped so inefficiently since I was fifteen. Once he saw me he never took another look at Sheila – good job – she finished off the champagne and was last seen in the gent's toilets flicking Quiche Lorraine over the cubicle doors.

Madge *(looming round a unit)* Are you looking for anything in particular?

Victoria I'm browsing.

Madge Well don't finger the bindings. *(She heads for the counter.)* John! What on earth are you doing with your sleeves rolled up? This isn't a massage parlour!

Sheila comes round the shelves, holding a book.

Victoria Got one!

They walk to the counter where John is being torn off a strip by Madge.

Sheila It's very difficult to find a book with no alcohol, no sex and no reference to men whatsoever.

Victoria What did you get?

Sheila *The Wincey Willis Book of Wholemeal Pasta.*

They wait to have the book stamped; Madge is still in full flow.

Madge And it isn't just your clothing, John – though heaven knows, training shoes are hardly compatible with a love of literature. It's your wishy-washy liberal attitude – video machines and Asian novels here, taped reminiscences there – mark my

---

became so familiar to the staff that they dubbed me, in kindly fashion, 'the young professor'.
Ralph Glasser, *Growing Up in the Gorbals* (1986)

words, John, make people welcome in the library and it's the thin end of the bookmark; before you can say 'Monica Dickens' they'll be drying their underwear on the radiators and doing boil-in-the-bag noodles behind the photocopier. Kindly digest. If anybody wants me I shall be in the stacks with a Jackie Collins and felt-tip pen.

She leaves.

John Just the one book, Sheila? Er – sorry about that –

Sheila Oh, she doesn't bamboozle me. I remember her when she first came – never seen so many kirbys in a French pleat.

John Cookery book, eh? Now that's my absolute blind spot, I'm afraid. I really am clueless.

Sheila Oh I'm nuts on cuisine. I really miss having somebody to cook for. There's a lovely thing in here with courgettes but it's not worth cooking for one.

John Well, if you ever need an extra mouth . . .

Sheila Well I was thinking of doing a little meal this evening if you've no plans afoot?

John No, I haven't but –

Victoria Sheila!

Sheila I'm not being forward, Victoria. I like to think of myself as liberated – I could have burnt my bra but it was longline and I didn't have the time. So would you care to accept my invitation to dinner?

John Certainly – and I very much appreciate it.

Sheila Eight o'clock then. Bye.

They leave.

Victoria You didn't give him your address.

Closing a library would have been unthinkable ten years ago. Now a richer society can't support it. Something is seriously wrong.

Joan Bakewell, *The Sunday Times* (1987)

Sheila He's a librarian. He'd find it sharp enough if I owed 8p on a Georgette Heyer.

Victoria and Sheila are walking along a quiet street of semis.

Victoria Just have somebody in the house with you – that's all I'm saying. Haven't you got an Auntie Lill or a Cousin Ida?

Sheila I've got an Auntie Lill *and* a Cousin Ida. One's in Toronto and the other's body-building in Hendon.

They stop outside the house.

Victoria Well, shall I do it?

Sheila Oh no, we've had the last twice.

Victoria I'll hide in the garden – keep an eye through the window.

Sheila You can't, we've got vigilantes. Mr Brewer's forever up and down the avenue with a beret and a ping-pong bat.

Victoria *(striding up the path)* I know! Come on!

Sheila Hang on – my Yale's under my Wincey Willis.

Sheila's house. The hall, stairs, and bathroom door at the top of the stairs. All is clean and neat and ten years out of date. Sheila stands anxiously outside the bathroom door.

Sheila Are you nearly ready?

Victoria *(Voice Over)* Yeah, I won't be a sec. Now, you know the plan?

Sheila I take him in the kitchen, introduce you, explain you won't be joining us for dinner then take him through into the dining room.

Victoria *(Voice Over)* And I'll be in the kitchen the whole time so just give us a shout if he gets frisky.

The major arena of my education became the Public Library, a white stone building of no architectural merit across the road from the [Sheffield] Town Hall. A flicker of grim romance was attached to that lobby, through which one entered the library, by the fact that a suicide had once hurled

Sheila If he gets what?

Victoria *(Voice Over)* Frisky!

Sheila *(pattering down the stairs)* Will do! I thought you said frisky!

Victoria's puzzled face appears round the door.

Sheila's hall. She opens the front door to a nervous John.

Sheila Oh, come in.

He trips.

Mind the mat. It's from the Philippines – and I'm not sure they always take quite the trouble.

John Well it's rather a corrupt society.

Sheila Oh I know. Take your coat off. I saw a documentary. It looked to be quite an uprising, even with the sound off.

John *(standing by the coatstand)* Shall I? *(He hangs his coat on a knob.)*

Sheila Yes do. *(All the coats fall down.)* Oh, that coatstand. I arranged to have it renovated but they lost interest when they heard it was just a knob.

John I could probably glue it back on for you.

Sheila Oh could you?

John If you have any glue, perhaps after dinner –

Sheila I may have some UHU left over from the Nativity. Anyway – come through to the kitchen . . .

Inside Sheila's kitchen. It is clean but dreary; lots of pots and pans are bubbling away. Victoria is at the kitchen table in old lady dress and woolly hat. Sheila and John come in.

---

himself down on to the tiles from the Art Gallery balcony, three floors above.

George MacBeth, *A Child of the War* (1987)

Sheila This is my auntie *(she casts around the room)* Marjoram – Marjorie.

John I'm very pleased to meet you.

Victoria 'Appen as mebbe. But you'll know what they say?

John No, what's that?

Victoria Pleased to meet is sorry to greet come Michaelmas.

John Now, I've never heard that; isn't that fascinating!

Victoria Now you don't want to waste your time with an old outhouse like mysen – get the knees under t' table and set to supping.

John You're not joining us for dinner then, Mrs –?

Victoria Witherstrop. Nay – I topped up long since. Nice plate of brains and a ginger nut. Tek him through, Sheila – I shall be all right here.

Sheila Right – John –?

John *(sitting down)* I'm sure there's time for a little chat, Sheila?

Victoria Oh, no, you get about your dining arrangements. Them as chat shall never grow fat.

John That's another lovely saying I've never come across.

Sheila *(at the stove)* I'll just finish off if you're all right, John?

John Certainly. Gosh, it's warm in here. Can I take your hat, Mrs Withersdrop?

Victoria I can't tek it off, lad. I lost every hair on my head the day they bombed Eccles.

John Blast.

I have these days when I feel really creative. Sometimes I don't. Sometimes I think I should have been a librarian.
                              Cher, *The Mail on Sunday* (1988)

Victoria That's what I said.

Sheila I'm sure John doesn't want to hear about that, Marjorie.

John No, I'd love to.

Victoria February the eleventh, 1941. I was clocking off from work – aye, from munitions – they had to convert when war broke out – they had been making liquorice torpedoes so it weren't too much of an upheaval. Vera Lynn were coming over the Gannex –

John I beg your pardon?

Victoria The tannoy. Big Ellen Mottershead turned to me – her crossover pinnie was wet with tears. 'It's a bomber's moon, Marjorie,' she said, 'It's a bomber's moon.'

John Look – I'm sorry to interrupt – this is absolutely fascinating and just what I need.

Victoria Eh?

John My taped reminiscence programme – it's been very hard to get it off the ground – a lot of opposition from Madge. These stories of yours are just what I need to get the ball rolling. Sheila – would you mind if I just fetched my tape recorder?

Sheila No.

John I won't be one sec.

He dashes out of the back door.

Sheila I thought you said no one could possibly have an interest in an old woman. What a marvellous evening I'm going to have.

Victoria Well, I'll keep it short.

Sheila How? He wants your life story.

Victoria I'll tell him I was killed in an air raid.

You grew up in a working-class suburb of Honolulu. Do you wonder what might have happened if you hadn't been able to sing?
Yes, and I thank God for that gift. Without it, I probably

John reappears with a tape recorder.

John Actually, Mrs Withersdrop, I've been thinking – it's awfully rude to suddenly conduct an interview with you when Sheila has this lovely meal already prepared?

Victoria Aye, well.

John So what I thought was, rather than me bombarding you with questions, if Sheila doesn't mind, my uncle's in the car outside – if he could perhaps come in, I'll set the machine going and you could both chat together, I should think you're pretty much of an age.

Sheila Bring him in, by all means.

John *(shouting from the doorway)* Uncle Ted! Come in then!

Sheila But what's he doing in the car? I don't follow.

John Well I'm sure you'll think I'm a bit of a weed – but you read such terrible things in the papers; men kidnapped by fanatical women, used as sex slaves – I brought Ted as a safety precaution.

Sheila I wouldn't kidnap a man for sex – I'm not saying I couldn't use someone to oil the mower.

Ted comes in.

Ted Hey up, fans!

John This is Mrs Withersdrop, Ted. She's going to tape her memories of the raid on Eccles.

Ted *(sitting down)* There never were a ruddy raid on Eccles –there were nowt worth bombing, bar two tarts at the bus station.

Victoria Aye, well – my memory's not what it was.

John Well I'll just leave the tape running – you two settle down and have a really good chat about the old days and Sheila and I can get stuck into our dinner.

---

would have . . . killed myself. No. I probably would have been a librarian – I like books. I like the company of books. I like the smell and feel. I like collating. You know, I have three librarians in my family, as a matter of fact. And I would

Sheila Lovely. If you'll just push the trolley, John.

John goes out with the laden trolley.

Sheila Offer Ted a Beer, Marjorie – you may be in for a long evening.

Sheila leaves with a bottle of wine. Victoria snaps open a beer for Ted. He slurps and belches.

Ted Pardon.

Victoria Right, well, let's get it over with. I was born in a one up one down. My mother washed everything by hand, and I didn't set eyes on a sprout till I was seventeen.

Ted switches off the tape.

Ted Never mind John's old rubbish. *(He hutches his chair up and lays a heavy hand on her leg.)* By! That's a leg and a half. I tell you what – I may be seventy-eight but I've still plenty of snap in my celery. You know what they say?

Victoria What?

Ted There's many a new piston under an old bonnet.

Mens Sana in Thingummy Doodah (Methuen, 1990)

CREDITS TO THE PROFESSION

Turn to the acknowledgments in any book, even this one, and you will find librarians fulsomely praised. To be a librarian is to be a foot soldier to book makers, ever the bridesmaid, never the bride. There is something saintly about librarians that brings out the best in writers. Yet for many growing up in poorer parts of the country, an encounter with a librarian was tantamount to being hauled over the coals by a headmaster. A librarian in the west of Scotland once recalled how when he went to the library, the librarian inspected his hands and sent him home to have them scrubbed. The shame kept him away from the place for years.

Mostly though, librarians are receptive and encouraging. They have, however, an unfortunate image, one that is perpetuated by newspapers and other media. Whenever television deigns to portray them it is always a mickey-take. One thinks of Ronnie Corbett in *Sorry* (ah, how indicative is the title), a tot in spectacles and woolly cardigan, still loding with his mother. The popular view of the librarian is of someone invariably uncommunicative and tight-laced, who always has the word 'shush' on his or her lips.

It is a view that is difficult to dislodge once it has entered the imagination. In the library press it continues to be a source of annoyance; among the professions it is hard to think of one that worries quite so much about image as librarians. Only a psychiatrist can say why. The truth is other. Librarians, being selfless, offer succour to the ignorant, a life-line to flounderers, hope to no-hopers. Money, time, health, sanity, all can be preserved by the judicious use of libraries. All human thought is there. It has been said that if only someone had known where to look, the key to the Watergate scandal was in papers lodged in the Library of Congress. Who needs Woodward or Bernstein? All you have to do is ask the librarian.

PHILIP LARKIN

Who is Borges?

Interviewer *How did you come to be a librarian? Had you no interest in teaching? What was your father's profession?*

Larkin Oh dear, this means a lot of autobiography. My father was a city treasurer, a finance officer. I never had the desire to 'be' anything when I was at school, and by the time I went to Oxford the war was on and there wasn't anything to 'be' except a serviceman or a teacher or a civil servant. In 1943 when I graduated I knew I couldn't be the first, because I'd been graded unfit (I suppose through eyesight), nor the second because I stammered, and then the Civil Service turned me down twice, and I thought, Well, that lets me out, and I sat at home writing *Jill*. But of course in those days the government had powers to send you into the mines or on to the land or into industry, and they wrote quite politely to ask what in fact I was doing: I looked at the daily paper (the *Birmingham Post*: we were living at Warwick then) and saw that a small town in Shropshire was advertising for a librarian, applied for it, and got it, and told the government so, which seemed to satisfy them.

Of course, I wasn't a real librarian, more a sort of caretaker – it was a one-man library – and I can't pretend I enjoyed it much. The previous librarian had been there about forty years, and I was afraid I should be there all my life too. This made me start qualifying myself professionally just in order to get away, which I did in 1946. By then I'd written *Jill*, and *The North Ship*, and *A Girl in Winter*. It was probably the 'intensest' time of my life.

Interviewer *Is Jorge Luis Borges the only other contemporary poet of note who is a librarian, by the way? Are you aware of any others?*

Larkin Who is Jorge Luis Borges? The writer-librarian *I* like is Archibald MacLeish. You know he was made Librarian of Congress in 1939, and on his first day they brought him some

---

The great guides were the books I discovered in the John Hopkins Library, where my student job was to file the books away. One was more or less encouraged to take a cart of books and go back into the stacks and not come out for

papers to sign, and he wouldn't sign them until he understood what they were all about. When he did understand, he started making objections and countersuggestions. The upshot was that he reorganised the whole Library of Congress in five years simply by saying, I don't understand and I don't agree, and in wartime, too. Splendid man.

The Paris Review Interviews: Writers at Work, Seventh Series, edited by George Plimpton (Secker & Warburg, 1987)

seven or eight hours. So I read what I was filing.
John Barth, quoted in *The Writer's Chapbook* (1989)

PHILIP LARKIN

Conference Going

Larkin's lugubriousness was never more pronounced than when his thoughts turned to meeting up with his professional peers.

Letter to Winifred Arnott, 2 August 1952
. . . My life is upside down at present: my mother is staying in my flat and I am living a nomadic existence among other tenants' property. No fewer than four people have left me their keys: if I were at all businesslike I should be putting up British Association members – or holiday makers, even – at five gns a week, nothing found. Once mother has gone (night of the 13th) workmen entirely empty my living-room, remove my skylight and start putting in a dormer window. This will take about four weeks. Only *then* shall I be at rest. And then that annual romp, that orgy of licence, that recollection of the worst excesses of 1789, the Conference of the University and Research Section of the Library Association. I suppose you're not by any chance going?

Letter to Barbara Pym, 8 April 1963
Today I have just come back from Bangor, where I have attended (these tenses seem all wrong) *two* conferences, the sentences to run consecutively as they say – the Standing Conference of National and University Libraries and then the University and Research Section of the Library Association. The first is a gentlemanly affair of about 40, the second a mob of some 150. I wouldn't have stayed, except I was helping to 'introduce a discussion', and in the event was not saved by a 'nasty turn', like A. Forbes [a character in Pym's novel, *No Fond Return of Love*]. Not that I mean to sound as if I thought (think?) myself above such things, but a couple of nights in a hall of residence bed with no bed light are really good enough for me. As it was, I had *five*. However, the hall was really very good as halls go, and the Warden very anxious that one should eat, drink and be merry. Not like the Warden in the hall here who makes the conference secretary's life a misery with

---

I am told by those who have made the experiment, that if you apply to read *The British Museum is Falling Down* in the very building itself, you are required to do so in the North Library, that inner sanctum which . . . is reserved for the perusal of books deemed to be either especially valuable or

'several tea pots and hot water jugs left standing on a polished table last night, instead of being replaced on the tray provided. The table was marked in consequence . . .'

Selected Letters of Philip Larkin, edited by Anthony Thwaite (Faber and Faber, 1992)

---

pornographic. I have not ventured to inquire which of these criteria has been applied to my novel.

David Lodge, author of *The British Museum is Falling Down*
(1990)

MARTYN HARRIS

Bring Back Lucy Finch

Lucy Finch was my first love. She was only four foot eight, and pushing 50, but she knew her way around. She turned me on to Arthur Ransome at the age of eight, introduced me to Rosemary Sutcliffe at 10, and Orwell and Golding by the time I was 11. Miss Finch was the Sketty librarian, my godmother and godmother also to all juvenile book junkies: 'Have you heard of Jack London? You might enjoy him. And perhaps this new writer called Roald Dahl . . .' I look back amazed at my younger self, swallowing seven books a week. Once it was four in a single head-buzzing day. When did I play, or eat – or breathe?

Saturation reading is the path to becoming a writer, and most writers have similar memories: the austere and orderly library with its clacking parquet floors and smell of beeswax polish; the soft-eared cardboard library pass that was the first badge of adulthood; the slithering armful of plastic-wrapped hardbacks, miraculously free, and as pregnant with possibility as Christmas.

This is all nostalgic rubbish according to a new report, *The Future of Public Libraries In The UK*, from Comedia market research: 'The public library's most vociferous defenders have focused on what the library was, rather than what it could be. The public interventions by writers and critics such as Margaret Drabble and Richard Hoggart, often defending a library ethos remembered affectionately and powerfully from childhood, are in danger of becoming counter productive.' So shut up all you middle-class sentimentalists, and listen to the voice of progress, which as usual speaks for the fashionable, the transient and the silly.

Aiming to be 'accessible and jargon-free' the report demands the libraries 'play a significant role in information policy and cultural renewal – with online business services, economic development initiatives, open learning . . .' From this welter of undefined terms emerges the familiar picture of the library as a right-on creche for latchkey children, the 'unwaged', single mothers and what the

---

I remember a time when I used to come here [the Biblioteca Nacional, Argentine] to read. I was a very young man, and I was far too timid to ask for a book. Then, I was rather, I won't say poor, but I wasn't too wealthy in those days – so I used to come here and pick out a volume of the *Encyclo-*

jargon-free report calls 'an entry point to the wider culture for many of Britain's ethnic minority communities'.

It is a familiar picture because it is what my own local library in Hornsey looks like: a decaying Sixties block with spray-can graffiti competing for space on the windows with 'Save Our Library' pictures by the local junior school. Around the council bottle banks, thoughtfully placed outside the children's playgroup, there is a carpet of splintered glass, while dandelions sprout in the pavement of the ornamental garden. 'It's the cuts,' library staff say in a laconic abdication of responsibility, but I've never understood, when the young librarian Philip Larkin stoked his own boiler, why 'cuts' prevent his modern counterpart from sweeping up a bit of glass.

The hugely successful Waterstone's bookshops are like old-fashioned libraries with wood shelving and sombre green paintwork and gilt signage, but Hornsey, of course, is beige tin and plastic with acres of tattered notices advertising Tai Chi, Feminist Massage, and *Practical Magic*. There is a single Jack London volume in stock and the only Orwell I can find is one copy of *Animal Farm*. I gave up on the place years ago for borrowing fiction.

I still use the reference section but as soon as I settle down with *Who's Who*, a fat man stamps up, shouting: 'The library shuts in five minutes.' The time is 4.45 and it shuts at 5.0 but fat man is unimpressed by this argument. The next morning, Friday, I find it is shut all day.

The Adam Smith Institute has argued that as it costs £1.24 to lend each book (a crude figure obtained by dividing library costs by books issued) it would be cheaper to close public libraries and give books away free. As book borrowing has dropped 15 per cent in 10 years (at a time of increased library building and unprecedented public interest in fiction) – and since libraries may now irrevocably be in the hands of fools more interested in social engineering – I have sympathy for this argument.

Before we get too drastic, however, there are other paths to explore. Appoint Tim Waterstone as library supremo to introduce proper management, strategic purchasing and promotion. Throw out the video libraries, the 'feminist book' sections, the fragile and expensive children's picture books, and the money-pit microcomputers. Concentrate on lending *books*, from libraries which are open at hours when people can visit them; sweep up the glass; kill the dandelions, and bring back Miss Finch.

The Daily Telegraph (26 June 1993)

---

paedia Britannica, the old edition. The eleventh or twelfth because those editions are far above the new ones. They were meant to be *read*. Now they are merely reference books. While in the eleventh or twelfth edition of the *Encyclopaedia Britannica*, you had long articles by Macaulay,

JIMMY REID

The Woman in Govan Library

Libraries played a very important part in my own education, if you can call it an education. In terms of formal scholastic qualifications I have none – not even an 'O' level. Not because I was a total 'bampot', as they say, but I left school at fourteen and, to tell you the truth, we did not take exams at that time. I passed my eleven plus. We still had the eleven plus in those days. I think it was out of 150, and I got 148½, which was not a bad pass mark. I am not indicating anything here, because I did not think much about the eleven plus at that time. When I grew to maturity I thought even less about it as any kind of guide for measuring the intelligence of human beings, because people, particularly children, develop at different levels.

Anyway, I passed the eleven plus. I don't know what it is like now, but they streamed you in those days, and in Govan we were streamed into the academic stream that was based on Oxford and Cambridge. I did Greek, French and Latin, but my expectations never involved higher education. I did not know anybody who went to university from the streets of Govan. You normally assumed that at the first opportunity you were out to work. I must confess I never found a smattering of knowledge about Latin verbs of great assistance in the shipyards, but do not knock it for that reason.

I must also add that I have no recollection of my formal education, particularly at secondary school, stimulating or generating the slightest interest in any subject, in any subject at all, yet at the age of twelve or thirteen I was a voracious reader and pestered the life out of the woman in Govan Library. She swore blind that I could not be reading all the books I was taking out! Now, I was not exactly a bookworm – I used to play football and do all the other things with the lads. The truth is that for whatever reason, I started reading and by the time I was thirteen or fourteen had read everything that Shaw had ever written, including his novels (which were not very good), and, to this day, I am still a voracious reader.

---

by Coleridge, De Quincey, and so on. So that I used to take any volume from the shelves – there was no need to ask for them: they were reference books – and then I opened the book till I found an article that interested me, for example about the Mormons or about any particular writer. I sat

The importance of the library to me then was considerable. But there is another factor which I want to raise with you this morning which I think is important. The best way of raising it is to ask you to jump forward in time to about 1972–73. I went down to London to do a literary programme for London Weekend Television and Jonathan Miller was there. I introduced the question of the decline and fall of the novel. All the evidence suggests, in my opinion, that that particular literary art form has gone over the apex of its development. I am saying that now, more in sorrow than in joy, because to me it has made a colossal contribution to human knowledge. Anyway, we went into this in detail and after the programme, having a drink, he said to me, 'Where did you study English Literature?' I said, 'Govan Library', and he said, 'Ah, come on. The library?' And I did realise then that because I had not been reading in order to increase job expectations, or career prospects, or to pass an examination, there was a catholicity in my reading for which I am eternally grateful.

There was another question which Miller raised which I want to raise. Miller and Bennett and some of the others from *Beyond the Fringe* years ago bought a Church of Scotland manse that was being sold off by the Kirk in Perthshire. He loves going up there, with three or four others, where they are away from all the pressures of the big city. Miller told us that they went down to the local pub with their big woolly jumpers on. (That is what intellectuals do. When workers come home they take off the woolly jumpers and put on a pin-stripe suit. When they take off the pin-stripe suit they put on big woollies!) Anyway, Jonathan had the big woollies on and was down in the local pub when a wee guy wearing a bonnet, rolling a fag, came over and said 'Are you Jonathan Miller?' and he said 'Yes, I am.' And the wee guy said 'I must say I disagree with your interpretation of Marlowe.' He was a maintenance engineer in a local distillery, and his critique was more effective than anything in *New Society*, the *New Statesman*, the *Guardian*, or *The Times*. The wee guy said it all, and Miller had to listen to him. There is nowhere in Britain where you are more likely to get working-class intellectuals than in Scotland. It could never happen in the East End of London.

I will tell you why I am raising this with you. There is a tradition, sadly, I think, diminishing, but still extant when I was a youth, a tradition of literacy among the Scottish people that goes back some centuries. The reason Scotland has a ploughman as its national bard is because two hundred years ago the ploughmen in

---

down and read it because those articles were really monographs, really books or short books. The same goes for the German encyclopaedias – Brockhaus or Meyers. When we got the new copy, I thought that was what they call the *Shorter Brockhaus*, but it wasn't. It was explained to

Scotland were more likely to be literate than the ploughmen in England. At that time we were among the most literate nations in the world. I do not know the historic reasons for this. Perhaps it was the Kirk, with its demand for a school in every village and a college in every town. But it is not without significance that at a time when Scotland had a ploughman as the national bard the equivalent south of the Border was more likely to be Lord Shelley, Lord Byron or Keats. Not because English ploughmen lacked potential literary merit, but because it was just a bit difficult to express such merit if you were illiterate.

I think the point I am making here is that literacy became a characteristic and a feature of the Scottish working class in the industrial era. I told Miller that there is another place in Britain where I have detected that characteristic, and that is in South Wales. There, the miners in 1880 and 1885 were deducting a half a penny and a penny a week to build their own libraries. Everyone in the Labour movement quotes Bevan now – people who would have spat on him if he was alive. They are always saying 'as Nye said', and everybody invokes his name as a kind of Holy Ghost that will bring Benediction to whatever interpretation of socialism they are advancing. But Bevan's rhetoric, analysis and manner and mode of speech sprang from a broadly based culture that was achieved in a working man's library when he was in his late teens. Now there are all those young boys in London trying to emulate Bevan by reading all the political memoranda, whereas Bevan's secret was his broad literary base.

In Clydeside, when I left school, this tradition of the pursuit of knowledge as a good thing in itself was still alive and I remember when I was fourteen or fifteen going to a place in Renfrew Street in Glasgow called the Workers' Open Forum. It was a bit of a misnomer because there were some guys in there who were fairly successful businessmen, but all of them were either working class or working class in origin and they were all a bit pedantic, and they loved arguing, particularly about philosophy. I would sit and listen, and someone would talk about Nietzsche. I would think 'Nietzsche? Get his name down!' and down I would go to the Govan Library to swot up about Nietzsche!

I came through that period between fourteen and sixteen when my education, for what it is, took off because I was stimulated and generated by that then extant, tremendously important, Scottish tradition of valuing the pursuit of knowledge for itself which was very prevalent in the area where I grew up. Maybe I was of the

---

me that because people live in small flats there is no longer room for books in thirty volumes. Encyclopaedias have suffered greatly; they have been packed in.
  Jorge Luis Borges, quoted in *The Writer's Chapbook* (1989)

generation at the tail end of that tradition.

I read and read, and if I got a good book, I could be up to three or four in the morning because I couldn't lay it down! It was a tremendous feeling, like a voyage of discovery every time you went to the library. And I pursued everything. Someone mentioned Marx, and I was away down to the library to see what Karl had to say. Now I hear people on television, trade unionists, saying, 'I am a Marxist'. I know them personally. I know one guy who said, 'I am a Marxist', and I tell you he hasn't read Heidi never mind Marx! You can be a communist without having read Marx but I don't see how you can call yourself a Marxist without having read Marx! It is like calling yourself a nuclear physicist without ever having examined or studied nuclear physics. I think people are getting away with murder, particularly in politics, by making claims to perceptions and knowledge which they cannot possibly possess, because they haven't done even the elementary homework to acquire the information. That alone would give them the authority to claim to be what they say they are.

All I am saying is that my knowledge was obtained outside the formal educational structures. It came from life, I suppose, the old cliché about the university of life or life being my university. The library was there for me, and to this day I believe that it is a fundamental element when people talk about establishing a society within which there is an increasing quality of life representing something beyond the rat race. That is my view of the importance of libraries, and why I think that a public relations job has got to be done for them.

First of all, in Scotland we should rekindle a respect for that tradition of which I have spoken. Too many youngsters, and students in particular, are encouraged to read only within an academic syllabus to get themselves academic qualifications. I have met too many well-educated people now ever to make the mistake of confusing a good education with understanding or intelligence. It is possible to have a highly educated, highly intelligent, highly perceptive person. It is equally possible, and I know it from my own experience, to have a highly educated, not so highly intelligent, and by no means highly perceptive person, and you can get an ill-educated, not so highly intelligent and by no means highly perceptive person. In other words, the equation of educational excellence with intelligence is wrong. I have met professors who, outside their own discipline, could hardly tie two bits of string together. Now, I am not saying that they are all like

---

Edmund [Blunden] had began to read voraciously and the [Christ's Hospital] school library became the centre of his enthusiasm. It was part library, part museum, with fossils and Leigh Hunt's flowered waistcoat sharing the company of the books. The headmaster's secretary, 'Ratty' Rathbone,

that. By no means. There are a few of them that are almost as intelligent as some boiler-maker shop stewards I used to know! The point is that we have got to regenerate and rekindle the interest in that tradition and maybe even take a pride in it.

The second reason is because of one of C.P. Snow's arguments about the two cultures. The most alarming thing in the post-war educational establishments of this country has been the divergence of the sciences and the humanities. It seems to me that the anthropologists have the only meaningful definition of culture. They use it to describe the totality of a human civilisation. They talk about a culture meaning everything, meaning the economics, the law, the jurisprudence, the socio-economic character and features of that society. They aren't talking about something for the Arts Council, something esoteric. They mean the totality, and I do not believe that anyone, in the latter part of the twentieth century, can genuinely be equipped in the humanities unless they have some knowledge of the technology. How can you understand the sociology of modern society without having some appreciation of the technology? Similarly with the science students. I have experienced some appalling examples of crass philistinism in faculties of science, and I am fearful of people with scientific qualifications who have no appreciation of the humanities. We should be insisting on the humanities as a basic for science disciplines, and a knowledge of science as an indispensable factor in the humanities. It seems to me to be an unanswerable case.

Because what is happening? From a working-class Labour movement point of view, I believe we have been criminally neglectful in failing to draw attention to a very vital area of deprivation – cultural deprivation. You know, at the end of the day, that cultural deprivation can be more pernicious in stunting development of the human personality than lack of proper nourishment from food. Many working men and women are scared with a lack of self-confidence that stems, in my opinion, from a cultural deprivation. That seems to me to be a tragedy which we must overcome, and the library system is a vital cog in that process.

Let me tell you about another form of deprivation which I have noticed only over the last ten or fifteen years. I am talking here about people I know – good people. You go into their houses, and clearly they have done well for themselves. Their houses look like a shop window in Buchanan Street – the big furniture is all there, with the Tretchikoff, the clock on the wall. There is not a book in

reluctantly opened the library for half an hour a day. This meagre ration was not enough for Edmund, eager to explore beyond the copies of the *Captain* and *Chums* (popular periodicals for boys) or the editions of G.A. Henty and Conan Doyle, to the enticing volumes beyond. One afternoon he

sight. Instead of books, they have expensive, glossy magazines costing about two-and-a-half quid, usually presenting a kind of predigested pap so that you can take a short cut to some area of knowledge. The kids are brought up in a house without books. There is a cultural deprivation becoming more and more evident among an emerging middle class whose education has focused almost exclusively on being equipped to make a few bob, and not for an appreciation of the qualities of life, which cannot be enjoyed without a cultural dimension to your upbringing, to your attitude, to your outlook and to your concepts.

Therefore, to me, a library system is not a luxury that should be subject to government economies. There are certain services which are fundamental and crucial to the development of proper social relations and the development of people, and I really do put libraries in that context. I think that libraries are not promoted as they should be. I think an emphasis on books, and a re-orientation to an educational system which tries to engender an interest in books and literature as one of the colossal delights of human life is essential. That, related to the availability of books through the library, is a very important cog in human society in the latter part of this century. If we are not to have a mass, permanent pool of unemployed, we can only find means of averting it by thinking of principles and concepts of work-sharing. That will mean, for many people, leisure time on a scale never previously conceived. If you could negotiate a thousand pounds a week take-home pay and a fifteen-hour working week for some men in our society, you would be virtually signing their death certificate. It isn't their fault. They have been given the most minimal education for work and no education at all for the enjoyment of life and for the creative use of leisure time. If you are serious about maximising the social benefits of modern technology, then it has got to be associated not only with education but the re-education of people for the creative use of leisure time. That is an impossible concept unless it relates, very substantially, to opening people's minds through the delights of reading.

I also believe that the library system in the new technology age has other important tasks to perform. Why should people be going to shops for videos? Why shouldn't there be an expanded library system in this area? Public services have to be accepted as much more desirable than privatised services. I do not see people queuing up to privatise the sewage system, although if they thought they could make a few bob from it they might do that as well! The

was struck by the possibility of breaking into the library alone. The windows were only a little above the grass outside and, when he tried one, it yielded. Unfortunately he was inside for only a few moments before he was detected by the House bobby and handed over to his housemaster.

important thing here is that public services have got to be excluded from market forces, because once market forces are applied I think any element of public service disappears. Of course, you then get the search for the lowest common denominator, the opposite of excellence.

As you can gather, because of the Election I have come totally unprepared to speak to you today. I will not pretend that my remarks are in any way some substantive, coherent contribution to your deliberations this week, but then I did not create the circumstances of the last couple of weeks in which, for obvious reasons, both professionally and otherwise, I have been very much involved. You have my thoughts. They have come from the top of my head but they are, by and large, based on and stem from my own experiences. If you are fighting for the library service, then I want to tell you that in me you not only have an ally but a zealot, because I believe that libraries are fundamental to the kind of society that I want to live in and in which I want my children to grow up. I think your service is, indeed, absolutely essential.

From an address to the Scottish Library Association Conference, 1983,
As I Please (Mainstream, 1984)

The civilised Mr Goodwin did not mete out the expected thrashing, but merely enquired whether Edmund had a wheelbarrow waiting outside the window.
Barry Webb, *Edmund Blunden: A Biography* (1990)

SAUL BELLOW

Him with His Foot in His Mouth

Dear Miss Rose: I almost began 'My Dear Child', because in a sense what I did to you thirty-five years ago makes us the children of each other. I have from time to time remembered that I long ago made a bad joke at your expense and have felt uneasy about it, but it was spelled out to me recently that what I said to you was so wicked, so lousy, gross, insulting, unfeeling, and savage that you could never in a thousand years get over it. I wounded you for life, so I am given to understand, and I am the more greatly to blame because this attack was so gratuitous. We had met in passing only, we scarcely knew each other. Now, the person who charges me with this cruelty is not without prejudice towards me, he is out to get me, obviously. Nevertheless, I have been in a tizzy since reading his accusations. I wasn't exactly in great shape when his letter arrived. Like many elderly men, I have to swallow all sorts of pills. I take Inderal and quinidine for hypertension and cardiac disorders, and I am also, for a variety of psychological reasons, deeply distressed and for the moment without ego defences.

It may give more substance to my motive in writing to you now if I tell you that for some months I have been visiting an old woman who reads Swedenborg and other occult authors. She tells me (and a man in his sixties can't easily close his mind to such suggestions) that there is a life to come – wait and see – and that in the life to come we will feel the pains that we inflicted on others. We will suffer all that we made them suffer, for after death all experience is reversed. We enter into the souls of those whom we knew in life. They enter also into us and feel and judge us from within. On the outside chance that this old Canadian woman has it right, I must try to take up this matter with you. It's not as though I had tried to murder you, but my offence is palpable all the same.

I will say it all and then revise, send Miss Rose only the suitable parts.

. . . In this life between birth and death, while it is still possible to make amends . . .

I wonder whether you remember me at all, other than as the

The only significant contribution I made during my time on the committee, suitably enough for a lavatory humorist, was to plead for the restoration of the upstairs Gents. That, like the library, is full of atmosphere, beyond a grained and varnished door halfway up the red-carpeted stairs from the

person who wounded you – a tall man and, in those days, dark on the whole, with a moustache (not worn thick), physically a singular individual, a touch of the camel about him, something amusing in his composition. If you can recall the Shawmut of those days, you should see him now. *Edad con Sus Disgracias* is the title Goya gave to the etching of an old man who struggles to rise from the chamber pot, his pants dropped to his ankles. 'Together with most weak hams,' as Hamlet wickedly says to Polonius, being merciless about old men. To the disorders aforementioned I must add teeth with cracked roots, periodontia requiring antibiotics that gave me the runs and resulted in a haemorrhoid the size of a walnut, plus creeping arthritis of the hands. Winter is gloomy and wet in British Columbia, and when I awoke one morning in this land of exile from which I face extradition, I discovered that something had gone wrong with the middle finger of the right hand. The hinge had stopped working and the finger was curled like a snail – a painful new affliction. Quite a joke on me. And the extradition is real. I have been served with papers.

So at the very least I can try to reduce the torments of the afterlife by one.

It may appear that I come grovelling with hard-luck stories after thirty-five years, but as you will see, such is not the case.

I traced you through Miss Da Sousa at Ribier College, where we were all colleagues in the late forties. She had remained there, in Massachusetts, where so much of the nineteenth century still stands, and she wrote to me when my embarrassing and foolish troubles were printed in the papers. She is a kindly, intelligent woman who *like yourself, should I say that*? never married. Answering with gratitude, I asked what had become of you and was told that you were a retired librarian living in Orlando, Florida.

I never thought that I would envy people who had retired, but that was when retirement was still an option. For me it's not in the cards now. The death of my brother leaves me in a deep legal–financial hole. I won't molest you with the facts of the case, garbled in the newspaper. Enough to say that his felonies and my own faults or vices have wiped me out. On bad legal advice I took refuge in Canada, and the courts will be rough because I tried to escape. I may not be sent to prison, but I will have to work for the rest of my natural life, will die in harness, and damn queer harness, hauling my load to a peculiar peak. One of my father's favourite parables was about a feeble horse flogged cruelly by its driver. A

Reading Room to English Literature. It is all cracked white tiles and glazed brick, with an old glass tumbler in a metal ring above the ancient washbasin, a worn piece of Imperial Leather soap, and an even more ancient hairbrush that

bystander tries to intercede: 'The load is too heavy, the hill is steep, it's useless to beat your old horse on the face, why do you do it?' 'To be a horse was *his* idea,' the driver says.

I have a lifelong weakness for this sort of Jewish humour, which may be alien to you not only because you are Scotch-Irish (so Miss Da Sousa says) but also because you as a (pre-computer) librarian were in another sphere-zone of quiet, within the circumference of the Dewey decimal system. It is possible that you may have disliked the life of a nun or shepherdess which the word 'librarian' once suggested. You may resent it for keeping you out of the modern 'action' – erotic, narcotic, dramatic, dangerous, salty. Maybe you have loathed circulating other people's lawless raptures, handling wicked books (for the most part fake, take it from me, Miss Rose). Allow me to presume that you are old-fashioned enough not to be furious at having led a useful life. If you aren't an old-fashioned person I haven't hurt you so badly after all. No modern woman would brood for forty years over a stupid wisecrack. She would say, 'Get lost!'

Who is it that accuses me of having wounded you? Eddie Walish, that's who. He has become the main planner of college humanities surveys in the State of Missouri, I am given to understand. At such work he is wonderful, a man of genius. But although he now lives in Missouri, he seems to think of nothing but Massachusetts in the old days. He can't forget the evil I did. He was there when I did it (whatever *it* really was), and he writes, 'I have to remind you of how you hurt Carla Rose. So characteristic of you, when she was trying to be agreeable, not just to miss her gentle intentions but give her a shattering kick in the face. I happen to know that you traumatised her for life.' (Notice how the liberal American vocabulary is used as a torture device: By 'characteristic' he means: 'You are not a *good person*, Shawmut.') Now, were you really traumatised, Miss Rose? How does Walish 'happen to know'? Did you tell him? Or is it, as I conjecture, nothing but gossip? I wonder if you remember the occasion at all. It would be a mercy if you didn't. And I don't want to thrust unwanted recollections on you, but if I did indeed disfigure you so cruelly, is there any way to avoid remembering?

So let's get back again to Ribier College. Walish and I were great friends then, young instructors, he in literature, I in fine arts – my speciality music history. As if this were news to you; my book on Pergolesi is in all libraries. Impossible that you shouldn't have

might, who knows, have disciplined the thinning hair of Eliot himself. There is a high urinal of suitable antique design, and three spacious cubicles in panelled wood, any one of which could have accommodated Lytton Strachey, H.G. Wells,

come across it. Besides, I've done those musicology programmes on public television, which were quite popular.

But we are back in the forties. The term began just after Labour Day. My first teaching position. After seven or eight weeks I was still wildly excited. Let me start with the beautiful New England setting. Fresh from Chicago and from Bloomington, Indiana, where I took my degree, I had never seen birches, roadside ferns, deep pinewoods, little white steeples. What could I be but out of place? It made me scream with laughter to be called 'Dr Shawmut'. I felt absurd here, a camel on the village green. I am a high-waisted and long-legged man, who is susceptible to paradoxical, ludicrous images of himself. I hadn't yet gotten the real picture of Ribier, either. It wasn't true New England, it was a bohemian college for rich kids from New York who were too nervous for the better schools, unadjusted.

Now then: Eddie Walish and I walking together past the college library. Sweet autumnal warmth against a background of chill from the surrounding woods – it's all there for me. The library is a Greek Revival building and the light in the porch is mossy and sunny – bright-green moss, leafy sunlight, lichen on the columns. I am turned on, manic, flying. My relations with Walish at this stage are easy to describe: very cheerful, not a kink in sight, not a touch of darkness. I am keen to learn from him, because I have never seen a progressive college, never lived in the East, never come in contact with the Eastern Establishment, of which I have heard so much. What is it all about? A girl to whom I was assigned as adviser has asked for another one because I haven't been psychoanalysed and can't even begin to relate to her. And this very morning I have spent two hours in a committee meeting to determine whether a course in history should be obligatory for fine-arts majors. Tony Lemnitzer, professor of painting, said, 'Let the kids read about the kings and the queens – what can it hoit them?' Brooklyn Tony, who had run away from home to be a circus roustabout, became a poster artist and eventually an Abstract Expressionist. 'Don't ever feel sorry for Tony,' Walish advises me. 'The woman he married is a millionairess. She's built him a studio fit for Michelangelo. He's so embarrassed to paint, he only whittles there. He carved out two wooden balls inside a birdcage.' Walish himself, Early Hip with a Harvard background, suspected at first that my ignorance was a put-on. A limping short man, Walish looked at me – looked upward – with real shrewdness and traces of disbelief about the mouth. From Chicago, a Ph.D.

---

out of Bloomington, Indiana, can I be as backward as I seem? But I am good company, and by and by he tells me (is it a secret?) that although he comes from Gloucester, Mass., he's not a real Yankee. His father, a second-generation American, is a machinist, retired, uneducated. One of the old man's letters reads, 'Your poor mother – the doctor says she has a groweth on her virginia which he will have to operate. When she goes to surgery I expect you and your sister to be here to stand by me.'

There were two limping men in the community, and their names were similar. The other limper, Edmund Welch, justice of the peace, walked with a cane. Our Ed, who suffered from curvature of the spine, would not carry a stick, much less wear a built-up shoe. He behaved with sporting nonchalance and defied the orthopaedists when they warned that his spinal column would collapse like a stack of dominoes. His style was to be free and limber. You had to take him as he came, no concessions offered. I admired him for that.

Now, Miss Rose, you have come out of the library for a breath of air and are leaning, arms crossed, and resting your head against a Greek column. To give himself more height, Walish wears his hair thick. You couldn't cram a hat over it. But I have on a baseball cap. Then, Miss Rose, you say, smiling at me, 'Oh, Dr Shawmut, in that cap you look like an archaeologist.' Before I can stop myself, I answer, 'And you look like something I just dug up.'

Awful!

The pair of us, Walish and I, hurried on. Eddie, whose hips were out of line, made an effort to walk more quickly, and when we were beyond our little library temple I saw that he was grinning at me, his warm face looking up into my face with joy, with accusing admiration. He had witnessed something extraordinary. What this something might be, whether it came under the heading of fun or psychopathology or wickedness, nobody could yet judge, but he was glad. Although he lost no time in clearing himself of guilt, it was exactly his kind of wisecrack. He loved to do the Groucho Marx bit, or given an S. J. Perelman turn to his sentences. As for me, I had become dead sober, as I generally do after making one of my cracks. I am as astonished by them as anybody else. They may be hysterical symptoms, in the clinical sense. I used to consider myself absolutely normal, but I became aware long ago that in certain moods my laughing bordered on hysteria. I myself could hear the abnormal note. Walish knew very well that I was subject to such seizures, and when he sensed that one of my fits was

There is [in the London Library], as in most libraries, a heavily charged erotic atmosphere in the Reading-Room: a girl undoing a button of her cardigan lifts her head from every armchair. It is hard not to imagine urgent ecstasies in

approaching, he egged me on. And after he had had his fun he would say, with a grin like Pan Satyrus, 'What a bastard you are, Shawmut. The sadistic stabs you can give!' He took care, you see, not to be incriminated as an accessory.

And my joke wasn't even witty, just vile, no excuse for it, certainly not 'inspiration'. Why should inspiration be so idiotic? It was simply idiotic and wicked. Walish used to tell me, 'You're a Surrealist in spite of yourself.' His interpretation was that I had raised myself by painful efforts from immigrant origins to middle-class level but that I avenged myself for the torments and falsifications of my healthy instincts, deformities imposed on me by this adaptation to respectability, the strain of social climbing. Clever, intricate analysis of this sort was popular in Greenwich Village at that time, and Walish had picked up the habit. His letter of last month was filled with insights of this kind. People seldom give up the mental capital accumulated in their 'best' years. At sixty-odd, Eddie is still a youthful Villager and associated with young people, mainly. I have accepted old age.

It isn't easy to write with arthritic fingers. My lawyer, whose fatal advice I followed (he is the youngest brother of my wife, who passed away last year), urged me to go to British Columbia, where, because of the Japanese current, flowers grow in midwinter, and the air is purer. There are indeed primroses out in the snow, but my hands are crippled and I am afraid that I may have to take gold injections if they don't improve. Nevertheless, I build up the fire and sit concentrating in the rocker because I need to make it worth your while to consider these facts with me. If I am to believe Walish, you have trembled from that day onward like a flame on a middle-class altar of undeserved humiliation. One of the insulted and injured.

From my side I have to admit that it was hard for me to acquire decent manners, not because I was naturally rude but because I felt the strain of my position. I came to believe for a time that I couldn't get on in life until I, too, had a false self like everybody else and so I made special efforts to be considerate, deferential, civil. And of course I overdid things and wiped myself twice where people of better breeding only wiped once. But no such programme of betterment could hold me for long. I set it up, and then I tore it down, and burned it in a raging bonfire.

Walish, I must tell you, gives me the business in his letter. Why was it, he asks, that when people groped in conversations I supplied the missing phrases and finished their sentences with

_____

the more secluded areas of Biography, but the only story I was told was of two American research students meeting in the library who have since married. Joan Bailey [a librarian] was convinced people used to jam the lift between floors in

greedy pedantry? Walish alleges that I was showing off, shuffling out of my vulgar origins, making up the genteel and qualifying as the kind of Jew acceptable (just barely) to the Christian society of T. S. Eliot's dreams. Walish pictures me as an upwardly mobile pariah seeking bondage as one would seek salvation. In reaction, he says, I had rebellious fits and became wildly insulting. Walish notes all this well, but he did not come out with it during the years when we were close. He saved it all up. At Ribier College we liked each other. We were friends, somehow. But in the end, somehow, he intended to be a mortal enemy. All the while that he was making the gestures of a close and precious friend he was fattening my soul in a coop till it was ready for killing. My success in musicology may have been too much for him.

Eddie told his wife – he told everyone – what I had said to you. It certainly got around the campus. People laughed, but I was depressed. Remorse: you were a pale woman with thin arms, absorbing the colours of moss, lichen, and limestone into your skin. The heavy library doors were open, and within there were green reading lamps and polished heavy tables, and books massed up to the gallery and above. A few of these books were exalted, some were usefully informative, the majority of them would only congest the mind. My Swedenborgian old lady says that angels do not read books. Why should they? Nor, I imagine, can librarians be great readers. They have too many books, most of them burdensome. The crowded shelves give off an inviting, consoling, seductive odour that is also tinctured faintly with something pernicious, with poison and doom. Human beings can lose their lives in libraries. They ought to be warned. And you, an underpriestess of this temple stepping out to look at the sky, and Mr Lubeck, your chief, a gentle refugee always stumbling over his big senile dog and apologising to the animal, 'Ach, excuse me!' (heavy on the sibilant).

Personal note: Miss Rose never was pretty, not even what the French call une belle laide, or ugly beauty, a woman whose command of sexual forces makes ugliness itself contribute to her erotic power. A belle Laide (it would be a French idea!) has to be a rolling-mill of lusts. Such force was lacking. No organic basis for it. Fifty years earlier Miss Rose would have been taking Lydia Pinkham's Vegetable Compound. Nevertheless, even if she looked green, a man might have loved her – loved her for her timid warmth, or for the courage she had had to muster to compliment me on my cap. Thirty-five years ago I might have bluffed out this embarrassment with compliments, saying, 'Only think, Miss Rose, how

---

order to make love, though Christopher Logue thought the lift was so slow you wouldn't have needed to jam it.

John Wells, ibid

many objects of rare beauty have been dug up by archaeologists – the
Venus de Milo, Assyrian winged bulls with the faces of great kings. And
Michelangelo even buried one of his statues to get the antique look and then
exhumed it.' But it's too late for rhetorical gallantries. I'd be ashamed.
Unpretty, unmarried, the nasty little community laughing at my crack,
Miss Rose, poor thing, must have been in despair.

Eddie Walish, as I told you, would not act the cripple despite his
spiral back. Even though he slouched and walked with an
outslapping left foot, he carried himself with style. He wore good
English tweeds and Lloyd & Haig brogans. He himself would say
that there were enough masochistic women around to encourage
any fellow to preen and cut a figure. Handicapped men did very
well with girls of a certain type. You, Miss Rose, would have done
better to save your compliment for him. But his wife was then
expecting; I was the bachelor.

Almost daily during the first sunny days of the term we went
out walking. I found him mysterious then.

I would think: Who is he, anyway, this (suddenly) close friend
of mine? What is this strange figure, the big head low beside me,
whose hair grows high and thick? With a different slant, like
whipcord stripes, it grows thickly also from his ears. One of the
campus ladies has suggested that I urge him to shave his ears, but
why should I? She wouldn't like him better with shaven ears, she
only dreams that she might. He has a sort of woodwind laugh,
closer to oboe than to clarinet, and he releases his laugh from the
wide end of his nose as well as from his carved pumpkin mouth.
He grins like Alfred E. Neuman from the cover of *Mad* magazine,
the successor to Peck's Bad Boy. His eyes, however, are warm and
induce me to move closer and closer, but they withhold what I
want most, I long for his affection, I distrust him and love him, I
woo him with wisecracks. For he is a wise guy in an up-to-date
post-modern existentialist sly manner. He also seems kindly. He
seems all sorts of things. Fond of Brecht and Weill, he sings
'Mackie Messer' and trounces out the tune on the upright piano.
This, however, is merely period stuff – German cabaret jazz of the
twenties, Berlin's answer to trench warfare and exploded human-
ism. Catch Eddie allowing himself to be dated like that! Up-to-
the-minute Eddie has always been in the avant-garde. An early fan
of the Beat poets, he was the first to quote me Allen Ginsberg's
wonderful line 'America I'm putting my queer shoulder to the
wheel'.

Eddie made me an appreciative reader of Ginsberg, from whom

When I was sixteen I found a book that did truly change my
life – *The Gambler* by Dostoyevsky. Not his best book, but
good enough for me at the time. I didn't know that
Dostoyevsky was a genius, I knew nothing about Russia,
but I found something in *The Gambler* that comforted and

I learned much about wit. You may find it odd, Miss Rose (I myself do), that I should have kept up with Ginsberg from way back. Allow me, however, to offer a specimen statement from one of his recent books, which is memorable and also charming. Ginsberg writes that Walt Whitman slept with Edward Carpenter, the author of *Love's Coming-of-Age*; Carpenter afterward became the lover of the grandson of one of our obscurer Presidents, Chester A. Arthur; Gavin Arthur when he was very old was the lover of a San Francisco homosexual who, when he embraced Ginsberg, completed the entire cycle and brought the Sage of Camden in touch with his only true successor and heir. It's all a little like Dr Pangloss's account of how he came to be infected with syphilis.

Please forgive me, Miss Rose. It seems to me that we will need the broadest possible human background for this inquiry, which may so much affect your emotions and mine. You ought to know to whom you were speaking on that day when you got up your nerve, smiling and trembling, to pay me a compliment – to give me, us, your blessing. Which I repaid with a bad witticism drawn, characteristically, from the depths of my nature, that hoard of strange formulations. I had almost forgotten the event when Walish's letter reached me in Canada. That letter – a strange *megillah* of which I myself was the Haman. He must have brooded with *ressentiment* for decades on my character, drawing the profile of my inmost soul over and over and over. He compiled a list of all my faults, my sins, and the particulars are so fine, the inventory so extensive, the summary so condensed, that he must have been collecting, filing, formulating, and polishing furiously throughout the warmest, goldenest days of our friendship. To receive such a document – I ask you to imagine, Miss Rose, how it affected me at a time when I was coping with grief and gross wrongs, mourning my wife (and funnily enough, also my swindling brother), and experiencing *Edad con Sus Disgracias*, discovering that I could no longer straighten my middle finger, reckoning up the labour and sorrow of threescore and ten (rapidly approaching). At our age, my dear, nobody can be indignant or surprised when evil is manifested, but I ask myself again and again, why should Eddie Walish work up my faults for thirty–some years to cast them into my teeth? This is what excites my keenest interest, so keen it makes me scream inwardly. The whole comedy of it comes over me in the night with the intensity of labour pains. I lie in the back

---

satisfied me. I was irritated by the Russian names and baffled by the references to historical events, but I liked the notion of duality; that good and evil exist in every human being. I looked on the market stalls for more Dostoyevskys but found nothing. I couldn't borrow more Dostoyevskys

bedroom of this little box of a Canadian house, which is scarcely insulated, and bear down hard so as not to holler. All the neighbours need is to hear such noises at three in the morning. And there isn't a soul in British Columbia I can discuss this with. My only acquaintance is Mrs Gracewell, the old woman (she is very old) who studies occult literature, and I can't bother her with so different a branch of experience. Our conversations are entirely theoretical . . . One helpful remark she did make, and this was: 'The lower self is what the Psalmist referred to when he wrote, "I am a worm and no man." The higher self, few people are equipped to observe. This is the reason they speak so unkindly of one another.'

More than once Walish's document (denunciation) took off from Ginsberg's poetry and prose, and so I finally sent an order to City Lights in San Francisco and have spent many evenings studying books of his I had missed – he publishes so many tiny ones. Ginsberg takes a stand for true tenderness and full candour. Real candour means excremental and genital literalness. What Ginsberg opts for is the warmth of a freely copulating, manly, womanly, comradely, 'open road' humanity which doesn't neglect to pray and to meditate. He speaks with horror of our 'plastic culture', which he connects somewhat obsessively with the CIA. And in addition to the CIA there are other spydoms, linked with Exxon, Mobil, Standard Oil of California, sinister Occidental Petroleum with its Kremlin connections (that *is* a weird one to contemplate, undeniably). Supercapitalism and its carcinogenic petrochemical technology are linked through James Jesus Angleton, a high official of the Intelligence Community, to T. S. Eliot, one of his pals. Angleton, in his youth the editor of a literary magazine, had the declared aim of revitalising the culture of the West against the 'so-to-speak Stalinists'. The ghost of T. S. Eliot, interviewed by Ginsberg on the fantail of a ship somewhere in death's waters, admits to having done little spy jobs for Angleton. Against these, the Children of Darkness, Ginsberg ranges the gurus, the bearded meditators, the poets loyal to Blake and Whitman, the 'holy creeps', the lyrical, unsophisticated homosexuals whose little groups the secret police track on their computers, against whom they plant provocateurs, and whom they try to corrupt with heroin. This psychopathic vision, so touching because there is, realistically, so much to be afraid of, and also because of the hunger for goodness reflected in it, a screwball defence of beauty, I value more than my accuser, Walish, does. I

---

from the library because I owed a fortune in fines (I could never bear to take the books back). I realised that I would have to *buy* a book.

Sue Townsend, *The Pleasure of Reading*, edited by Antonia Fraser (1992)

truly understand. To Ginsberg's sexual Fourth of July fireworks I say, Tee-hee. But then I muse sympathetically over his obsessions, combing my moustache downward with my fingernails, my eyes feeling keen as I try to figure him. I am a more disinterested Ginsberg admirer than Eddie is. Eddie, so to speak, comes to the table with a croupier's rake. He works for the house. He skims from poetry.

One of Walish's long-standing problems was that he looked distinctly Jewy. Certain people were distrustful and took against him with gratuitous hostility, suspecting that he was trying to pass for a full American. They'd sometimes say, as if discovering how much force it gave them to be brazen (force is always welcome), 'What was your name before it was Walish?' – a question of the type that Jews often hear. His parents were descended from north of Ireland Protestants, actually, and his mother's family name was Ballard. He signs himself Edward Ballard Walish. He pretended not to mind this. A taste of persecution made him friendly to Jews, or so he said. Uncritically delighted with his friendship, I chose to believe him.

It turns out that after many years of concealed teetering, Walish concluded that I was a fool. It was when the public began to take me seriously that he lost patience with me and his affection turned to rancour. My TV programmes on music history were what did it. I can envision this – Walish watching the screen in a soiled woollen dressing-gown, cupping one elbow in his hand and sucking a cigarette, assailing me while I go on about Haydn's last days, or Mozart and Salieri, developing themes on the harpsichord: 'Superstar! What a horseshit idiot!' 'Christ! How phony can you get!' 'Huckleberry Fink!'

My own name, Shawmut, has obviously been tampered with. The tampering was done long years before my father landed in America by his brother Pinye, the one who wore a pince-nez and was a music copyist for Sholom Secunda. The family must have been called Shamus or, even more degrading, Untershamus. The *untershamus*, lowest of the low in the Old World synagogue, was a quasi-unemployable incompetent and hanger-on, tangle-bearded and cursed with comic ailments like a large hernia or scrofula, a pauper's pauper. 'Orm,' as my father would say, '*auf steiffleivent.*' *Steiffleivent* was the stiff linen-and-horsehair fabric that tailors would put into the lining of a jacket to give it shape. There was nothing cheaper. 'He was so poor that he dressed in dummy cloth.' Cheaper than a shroud. But in America Shawmut turns out to be

---

I discovered a new ruse. I was given a job at the public library which my mother approved of because (a) she reckoned that I couldn't read and work at the same time, and (b) it meant she could have unlimited number of large print mysteries. I think too that she hoped that simply being

the name of a chain of banks in Massachusetts. How do you like
them apples! You may have heard charming, appealing, sentimental things about Yiddish, but Yiddish is a *hard* language, Miss
Rose. Yiddish is severe and bears down without mercy. Yes, it is
often delicate, lovely, but it can be explosive as well. 'A face like a
slop jar,' 'a face like a bucket of swill.' (Pig connotations give
special force to Yiddish epithets.) If there is a demiurge who
inspires me to speak wildly, he may have been attracted to me by
this violent unsparing language.

As I tell you this, I believe that you are willingly following, and I
feel the greatest affection for you. I am very much alone in
Vancouver, but that is my own fault, too. When I arrived, I was
invited to a party by local musicians, and I failed to please. They
gave me their Canadian test for US visitors: was I a Reaganite? I
couldn't be that, but the key question was whether El Salvador
might not be another Vietnam, and I lost half of the company at
once by my reply: 'Nothing of the kind. The North Vietnamese
are seasoned soldiers with a military tradition of many centuries –
really tough people. Salvadorans are Indian peasants.' Why
couldn't I have kept my mouth shut? What do I care about
Vietnam? Two or three sympathetic guests remained, and these I
drove away as follows: a professor from UBC observed that he
agreed with Alexander Pope about the ultimate unreality of evil.
Seen from the highest point of metaphysics. To a rational mind,
nothing bad ever really happens. He was talking high-minded
balls. Twaddle! I thought. I said, 'Oh? Do you mean that every gas
chamber has a silver lining?'
    That did it, and now I take my daily walks alone.
    It is very beautiful here, with snow mountains and still
harbours. Port facilities are said to be limited and freighters have to
wait (at a daily fee of $10,000). To see them at anchor is pleasant.
They suggest the 'Invitation au Voyage', and also 'Anywhere,
anywhere, Out of the world!' But what a clean and civilised city
this is, with its clear northern waters and, beyond, the sense of an
unlimited wilderness beginning where the forests bristle, spread-
ing northward for millions of square miles and ending at ice
whorls around the Pole.
    Provincial academics took offence at my quirks. Too bad.
    But lest it appear that I am always dishing it out, let me tell you,
Miss Rose, that I have often been on the receiving end, put down
by virtuosi, by artists greater than myself, in this line. The late

around books would cure me of my obsession for them,
rather in the way that retired astronauts are advised to lie
and look at the stars. In practice, I went to the library even
when I wasn't working, and sat uninterrupted in the reading
room under a stained-glass window bearing the legend,

Kippenberg, prince of musicologists, when we were at a conference in the Villa Serbelloni on Lake Como, invited me to his
rooms one night to give him a preview of my paper. Well, he
didn't actually invite me. I was eager. The suggestion was mine
and he didn't have the heart to refuse. He was a huge man dressed
in velvet dinner clothes, a copious costume, kelly green in colour,
upon which his large, pale, clever head seemed to have been
deposited by a boom. Although he walked with two sticks, a sort
of *diable boiteux*, there was no one faster with a word. He had
published *the* great work on Rossini, and Rossini himself had made
immortal wisecracks (like the one about Wagner: '*Il a de beaux
moments mais de mauvais quarts d'heure*'). You have to imagine also
the suite that Kippenberg occupied at the villa, eighteenth-century
rooms, taffeta sofas, brocades, cool statuary, hot silk lamps. The
servants had already shuttered the windows for the night, so the
parlour was very close. Anyway, I was reading to the worldly-
wise and learned Kippenberg, all swelled out in green, his long
mouth agreeably composed. Funny eyes the man had, too, set at
the sides of his head as if for bilateral vision, and eyebrows like
caterpillars from the Tree of Knowledge. As I was reading he
began to nod. I said, 'I'm afraid I'm putting you to sleep,
Professor.' 'No, no – on the contrary, you're keeping me awake,'
he said. That, and at my expense, was genius, and it was a
privilege to have provoked it. He had been sitting, massive, with
his two sticks, as if he were on a slope, skiing into profound sleep.
But even at the brink, when it was being extinguished, the unique
treasure of his consciousness could still dazzle. I would have gone
around the world for such a put-down.

Let me, however, return to Walish for a moment. The Walishes
lived in a small country house belonging to the college. It was
down in the woods, which at that season were dusty. You may
remember, in Florida, what New England woods are in a dry
autumn – pollen, woodsmoke, decayed and mealy leaves, spider
webs, perhaps the wing powder of dead moths. Arriving at the
Walishes' stone gateposts, if we found bottles left by the milkman
we'd grab them by the neck and yelling, hurl them into the bushes.
The milk was ordered for Peg Walish, who was pregnant but hated
the stuff and wouldn't drink it anyway. Peg was socially above her
husband. Anybody, in those days, could be; Walish had below him
only Negroes and Jews, and owing to his Jewy look, was not
secure even in this advantage. Bohemianism therefore gave him
strength. Mrs Walish enjoyed her husband's bohemian style, or

'Industry and Prudence Conquer'.
                    Jeanette Winterson, *The Pleasure of Reading*,
                              edited by Antonia Fraser (1992)

said she did. My Pergolesi and Haydn made me less objectionable
to her than I might otherwise have been. Besides, I was lively
company for her husband. Believe me, he needed lively company.
He was depressed; his wife was worried. When she looked at me I
saw the remedy-light in her eyes.

Like Alice after she had emptied the DRINK · ME bottle in
Wonderland, Peg was very tall; bony but delicate, she resembled a
silent-movie star named Colleen Moore, a round-eyed ingenue
with bangs. In her fourth month of pregnancy, Peg was still
working at Filene's, and Eddie, unwilling to get up in the morning
to drive her to the station, spent long days in bed under the faded
patchwork quilts. Pink, when it isn't fresh and lively, can be a
desperate colour. The pink of Walish's quilts sank my heart when I
came looking for him. The cottage was panelled in walnut-stained
boards, the rooms were sunless, the kitchen especially gloomy. I
found him upstairs sleeping, his jaw undershot and his Jewish lip
prominent. The impression he made was both brutal and innocent.
In sleep he was bereft of the confidence into which he put so much
effort. Not many of us are fully wakeful, but Walish took
particular pride in being alert. That he was nobody's fool was his
main premise. But in sleep he didn't look clever.

I got him up. He was embarrassed. He was not the complete
bohemian after all. His muzziness late in the day distressed him,
and he grumbled, putting his thin legs out of bed. We went to the
kitchen and began to drink.

Peg insisted that he see a psychiatrist in Providence. He kept this
from me awhile, finally admitting that he needed a tune-up, minor
internal adjustments. Becoming a father rattled him. His wife
eventually gave birth to male twins. The facts are trivial and I don't
feel that I'm betraying a trust. Besides, I owe him nothing. His
letter upset me badly. What a time he chose to send it! Thirty-five
years without a cross word. He allows me to count on his
affection. Then he lets me have it. When do you shaft a pal, when
do you hand him the poison cup? Not while he's still young
enough to recover. Walish waited till the very end – *my* end, of
course. *He* is still youthful, he writes me. Evidence of this is that he
takes a true interest in young lesbians out in Missouri, he alone
knows their inmost hearts and they allow him to make love to
them – Walish, the sole male exception. Like the explorer
McGovern, who went to Lhasa in disguise, the only Westerner to
penetrate the sacred precincts. They trust only youth, they trust
him, so it's certain that he can't be old.

Him with His Foot in His Mouth and Other Stories
(Secker and Warburg, 1974)

RETURNING THE FAVOUR

Authors express their thanks to librarians in the acknowledgment to their books. It is gratefully received. The public can be rude, uncomprehending, dumb as oxen. They use libraries like council tips and librarians like dishwashers. Readers leave the strangest things in books: bus tickets, cigarette stubs, one had the temerity to use a potato chip as a bookmark. Librarians mop up behind them like a mother cleaning the hamster cage for the kids; it's not a pleasant job but someone has got to do it.

This is what is called a profession. 'Why do you need to go to college to be a librarian?' people used to ask me before I went. I didn't have an answer. In the branch library where I first worked I spent more time tidying up than a chambermaid. This was all that the public saw of those who worked in libraries, so who could blame them for thinking that librarians were glorified skivvies. The senior librarian hid in his office. Who knows what he was doing all day? Paperwork, I suppose, and sorting out the holiday roster. Then there was the choosing of new stock, an infinitely time-consuming task if you felt up to reading every book that came out. When he did appear he strode around his policies looking for books that were shelved out of alphabetical order.

Even in such unpromising circumstances good librarians worked wonders, especially with children. Bad librarians inspected hands, said 'shush' if you whispered, and chased kids away from so-called unsuitable books; good librarians were forever pressing books into your hands, waiving fines and letting you take out books that were so risqué that you had to read them in bed with a torch. As John Updike recalls, to be allowed into the stacks by an enlightened librarian such as Miss Ruth, the *maître d'* of Shillington library, was to be given access to an unexplored country. It is the kind of privilege that turns a shy young man into an internationally renowned writer. It is a demonstration of society's acceptingness of him.

The best librarians understand 'acceptingness'. Philip Roth, Updike's contemporary, realises this, and showed his gratitude in his trenchant defence of Newark library when it was threatened with closure. Other writers, such as Dervla Murphy and Hugh MacDiarmid, grew up in the shadow of a library, the former being the daughter of a county librarian, the latter spending his formative years above a library in Langholm. Such proximity to books and libraries made them both lifelong users. Thereafter they were incurable addicts, the kind of eclectic readers any librarian would give his eye-teeth to have as members of his library.

DERVLA MURPHY

One Priceless Perk

Having been born with a 'weak chest' I was accustomed to enjoying a few weeks of invalidism each winter and I revelled in being free to read, almost without interruption, for fourteen hours a day seven days a week. Whatever the theologians might say about Heaven being a state of union with God, I knew it consisted of an infinite library; and eternity, about which my parents were wont to argue with amusing vehemence, was simply what enabled one to read uninterruptedly forever.

The only interruptions I welcomed during these withdrawals from the world were Dr White's visits. He treated me with the sort of rough affection one bestows on a large dog and gave me delicious syrup from a bottle excavated with difficulty from the depths of his greatcoat pocket and told heart-stopping stories about his soldiering days in India and South Africa. Sometimes he advised me to rest my eyes, but this advice went unheeded as I took no interest whatever in any of the standard children's games or pastimes. (A serious handicap nowadays, when I have a more versatile child of my own.)

I remember the perfection of my happiness – a perfection not often attained in this life, as I realised even then – when I woke on a dark winter's morning and switched on the light to see a tower of unread library books by my bed. From then I would look caressingly towards my own books on their shelves around the wall and reflect that now I had time to reread; I could never decide which was the greater pleasure, rereading old favourites or discovering new ones. For a moment I would lie still, ecstatically anticipating the day's bliss. And sometimes it would cross my mind that only Pappa could fully understand how I felt.

There is a difference between the interest taken in books by normal readers (people like my parents) and the lunatic concern of bibliomaniacs (people like Pappa and myself). Everything to do with books mattered to me and I fretted much more over their wartime deterioration – that squalid gravy-coloured paper! – than I

I joined the library thirsting after more *William* books. I read one a day and then two a day, then I ran out and fumbled along the library shelves pulling out books at random. Nothing was ever as good as William, but the die was cast, I

did over butter rationing or inedible bread. (Clothes rationing I of course considered a blessing in disguise.) After a quick glance at any open page I could by the age of nine have told you the publisher of most children's books – and often the printer and illustrator, too. One of my hobbies was rewriting blurbs which seemed inadequate and I collected publishers' lists as other children collect stamps. During June and July I often prayed for rain; on fine days I was supposed to be out in the fresh air, but on wet days I could go to the county library headquarters and help unpack the new books that came by the hundred, in tea-chests, at that season. The sight, smell and feel of these books so intoxicated me that I often refused to go home at lunch time. I had an agreement with my parents that when the children's books came I could always help unpack, regardless of climatic conditions. I would then – to my father's sensibly silent disgust – seize on the least worthy volumes (Biggles and so forth) and beg to be allowed to borrow them even before they had been initiated into the public circulation. But my father did not believe in Privilege so I had to bide my time – very sulkily. It must have exasperated my parents that for so long I preferred exciting stories to good writing. At every stage of childhood I completely rejected all the classical fairy stories, and Lewis Carroll, Captain Marryat, Louisa Alcott, Kipling, E. Nesbit and any volume that I suspected might be intended to improve my mind. But neither, to be fair to myself, would I read Enid Blyton when she began to pollute the literary atmosphere. I was uncompromisingly middlebrow; and so, with minor modifications, I have remained to this day.

As the librarian's daughter I did have one priceless perk. When public library books become too battered and disgusting for rebinding or recirculation they are 'Withdrawn From Circulation', stamped to that effect and despatched either to fever hospitals or to the pulpers. And among those glorious, revolting heaps of 'Withdrawn' books – their pages interlarded with evidence of the diet of the rural reader – I was free to wander and take my pick and carry the noisome volumes home by the armful to be mine forever. (Many of them are still mine; no one ever steals them.)

I went through one appalling crisis in relation to 'Withdrawn' books. At the age of eight or so I had a compulsive secret vice – crossing out the author's name on the title page of old books and substituting my own. This could be done without fear of detection in unfrequented corners of the library; but then, in bed one ghastly evening, I suddenly realised that some of the books I had been

---

was addicted to print.
Sue Townsend, *The Pleasure of Reading*,
edited by Antonia Fraser (1992)

abusing might go, not to the pulpers but to a fever hospital. If this happened both my iniquitous vandalism and my vain ambitions would be exposed to a shocked and derisive public. This hideous possibility so tormented me that I could not sleep. As my parents were listening to the late news I crept downstairs and confessed all to my mother – who remained astonishingly unperturbed. She assured me that the defacement of such books was forgivable and that no fever hospital patient was likely to report on my little weakness to the world's press – which would in any case be disinclined to take the matter up. I always enjoyed the irony with which she put things in perspective; curiously enough, it never made me feel foolish.

Wheels Within Wheels (John Murray, 1979)

A public library is the most democratic thing in the world. What can be found there has undone dictators and tyrants: demagogues can persecute writers and tell them what to write as much as they like, but they cannot vanish what has been written in the past, though they try often enough. In

JOHN UPDIKE

I Was a Teen-Age Library User

Reading – the Pennsylvania city, not the activity – seemed a considerable distance from Shillington in the 1940s; you boarded a trolley car in front of Ibach's Drug Store and for twenty minutes jerked and swayed down Lancaster Avenue through Kenhorst and Eighteenth Ward, up over the Bingaman Street Bridge, along Fourth Street. If you wanted to get off north of Penn on Fifth Street, you bucked one-way traffic for a block of Washington Street, with much honking of automobile horns and clanging of the trolley bell. If you were going to the public library, you could get off at Franklin and walk a block to where the stately building, one of sainted Andrew Carnegie's benefactions, was located along Fifth, with Schofer's sweet-smelling bakery on one side and the Elks on the other. The Elks had a bronze elk in their front yard. As a boy I was fascinated by the little sharp points that had been placed on the metal animal's back; the purpose was to prevent bad boys from sitting on the statue, but for a long time I thought they might be part of the elk's anatomy.

Inside the library, there was a whispering quiet and walls of books. The great central space now occupied by a big box of central shelves was empty, and to my young eyes the ceiling seemed infinitely far away, and the balconies cosmically mysterious. My mother was a keen reader and my early trips there were at her side. An attempt was made to enroll me in the children's library downstairs, but I found children's books depressing, with their webby illustrations of historical costumes and crumbling castles, and by the age of twelve, I think, I was allowed to have my own adult card, and to check out whatever books I wanted. Miss Ruth, who had been (I later discovered) a high-school classmate of Wallace Stevens, was the head librarian, and very kind. I used to check out stacks, and she never blinked.

Stacks of what? P.G. Wodehouse is the author that first comes to mind: the library owned close to all the master's titles, around fifty of them at that time, and they all struck me as hilarious and

---

my paranoid moments I wonder if the neglect, amounting to persecution, of libraries in this country now is because people who have access to good libraries, to history, ideas, information, cannot be told what to think. People who love literature have at least a part of their minds immune from

enchanting. They admitted me to a privileged green world of English men's clubs, London bachelor flats, country weekends, golf courses, roadsters, flappers, and many other upper-crust appurtenances fabulous to think of in wartime Berks County. A real reader, reading to escape his own life thoroughly, tends to have runs on authors; besides Wodehouse, I pretty well ploughed through Erle Stanley Gardner, Ellery Queen, Agatha Christie, and Ngaio Marsh, whose mystery novels stood in long orderly rows on the library shelves. Books cost two dollars then, and must have cost libraries rather less, and in pinched times seemed in abundant supply. The libraries and the railroad stations were the monumental structures that a citizen of Roosevelt's America was most apt to enter, and the era of television and the airplane has yet to construct with a comparable dignity. The movies and the radio were offering their own styles of popular entertainment without seizing, as does television for its addicts, all the day, every day. Department stores like Whitner's and Pomeroy's and many corner drugstores ran their own rental libraries – the cellophane-wrapped books available for (can it be?) as little as two cents a day. The public-library books had shed their jackets and in many cases had worn out their covers, and the sturdy look of a book that had been redone at the bindery was so pleasing to me that, in my late teens, I had some collected pages of my own composition professionally bound, for some modest charge like five dollars.

I loved the peace and patience of the library. Now, amazingly, some libraries have music in the background, and permit animated conversations; but silence was a sacred rule then, and one could hear with the distinctness of forest sounds at night a newspaper page being turned, or the drinking fountain by the front door being operated. A young man is perforce a somewhat distrusted creature, full of noisy tendencies and inconvenient impulses and what I remember of the library is its acceptingness of me – tiny Miss Ruth's friendly smile, the walls of books waiting to be opened, the august long tables with their mellow green-shaded lamps glowing. When I went away to college, I discovered that the Reading Public Library functioned surprisingly well as a research centre, and I was able to do at least one college paper (on Heloise and Abelard) with the resources upstairs in the mysterious balconies, where the more scholarly books were stashed, unruffled by the greedy hands of collegiate competition.

Aside from my beloved mystery writers and humorists (have I mentioned Thurber and Benchley, and the Mr Tutt stories of

indoctrination. If you read, you can learn to think for yourself.
Doris Lessing, *The Pleasure of Reading*,
edited by Antonia Fraser (1992)

Arthur Train?) I did now and then stab randomly toward culture: Eliot's *Waste Land* and Wells's *Time Machine* and Shaw's *Back to Methuselah* are three books that I pondered at these glowing tables, along with Edmund Wilson's *Memoirs of Hecate County*, James Cain's *Serenade*, and something by Irving Schulman about New York teen-age gangs – all of them offering a stimulating glimpse into the strange realities of sex. It saddens me to hear of books being pulled from library shelves because of their alleged lubricity of radicalism or racism; surely the great thing about books as instruments of education is that one reads no more than one is ready to understand. One is always free to stop and read a book of different quality or an opposed opinion. A book doesn't trap a reader, it is there to be taken or left. I remain grateful to the Reading Public Library and its personnel for the freedom given me in those formative years when we, generally speaking, become lifelong readers or not. A kind of heaven opened up for me there. As a writer, I imagine my books' ideal destination to be the shelves of a place like the Reading Public Library, where they can be picked up without prejudice, by a reader as innocent as I was, and read for their own sake, as ways out of reality and back into it.

Written originally for *Bookends*, the journal of the Friends of the Reading–Berks Public Libraries, and reprinted in *Odd Jobs* (Deutsch, 1992)

This guy [Philip Larkin], this mid-century librarian who publishes poems about his sexual frustration, didn't just buy one dirty mag and look at it, and decide it was boring and

PHILIP ROTH

The Newark Public Library

What will the readers of Newark do if the City Council goes ahead with its money-saving plan to shut down the public library system on April 1? Will they loot the stacks the way Newarkers looted appliance stores in the riot of 1967? Will police be called in to Mace down thieves racing off with the *Encyclopaedia Britannica*? Will scholars take up sniping positions at the reference-room windows and school-children seize the main Washington Street building in order to complete their term papers? If the City Council locks up the books, will library card holders band together to 'liberate' them?

I suppose one should hope not. Apparently there must be respect for Law and Order, even when there is none for aspiration and quiet pleasure, for language, learning, scholarship, intelligence, reason, wit, beauty, and knowledge.

When I was growing up in Newark in the forties, we assumed that the books in the public library belonged to the public. Since my family did not own many books, or have the money for a child to buy them, it was good to know that solely by virtue of my municipal citizenship I had access to any on Washington Street, or from the branch library I could walk to in my neighbourhood. No less satisfying was the idea of communal good. Why I had to care for the books I borrowed, return them unscarred and on time, was because they weren't mine alone, they were everybody's. That idea had as much to do with civilising me as any I was ever to come upon in the books themselves.

If the idea of a *public* library was civilising, so was the place with its comforting quiet, its tidy shelves, its knowledgeable, dutiful employees who weren't teachers. The library wasn't simply where one had to get the books, it was the kind of exacting haven to which a city youngster willingly went for his lesson in restraint and his training in self-control. And then there was the lesson in order, the enormous institution itself serving as instructor. What trust it inspired – in both oneself and in systems – first to decode

---

chuck it away. Oh *no* – he bought *one after another!* And he . . . kept them in a box!
William Leith, *The Independent on Sunday* (April 1993)

the catalogue card, then to make it through the corridors and stairwells into the open stacks, and there to discover, exactly where it was supposed to be, the desired book. For a ten-year-old to find he actually can steer himself through tens of thousands of volumes to the very one he wants is not without its satisfactions. Nor did it count for nothing to carry a library card in one's pocket; to pay a fine; to sit in a strange place, beyond the reach of parent and school, and read whatever one chose, in anonymity and peace; finally to carry home across the city and even into bed at night a book with a local lineage of its own; a family tree of Newark readers to which one's name had now been added.

In the forties, when the city was still largely white, it was simply an unassailable fact of life that the books were 'ours' and that the public library had much to teach us about the rules of civilised life, as well as civilised pleasures to offer. It is strange (to put it politely) that now, when Newark is mostly black, the City Council (for fiscal reasons, we are told) has reached a decision that suggests that the books don't really belong to the public after all, and that what a library provides for the young is no longer essential to an education. In a city seething with social grievances there is, in fact, probably little that could be *more* essential to the development and sanity of the thoughtful and ambitious young than access to those books. For the moment the Newark City Council may have solved its fiscal problem; it is too bad, however, that the councilmen are unable to calculate the frustration, cynicism, and rage that this insult must inevitably generate, and to imagine what shutting down its libraries may cost the community in the end.

First published in the *New York Times*, 1 March 1969; Penguin, 1985

A survey of unusual bookmarks discovered by librarians included a used condom, a kipper, bacon rashers, and an old jam sandwich.

The Independent (May 1993)

HUGH MacDIARMID

A Basketful of Books

It was that [Langholm] library, however, that was the great determining factor. My father was a rural postman, his beat running up the Ewes Road to Fiddleton Toll, and we lived in the post office buildings. The library, the nucleus of which had been left by Thomas Telford, the famous engineer, was upstairs. I had constant access to it, and used to fill a big washing-basket with books and bring it downstairs as often as I wanted to. My parents never interfered with or supervised my reading in any way, nor were they inclined to deprecate my 'wasting all my time reading'. There were upwards of twelve thousand books in the library (though it was strangely deficient in Scottish books) and a fair number of new books, chiefly novels, was constantly bought. Before I left home (when I was fourteen) I would go into the library in the dark and find any book I wanted. I could do so still if the arrangement of the shelves has not been altered, although I have not been in it for thirty years now; and I can still remember not only where about on the shelves all sorts of books were, but whereabouts in the books themselves were favourite passages or portions that interested me specially for one reason or another, so that I could still go straight to them and open them – hundreds of them – at or about the very place in question.

Lucky Poet (Methuen, 1943)

Go and ask the lady who checks out the videos and ask her where the books are.
Roseanne to her son DJ , *Roseanne*, Channel 4 (May 1993)

MASSAGING THE MEDIUM

Throughout the sixties iconoclasts liked to parrot the preachings of Marshall McLuhan, a Canadian savant who declared that 'the medium is the message'. Apropos libraries, this was taken to mean that the end of the book was nigh. Books, opined McLuhan, are too slow. In his speeded-up world books would be redundant, a notion that regularly does the rounds.

Absurd as this seems, even at this early remove, the problem of a world continually producing books is one that librarians have always had to grapple with. No sooner is a library built than it starts to run short of space; how do you deal with such a problem?

Stock control is an obvious but potentially dangerous way of coping with the print explosion. In the early seventies in the stacks of a Camden reference library I came across a set of the Caxton edition of Balzac. There was a note in *Père Goriot*: 'Discard when the reader going through the lot has had enough.' I could have wept.

Circumstances change, which makes stock control such an inexact science; Eden Phillpotts may not be read today but then Trollope wasn't much read yesterday. Cost rather than availability determines which books are on the shelves. This is not an option for academic and national libraries which cannot predict what books of the past scholars of the future will want to consult. The easy answer is to collect everything, thus catering for any eventuality.

Jorge Luis Borges, the blind writer and national librarian of Argentina, knew that ultimately this was an unsatisfactory solution. He considered the Total Library, which has a long history, though most librarians are unaware of it, and it was not on the syllabus when I was a student at library school. In essence, the total library is the alphabet; give half a dozen monkeys typewriters and in a few eternities they would produce all the books in the British Museum. Which is why it was very clever of Terry Pratchett to have an ape preside over the library in Discworld.

JORGE LUIS BORGES

The Total Library

The caprice or fancy or utopia of the Total Library contains certain traits that can be confused with virtues. Actually, it is astonishing how long it took man to dream up the idea. Certain examples Aristotle attributes to Democritus and to Leucippus clearly prefigure it, but its late inventor is Gustav Theodor Fechner and its first expounder is Kurd Lasswitz. (Between Democritus of Abdera and Fechner flow – heavily laden – almost twenty-four centuries of European history.) Its connections are illustrious and multiple: it is related to atomism and combinatory analysis, to typography and to chance. In *The Race with the Tortoise* (Berlin, 1929), Dr Theodor Wolff suggests that it is either a derivation from or a parody of Raymond Lull's mental machine; I would add that it is a typographical avatar of the doctrine of the eternal return which, adopted by the Stoics or by Blanqui, by the Pythagoreans or by Neitzsche, eternally returns.

The most ancient of the texts that hints at it is alluded to in the first book of Aristotle's *Metaphysics*. I refer to the passage about Leucippus's cosmology: the formation of the world by the fortuitous conjunction of atoms. The writer observes that the atoms required by this conjecture are homogeneous and that their differences derive from position, order or form. To illustrate those distinctions he adds: 'A is different from N in form; AN and NA in order; Z from N in position.' In his treatise *De Generatione et Corruptione*, he attempts to bring the variety of visible things into accord with the simplicity of the atoms and he reasons that a tragedy is made up of the same elements as a comedy – that is, the twenty-six letters of the alphabet.

Three hundred years pass and Cicero composes an indecisive, sceptical dialogue and entitles it, ironically, *De Natura Deorum*. In the second book, one of the speakers argues:

'At this point must I not marvel that there should be anyone who can persuade himself that there are certain solid and indivisible particles of matter borne along by the force of gravity,

---

Free or open access can hardly be practised in so large a library as this. As it was once put, the danger would be not merely of losing the books, but also of losing readers.
    Arundell Esdaile, former secretary to the British Museum
When people say to me, oh yeah, comedy, rock and roll,

and that the fortuitous collision of those particles produces this elaborate and beautiful world? I cannot understand why he who considers it possible for this to have occurred should not also think that, if a countless number of copies of the one-and-twenty letters of the alphabet, made of gold or what you will, were thrown together in some receptacle and then shaken out on to the ground, it would be possible that they should produce the *Annals* of Ennius, all ready for the reader. I doubt whether chance could possibly succeed in producing a single verse!' (Loeb Classical Library, pages 212–213.)

Cicero's typographical image was long-lived. Toward the middle of the seventeenth century, it appears in an academic discourse by Pascal; Swift, at the beginning of the eighteenth, stresses it in the preamble to his indignant 'Trivial Essay on the Faculties of the Soul', which is a museum of commonplace – as is the future *Dictionnaire des idées reçues* by Flaubert.

A century-and-a-half later, three men vindicate Democritus and refute Cicero. Because such a huge period of time separates the litigants, the vocabulary and the metaphors of the polemic are different. Huxley (one of the men) does not say that the 'golden letters' would finally compose a Latin verse if they were thrown a sufficient number of times; he says that a half-dozen monkeys, supplied with typewriters, would produce in a few eternities all the books in the British Museum. Lewis Carroll (one of the other refuters) observes in the second part of his extraordinary dream novel *Sylvie and Bruno* (1893) that since the number of words in a language is limited, so is the number of their possible combinations, that is, of their books. 'Soon [he says] literary men will not ask themselves, "What book shall I write?" but "Which book?".' Lasswitz, stimulated by Fechner, imagined the Total Library. He published his invention in the volume of fantastic tales *Traumkristalle*.

Lasswitz's basic idea is the same as Carroll's, but the elements of his game are the universal orthographic symbols, not the words of a language. The number of such elements – letters, spaces, punctuation marks – is reduced and can be reduced even further. The alphabet can do without the 'q' (which is completely superfluous) the 'x' (which is an abbreviation), and all the capital letters. The algorithms in the decimal system of enumeration can be eliminated or reduced to two, as they are in Leibniz's binary notation. Punctuation could be limited to the comma and the period. There would be no accents, as in Latin. By means of

---

boxing and football, that's the way out of the working class, they always forget to say the library; *that's* the best way out of all. We're the outstanding examples – Sean Connery and me and people like that – coming from the working class

similar simplifications, Kurd Lasswitz arrives at twenty-five symbols (twenty-two letters, the space, the period, the comma), whose recombination and repetition would include everything it is possible to express: in all languages. The totality urges mankind to construct that inhuman library, which chance would organise and which would itself eliminate intelligence. (*The Race with the Tortoise* by Wolff expounds the execution and the dimensions of that impossible enterprise.)

Everything would be in its blind volumes. Everything: the detailed history of the future, Aeschylus's *Egyptians*, the exact number of times the waters of the Ganges have reflected the flight of a falcon, the secret and true name of Rome, the encyclopedia Novalis would have been composed, my dreams and musings at dawn on August 14, 1934, the proof of Pierre Fermat's theorem, the unwritten chapters of *Edwin Drood*, those same chapters translated into the language spoken by the Garamantes, the paradoxes Berkeley dreamed up about time and which he didn't publish, the iron books of Urizen, the premature epiphanies of Stephen Dedalus which before a cycle of 1000 years would be meaningless, the gnostic preachings of Basilides, the song the sirens sang, the accurate catalogue of the library, the proof that the catalogue is fallacious. Everything: but because of a reasonable line or a reliable piece of news there would be millions of mad cacophonies, of verbal farragoes, and incoherences. Everything: but all of the generations of men will die out before the vertiginous shelves – the shelves which obliterate the daylight and in which chaos resides – ever grant them an acceptable page.

One of the mind's habits is the invention of horrible fancies. It has invented Hell, predestination, being predestined to Hell, the Platonic ideas, the chimera, the sphinx, the abnormal transfinite numbers (where the parts are no less abundant than the whole), masks, mirrors, operas, the monstrous Trinity: the Father, the Son, and the unresolved Ghost, all articulated into one single organism . . . I have tried to save from oblivion a minor horror: the vast, contradictory library, whose vertical deserts of books run the incessant risk of metamorphosis, which affirm everything, and confuse everything – like a raving god.

'The Total Library' in *Borges: A Reader*, edited by Emir Rodriguez Monegal
and Alastair Reid (Dutton, 1981)

---

and getting into the big stuff. But we're the minority. The people who are in banking and law and commerce who came from the working class did it through the library.

Billy Connolly (August 1993)

TERRY PRATCHETT

Worse Than Murder

Carrot looked around him. Shelves stretched away in every direction. On those shelves, books. He made a calculated guess.

'This is the Library, isn't it?' he said.

The Librarian maintained his gentle but firm grip on the boy's hand and led him along the maze of aisles.

'Is there a body?' said Carrot. There'd have to be. Worse than murder! A body in a library. It could lead to anything.

The ape eventually padded to a halt in front of a shelf no different than, it seemed, a hundred others. Some of the books were chained up. There was a gap. The Librarian pointed to it.

'Oook.'

'Well, what about it? A hole where a book should be.'

'Oook.'

'A book has been taken. A book has been taken? You summoned the Watch,' Carrot drew himself up proudly, 'because someone's taken a *book*? You think that's worse than murder?'

The Librarian gave him the kind of look other people would reserve for people who said things like 'What's so bad about genocide?'

'This is practically a criminal offence, wasting Watch time,' said Carrot. 'Why don't you just tell the head wizards, or whoever they are?'

'Oook.' The Librarian indicated with some surprisingly economical gestures that most wizards would not find their own bottoms with both hands.

'Well, I don't see what we can do about it,' said Carrot. 'What's the book called?'

The Librarian scratched his head. This one was going to be tricky. He faced Carrot, put his leather-glove hands together, then folded them open.

'I *know* it's a book. What's its name?'

The Librarian sighed, and held up a hand.

'Four words?' said Carrot. 'First word.' The ape pinched two

The record for an unreturned and overdue library book was set when a book in German on the Archbishop of Bremen, published in 1609, was borrowed from Sidney Sussex College, Cambridge, by Colonel Robert Walpole in 1667–8. It was found by Prof. Sir John Plumb in the library of the

wrinkled fingers together. 'Small word? A. The. Fo–'

'Oook!'

'The? The. Second word . . . third word? Small word. The? A? To? Of? Fro – Of? Of. The something Of something. Second word. What? Oh. First syllable. Fingers? Touching your fingers. Thumbs.'

The orang-utan growled and tugged theatrically at one large hairy ear.

'Oh, *sounds* like. Fingers? Hand? Adding up. Sums. Cut off. Smaller word . . . Sum. Sum! Second syllable. Small. Very small syllable. A. In. Un. On. On! Sum. On. Sum. On. Summon! Summon-*er*? Summon-*ing*? Summoning. Summoning. The Summoning of Something. This is fun, isn't it! Fourth word. Whole word–'

He peered intently as the Librarian gyrated mysteriously.

'Big thing. Huge big thing. Flapping. Great big flapping leaping thing. Teeth. Huffing. Blowing. Great big huge blowing flapping thing.' Sweat broke out on Carrot's forehead as he tried obediently to understand. 'Sucking fingers. Sucking fingers thing. Burnt. Hot. Great big hot blowing flapping thing . . .'

The Librarian rolled his eyes. Homo sapiens? You could keep it.

---

then Marquess of Cholmondeley at Houghton Hall, Norfolk, and returned 288 years later. No fine was exacted.

The Guinness Book of Records (1993)

LONG OVERDUE

The fact that many libraries in medieval times were chained says more about the value that was placed on manuscript books than it does about the character of the users. Individually scripted and illuminated, such books were not cheap and those that were produced so painstakingly by monks were guarded like incarcerated royalty. Those who stole from such libraries could expect to be fined with their lives.

Until libraries became open access it was easy enough to keep track of who had what out. Occasionally, overtrusting librarians allowed privileged members of the public access to the inner sanctum, sometimes with unfortunate results. The most notable case is perhaps that of Thomas Wise who took advantage of his status as one of Britain's foremost bibliographers to vandalise pamphlets in the British Museum collection, copy them and sell his forgeries to collectors. He was not unmasked until 1934, three years before he died. After his death, the BM bought his library.

Joe Orton likewise defaced books but it was a schoolboy prank which went disastrously wrong when he was prosecuted and jailed, an unfortunate example of municipal humourlessness.

Until quite recently though, librarians were often seen as custodians of books rather than their willing dispensers. For the forgetful fines could amount to a substantial sum and many mothers regretfully withdrew their children's library cards because they could not afford the penalties incurred with the late return of books. At the cost of a penny a day for each book overdue, it did not take long to mount up. If by chance you went on holiday and forgot to return your books it could be cheaper to lie and say the book was lost and pay for its replacement; it might cost a bit more but at least you had the book.

In Edinburgh, as in other well-policed library authorities, it was the practice to send a caretaker out to retrieve books that were long overdue. The caretakers could be gone for days and when they returned they had more tales to tell than Hans Christian Andersen. One yarn spinner claimed to have helped a woman give birth; another knew the city's bus timetables better than those who drove them. On a quiet Friday night I was sent out to see if I could retrieve books from a family living in a rough part of town. I went up a stair with walls covered in graffiti. The smell of frying was pervasive. Behind every door seemed to lurk a slavering Rottweiler. I rang the bell. A man in a string vest with a pot belly and an armful of tattoos appeared in the doorway. 'What do you want?' he growled. 'Wrong address,' I whispered and retreated at a lick.

ERIC WAS NOW BEGINNING TO WISH HE'D
RETURNED HIS OVERDUE LIBRARY BOOKS

© Glen Baxter

SELECTIVE INDEX